MONOGRAPH 50

Settlement Archaeology and Political Economy at Tres Zapotes, Veracruz, Mexico

Edited by Christopher A. Pool

THE COTSEN INSTITUTE OF ARCHAEOLOGY

UNIVERSITY OF CALIFORNIA, LOS ANGELES

2003

Editorial Board of The Cotsen Institute of Archaeology at UCLA
Jeanne E. Arnold, Marilyn Beaudry-Corbett, Elizabeth Carter, Christopher Donnan, Susan Downey, Ernestine S. Elster, Lothar von Falkenhausen, John Papadopoulos, Judith Rasson, James Sackett, Julia L.J. Sanchez, Charles Stanish, Thomas Wake, and Willeke Wendrich

The Cotsen Institute of Archaeology at UCLA
Charles Stanish, Director
Julia L.J. Sanchez, Director of Publications
Brenda Johnson-Grau, Managing Editor

Edited by Rita Demsetz, Marilyn Gatto, and Brenda Johnson-Grau
Designed by Brenda Johnson-Grau
Production by Merlin Ramsey, Karla Saenz, Keomanee Vilaythong, and Alice Wang

Library of Congress Cataloging-in-Publication Data

Settlement archaeology and political economy at Tres Zapotes, Veracruz,
Mexico / edited by Christopher A. Pool.
p. cm. -- (Monograph series ; v. 50)
Includes bibliographical references.
ISBN 1-931745-07-2
1. Trez Zapotes Site (Mexico) 2. Olmecs--Antiquities. 3. Olmec
architecture--Mexico--Veracruz (State) 4. Olmec
pottery--Mexico--Veracruz (State) 5. Human
settlements--Mexico--Veracruz (State) 6. Social
archaeology--Mexico--Veracruz (State) 7. Veracruz (Mexico :
State)--Antiquities. I. Pool, Christopher A. II. Monograph (Cotsen
Institute of Archaeology at UCLA) ; 50.
F1219.8.O56 S47 2003
972'.62--dc21
2002012658

CONTENTS

For
Robert S. Santley
and
Marion Stirling Pugh

ACKNOWLEDGMENTS

THE *RECORRIDO ARQUEOLÓGICO DE TRES ZAPOTES* WAS INITIATED by Ithaca College and continued by the University of Kentucky with funding from the National Science Foundation (Grants SBR-9405063 and SBR-9615031). The National Science Foundation also funded Charles Knight's dissertation fieldwork at the outlying site of Palo Errado with a grant to the University of Pittsburgh (Grant SBR-9615365). Supported by a National Science Foundation grant to the University of Missouri Research Reactor (MURR), instrumental neutron activation analysis of obsidian from Palo Errado, conducted by Michael Glascock, identified sources of visual categories at Tres Zapotes. The Instituto Nacional de Antropología e Historia (INAH) granted permission to conduct both field projects.

Many individuals have contributed to the success of the project. We particularly appreciate the support of Joaquín García-Bárcena, president of the Consejo de Arqueología of INAH, and Daniel Goeritz, director of the Centro Regional INAH Veracruz. We owe a great debt of gratitude to the late Juan Carlos Sánchez and Miguel Angel Colmenero Castañeda of the Centro Regional for their unflagging aid in securing the cooperation of the Tres Zapotes ejido. Special thanks go to Ponciano Ortiz Ceballos of the Universidad Veracruzana, who lent his counsel and expertise in the early weeks of the project and his enduring friendship throughout. Participants in the 1995 season included students from several institutions: Luis Heredia Barrera, Zenaido Salazar Buenrostro, Maria de Lourdes Hernández-Jiménez, and Mireya Rodriguez Cruz of the Universidad Veracruzana; Michael Ohnersorgen of Arizona State University, and Charles Knight and Mark Kruszczynski of the University of Pittsburgh; Georgia Mudd Britt of Washington University; Elizabeth Hoag, then of the University of Cincinnati; Eileen Corcoran and Tina Farkas of Ithaca College; and University of Kentucky alumnus Tim Sullivan. Ingeniero Rodolfo A. García Morales conducted the topographic survey. Ithaca College undergraduates Jan Stephenson, Shannon Muillesseaux, Jason Kerschner, and Shannon Daly assisted in the data entry of the 1995 ceramic material. In the 1996 season, Knight, Kruszczynski, Hoag, and Corcoran were joined by Jorge Villegas and Maria Eugenia Maldonado of the Universidad Veracruzana, Kurt Rademaker and Carl Wendt of the University of Kentucky, and Dr. Yamile Lira Lopez of INAH. Participants in the 1997 season included Wendt, Maldonado, Britt, and Hoag, as well as Marcie Venter, Ellen Christina Lee, and Brian King of the University of Kentucky; Heidi Pullen of the University of Illinois; Michael Loughlin of the University of Alabama; and Shannon Wills of Stockton State College. Throughout the three seasons of survey, these students and archaeologists were assisted in the surface collection program and laboratory processing by over a hundred residents of Tres Zapotes. Though they are too numerous to mention here, the project would have been impossible without their aid.

This volume benefited greatly from the critical comments of several people. Barbara Stark served as the discussant for the symposium upon which most of these chapters are based and commented on an earlier draft of chapter 5, which was written especially for this volume. Hoag thanks Mike Marron of the Institute for Data Sciences at the University of Cincinnati and Scott Stewart for facilitating the statistical analysis in chapter 4. She also gratefully acknowledges Scott Stewart and Marilyn Masson for enhancing the clarity of the chapter with their comments. As volume editor, I particularly appreciate the helpful reviews by David Grove, Brandon Lewis, and Marilyn Beaudry-Corbett. I also thank Dr. Beaudry-Corbett for inviting us to submit the manuscript and for her patience during its preparation.

We dedicate this volume to Robert S. Santley, whose research at Matacapan has inspired much of our own, and to the memory of Marion Stirling Pugh, who helped blaze the archaeological trail at Tres Zapotes.

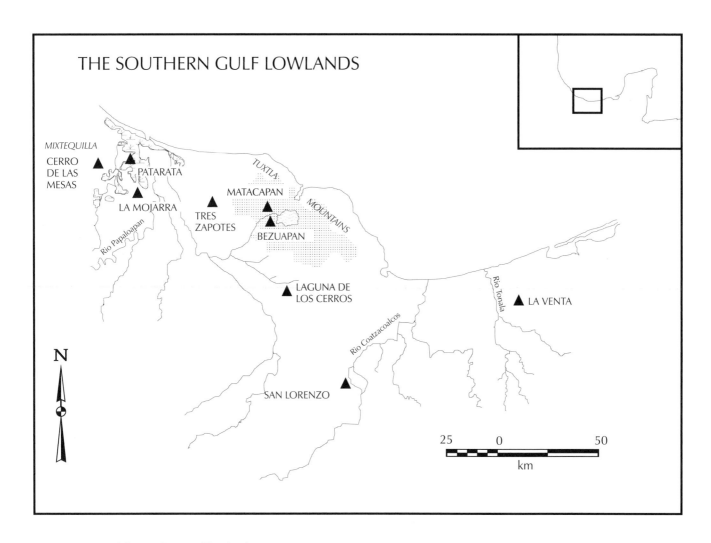

THE SOUTHERN GULF LOWLANDS

MIXTEQUILLA
CERRO
DE LAS
MESAS

PATARATA

LA MOJARRA

TRES
ZAPOTES

TUXTLA

MATACAPAN

BEZUAPAN

MOUNTAINS

Rio Papaloapan

LAGUNA DE
LOS CERROS

Rio Tonala

LA VENTA

Rio Coatzacoalcos

N

SAN LORENZO

25   0   50
km

Figure 1.1 Map of the southern Gulf lowlands. *Illustration prepared by Christopher A. Pool. After Coe 1965a:Fig. 1*

1.

INTRODUCTION

Christopher A. Pool

Heading southeastward from the port of Veracruz along the coastal Highway 180, the visitor to Mexico's Gulf Coast first passes through the cow pastures and pineapple farms of the semiarid zone of south-central Veracruz State, which encompasses the area called the Mixtequilla (figure 1.1). Soon the road emerges onto the long Alvarado sand bar, which separates the mangrove-lined estuaries of the lower Papaloapan basin from the Gulf of Mexico on the north. At the eastern end of the bar, swamps give way to fields of sugarcane watered by small streams descending from the Tuxtla Mountains which loom in the distance. Cutting through layers of volcanic ash and ancient marine sediments on the flanks of the mountains, the streams deposit fertile soils on the broad coastal plain. During the Formative period, the major center of Tres Zapotes arose along the banks of one of these streams, the Arroyo Hueyapan. In pre-Hispanic times, this location lay at the western entrance to the land the Aztecs called Olman, the "land of rubber," from which the historical and archaeological Olmecs take their name.

Lying in a slight rain shadow created by the Sierra de los Tuxtlas, the climate at Tres Zapotes is subhumid and hot (Aw$_1$ or Aw$_2$ in the Koeppen system, as modified by García (1981; Soto and Gama 1997:Fig. 1.12). About 1900 mm of rain falls each year, most of it from June through December, and freezing temperatures are unknown (Soto and Gama 1997:Appendix 1.2; compare Gomez-Pompa 1973:Fig. 6). The natural vegetation supported by this climate was probably a high evergreen or semi-evergreen selva (Gomez Pompa 1973:106, 110–111, 114).

Locally, the site lies at an interface between two distinct physiographic zones (figure 1.1). To the west stretches the broad deltaic plain of the lower Papaloapan basin. To the east, dissected, Tertiary marine sediments and younger

volcanic tephra form a region of low uplands around the heavily eroded slopes of the extinct volcano, Cerro el Vigía, which rises steeply to an altitude of 850 m. This physiographic, geologic, and hydrologic variation has created a diverse assemblage of soils, which are classified following the FAO/UNESCO system of soil nomenclature (INEGI 1984a) (figure 1.2). The Arroyo Hueyapan valley forms a pocket of fertile, easily worked, luvic phaeozem soils 11 km long by 4 km wide. Because of the high productivity of these soils, modern sugarcane cultivation closely parallels the distribution of luvic phaeozems (INEGI 1984b), and the same areas supported some of the densest pre-Hispanic settlement in the region (Coe 1965a:679; Stirling 1943:26-30). In contrast, the vertic gleysols of the deltaic plain suffer from high water tables; the dense, clayey vertisols of the sedimentary uplands are difficult to work; and the steep slopes on Cerro el Vigía make that area of luvic phaeozems and rocky orthic luvisols susceptible to erosion. Consequently, these less productive soils are currently exploited more frequently as pasture rather than as cropland. This is not to say that cultivation was impossible in any of these soils using ancient techniques, but it does suggest that Tres Zapotes lay within a moderately extensive area of prime agricultural land.

Tres Zapotes's location gave it access to a wide variety of resources in pre-Hispanic times. As we have seen, fertile agricultural land was abundant within the Arroyo Hueyapan valley. If, as Drucker (1943:8) believed, the uplands were less intensively cultivated, they would have provided fruits, nuts, game, pelts, feathers, timber, firewood, and other forest resources, including the rubber that gave the region its Aztec name. In addition, the rivers, lakes, and swamps of the Papaloapan basin would have supported a rich bounty of fish, shellfish, and aquatic plants. The geological setting also provided economically important mineral resources. The porphyritic basalt of Cerro el Vigía was used extensively for monuments and groundstone utensils (Williams and Heizer 1965:15-16), and the high-quality clays of the dissected sedimentary uplands evidently provided the material for pottery, then as in the recent past (Krotser 1974). Moreover, Tres Zapotes is well situated to take advantage of water transport for distribution of these products via the Arroyo Hueyapan and the larger rivers of the Papaloapan Basin.

History of Research

Tres Zapotes holds a prominent place in the history of Mesoamerican archaeology. Here on the lands of the old Hacienda Hueyapan a worker discovered the first of the colossal heads now recognized as hallmarks of Olmec culture. Seventy years after José Melgar's (1869) first report of the monument's discovery, Matthew Stirling (1940; 1943) initiated the first systematic investigation of an Olmec site at Tres Zapotes, completing two field seasons with the support of the Smithsonian Institution and the National Geographic Society. Stirling's pioneering excavations focused on finding and clearing stone monuments and trenching several of the more prominent mounds. In addition, stratigraphic excavations overseen by his field assistant, Philip Drucker, provided the first useful ceramic chronology from the Olmec heartland and identified deeply buried deposits of the Formative period (Drucker 1943a). Stirling's most exciting discovery, however, was the lower portion of the fragmented stela C. The stela's reconstructed Long Count date of (7).16.6.16.18.6, 6 Eznab, (1 Uo), or September 3, 32 BC, provided the first strong evidence that the Olmec culture predated the Classic Maya (Pugh 1981:6; Stirling 1940). Led by Sir J. Eric S. Thompson (1941), Mayanists vehemently opposed Marion Stirling's reconstruction of the missing baktun coefficient as too early. The Stirlings realized their ultimate vindication around 1970 when a local resident, Esteban Santo, found the upper portion of the monument with its baktun 7 coefficient intact (Porter 1989:41; Pugh 1981:6). By that time the issue of Olmec antiquity had been resolved by radiocarbon dates from La Venta (Drucker et al. 1959), and Stela C was shown to postdate the site's Olmec occupation.

Following Stirling's excavations, fieldwork at Tres Zapotes proceeded sporadically. In 1970, Ponciano Ortiz (1975) excavated a deep trench next to Drucker's (1943) trench 26 to refine the ceramic chronology of the Formative period. Eight years later, salvage operations for the construction of a gas pipeline resulted in the excavation of a small basalt column enclosure of probable Olmec vintage (Millet 1979).

Despite the limited quantity of fieldwork conducted since 1940, Tres Zapotes has continued to figure prominently in discussions of the Olmec heartland by Coe (1965a, 1965b), Bernal (1969), Drucker (1981), and Lowe (1989), among others. The Tres Zapotes sculptural corpus was catalogued by de la Fuente (1973), and it has been the subject of a detailed study by Porter (1989), who provides an updated catalog. Other important discussions of Tres Zapotes monuments appear in the works of Clewlow (1974; Clewlow et al. 1967), Drucker (1952a:204–215), Milbrath (1979), and Stirling (1965). Williams and Heizer included the monuments of Tres Zapotes in their 1965 petrographic sourcing study, and Hester, Jack, and Heizer (1971) made the obsidian recovered by Stirling the subject of a sourcing and technological study.

Research Objectives

As we began our reexamination of Tres Zapotes in 1995, several important questions remained about the site. Prior research had suggested that the site was first occupied some time in the Early Formative period (1500–900 BC) and that occupation continued through the Late Classic (AD 600–1000), with a sparse reoccupation in the Early Postclassic (AD 1000–1250) (Coe 1965a; Drucker 1943a; Ortiz 1975; Weiant 1943). Fascination with the site's Olmec and Epi-Olmec sculpture, however, had focused attention on the earlier part of the chronological sequence. Moreover, previous investigations had failed to produce an accurate site map, to establish the limits of the site, or to gather information on residential settlement patterns or craft production. To fill these gaps in our knowledge, I initiated the Tres Zapotes Archaeological Survey, which we call by its Spanish acronym, RATZ (*Recorrido Arqueológico de Tres Zapotes*).

Settlement and craft production data from Tres Zapotes are particularly important for understanding political and economic processes in the transition from Olmec to Classic period society. The long sequence of nearly continuous occupation at the site spans the poorly understood Late and Terminal Formative periods (400 BC–AD 300). This Epi-Olmec stage constituted a crucial episode in the development of Mesoamerican state-level societies during which Gulf Coast and Isthmian societies developed a hieroglyphic writing system and the Long Count calendar. These advances are associated with a sculptural style that suggests the development of new bases for political authority while maintaining continuity in thematic elements with late Olmec sculpture (Pool 2000a:152). As the largest known Epi-Olmec site in the Olmec heartland, Tres Zapotes provides a key link in this transition. In addition, the upland setting of Tres Zapotes contrasts

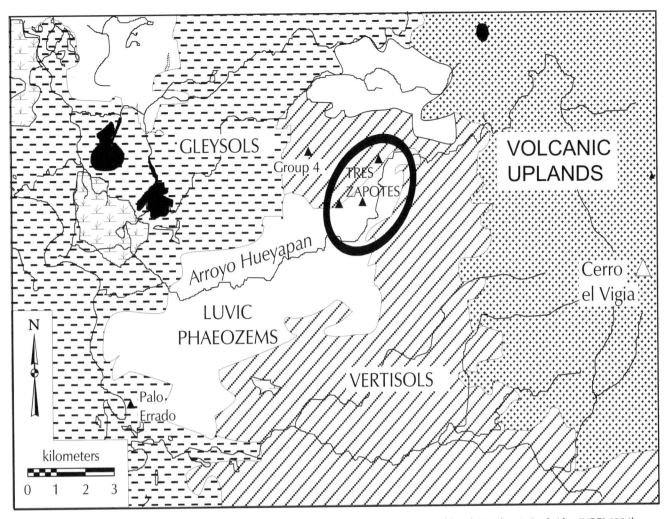

Figure 1.2 Map of the Tres Zapotes region showing distribution of soils *Illustration prepared by Christopher A. Pool. After INEGI 1984b*

markedly with the riverine and estuarine environments of the more intensively investigated eastern centers of Olmec culture, La Venta and San Lorenzo (figure 1.1). Consequently, ecological explanations for the emergence of Olmec society developed for the eastern centers are less applicable to the western Olmec heartland (Coe 1981b; Grove 1994). Moreover, the Early to Middle Formative sculpture of the site, which clearly falls within the Olmec style, diverges somewhat in its adherence to Olmec sculptural canons (de la Fuente 1981:94). To the extent that settlement patterns reflect adaptations to ecological, political, and economic systems, archaeological survey of Tres Zapotes is important for understanding variation in Olmec economic and political organization.

Tres Zapotes also provides a remarkable opportunity to inform models of political economy for the southern Gulf Coast. The site is located in an ecologically transitional zone between the Tuxtla Mountains and the Mixtequilla, a pre-Hispanic cultural subarea on the western margin of the lower Papaloapan basin (figure 1.1). Current explanations for differences in settlement organization between these two areas emphasize adaptations to low microtopographic diversity in lowland environments (Stark 1992:203–204; Stark and Heller 1991b:55–57) and participation in Classic period political economies, the latter focusing on interaction with the Central Mexican city of Teotihuacan (Santley 1994). In the Tuxtla Mountains, Matacapan was a primate center, which experienced substantial Teotihuacan influence and developed an internally differentiated ceramic production system that included intensive production in nucleated industries (Coe 1965a:704; Santley 1994; Santley, Arnold, and Pool 1989; Valenzuela 1945). Santley interprets Matacapan as a colonial enclave, which served as the primate center in a dendritic central place system geared toward the bulking and transport of goods to Teotihuacan (Pool and Santley 1992; Santley 1989a, 1994; Santley and Pool 1993). In contrast, the Classic

3

period occupation in the Mixtequilla appears to exhibit more even and continuous residential settlement and less intensive, more dispersed ceramic production (Stark 1990, 1991, 1992; Stark and Curet 1994). Formal architecture groups are closely spaced, but no one group dominates the others to the extent that many lowland Maya centers do, prompting Stark (1999) to speculate that the Mixtequilla may have constituted a persistent "capital zone" for the region. Teotihuacan influence, though present, is far less pronounced than at Matacapan. Stark and her associates attribute these characteristics to a variety of interrelated ecological and sociopolitical factors. These factors include more symmetrical political and economic interaction with Central Mexico (Stark 1990; Stark and Curet 1994:281–283), regional centralization of wealth through early cotton production and export to the highlands (Stark 1999:221), and an environment of low microtopographic diversity that encouraged considerable household self-sufficiency and discouraged strong social hierarchies (Stark 1992:204). Unclear, however, is the extent to which the different survey methods employed in the Mixtequilla and the Tuxtla Mountains have affected the interpretations of their respective archaeological records.

To summarize, the principal aim of RATZ has been to collect settlement data relevant to changes in political and economic organization during the Epi-Olmec stage in the Olmec heartland. We also expect data obtained by RATZ to provide a better understanding of variability in Olmec settlement systems and a more complete picture of Classic period political economy in the southern Gulf Coast region. These interests determined our three main research objectives: reconstructing the settlement history of Tres Zapotes, charting changes in its size and internal organization over its two thousand year history of occupation; investigating the organization of craft production at the site; and examining the effects of different survey and surface collection methods on the interpretation of settlement patterns.

Organization of this Volume

Using the data gathered by RATZ, the contributors to this volume have produced a series of new studies on intrasite settlement patterns, craft production, political economy, and urbanism at Tres Zapotes. In chapter 2, Michael Ohnersorgen and I discuss our surface survey methods and provide an overview of the site organization and settlement history they reveal. Surface data alone were inadequate to document settlement history at Tres Zapotes, however, because a large portion of the ancient site lies buried beneath the alluvium of the Arroyo Hueyapan floodplain. Consequently, we conducted an extensive auger testing program in the 1996 and 1997 field seasons. In chapter 3, Carl Wendt presents his analysis of the data recovered by the auger tests. These tests document the growth of the site in the Late Formative period and confirm that the site was significantly affected by a Terminal Formative volcanic eruption, which contributed to the subsequent abandonment of much of the floodplain.

Archaeological investigations in Mesoamerica frequently encounter, but less often collect, burned earthen artifacts (fired lumps of mud) that are usually interpreted as daub used in house construction. Recent investigations in the southern Gulf lowlands, especially at Matacapan (Pool 1990, 1997a; Santley, Arnold, and Pool 1989), have shown that tempered mud was also used to build ceramic kilns. In chapter 4, Elizabeth Hoag's detailed quantitative analysis of attributes in burned earthen materials evaluates criteria for distinguishing daub from kiln debris. Her analysis of the distribution of these materials across the site helps clarify patterns of residential settlement and documents the predominately household context of ceramic production.

In chapter 5, I assess the organization of specialized ceramic production at Tres Zapotes, drawing on Hoag's work on kiln debris in conjunction with other production indicators. Using a characterizational approach, I assess ceramic production along multiple dimensions of variation. In contrast to typological approaches, which attempt to assign production areas to predefined production modes, the characterizational approach is better able to capture the multivariate quality of production organization and permits the recognition of organizational arrangements not documented in the ethnographic and historical literature. Most Terminal Formative ceramic production at Tres Zapotes was carried out in domestic contexts, although there was considerable variability in the size and intensity of ceramic production areas. About one-third of the identified production areas were associated with elite residential or civic-ceremonial architecture. During the Classic period, specialized ceramic production contexts became more widely dispersed and more heavily geared toward the production of specific wares, while elite reliance on attached specialists appears to have declined. Comparison with comparable data sets from the Classic-period site of Matacapan in the Tuxtla Mountains reveals regional variation in the organization of ceramic production, which is best explained with respect to differences in their political economies.

In chapter 6, Charles Knight further develops the theme of political economy in his analysis of intrasite patterns of obsidian production and consumption. Prepared polyhedral cores were the principal obsidian import into Tres Zapotes, and prismatic blades were the primary artifacts used by consumers in the Late Formative through Classic periods. Comparison of the obsidian assemblages from selected zones of the site suggests that the manufacture of prismatic blades occurred in elite and nonelite contexts and that, with the exception of the apparently highly valued green obsidian from the Pachuca source, there was little difference in access to obsidian by elites and their subjects. Knight concludes that differential access to obsidian and its attendant technology did not play a prominent role in structuring and maintaining sociopolitical differences at Tres Zapotes.

The final chapter draws together the diverse lines of evidence presented in the volume to assess the political organization of Tres Zapotes at its height. Making an analytical distinction between the spatial nucleation of population, architecture, and activities on the one hand and the organizational centralization of functions, services, and authority on the other, I examine patterns of residential settlement, formal architecture, and craft production. During the Late and Terminal Formative periods, residential occupation exhibited a concentric structure, consisting of a nucleated residential core surrounded by a dispersed residential periphery. In contrast, formal groups of civic-ceremonial mounds surrounding plazas were widely dispersed, with three of the four plaza groups located in the residential periphery. Craft production was mainly carried out in domestic contexts, although elites ap-

pear to have relied to some degree on attached specialists for the production of their ceramic vessels and obsidian blades. Specialized ceramic production was more nucleated in the site's residential core than was obsidian production, but nonspecialized ceramic production apparently occurred in the residential periphery as well. Overall, administrative and ritual functions do not appear to have been highly centralized in the Late to Terminal Formative Period, and elites do not appear to have been able to exert strong control over the economic bases of political authority. The weak centralization of authority argues for an alliance among elites with competing claims to political power.

Though not intended as the final, comprehensive report of the RATZ project, this volume is not merely a compendium of preliminary, tentative interpretations. Instead, our aim in this volume is to present new data and inferences from a series of studies on specific questions regarding the archaeological record at Tres Zapotes and to contextualize these with discussions of our survey methods and the intrasite settlement patterns they reveal. In so doing, we hope to provide our colleagues with information that will help them frame new hypotheses about the evolution of complex society in a key region of Mesoamerica, particularly as regards the crucial transition from the Formative to the Classic period.

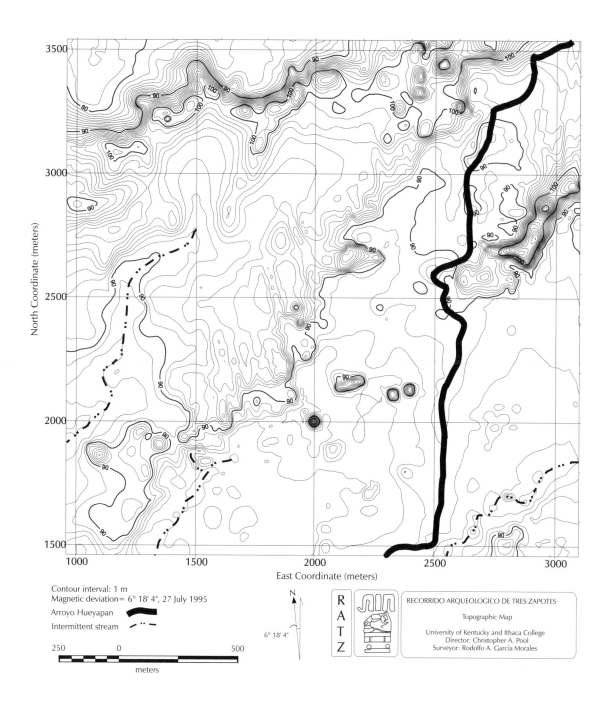

Figure 2.1 Topographic map of Tres Zapotes. *Illustration prepared by Christopher A. Pool*

ARCHAEOLOGICAL SURVEY AND SETTLEMENT AT TRES ZAPOTES

Christopher A. Pool and Michael A. Ohnersorgen

As described in the preceding chapter, the Recorrido Arqueológico de Tres Zapotes sought to document changes in the organization of settlement and craft production at the site and to investigate the interpretive effects of different survey and surface collection methods previously employed in the southern Gulf lowlands. Realizing these objectives was complicated by the fact that the archaeological site of Tres Zapotes sprawls across the terraces and alluviated floodplain of the Arroyo Hueyapan, and contemporary land use for cultivation and pasturage creates widely variable conditions of surface visibility. Consequently, the RATZ survey utilized a multistage research design. The 1995 season was devoted to topographic survey, intensive surface collection of the central and western portions of the site, extensive reconnaissance to define site boundaries, and ground verification of sites and landforms detected on aerial photographs of the surrounding region. In 1996 we completed intensive surface collection of the north, east, and south margins of the site and initiated an auger testing program to evaluate the extent of deeply buried occupational deposits beneath the floodplain of the Arroyo Hueyapan. The 1997 survey was devoted to completing the auger testing and artifact analysis. Two spin-off projects conducted by project members Charles Knight and Mark Kruszczynski in 1997 focused on obsidian production at the Late Formative to Classic period secondary center of Palo Errado (Knight 1999) and settlement patterns and basalt tool production on the slopes of Cerro el Vigía (Kruszczynski 1998).

Survey and Surface Collection

The 1995 field season began with the establishment of a site grid, oriented to magnetic north, which lay 6°18'04" east of true north. The primary site datum was established at the summit of mound 7, the principal mound of Group 2, which is located approximately at UTM coordinates N2044650-E242800. The primary datum was arbitrarily assigned grid coordinates of N 2000 E 2000 and an elevation of 100 m. The true elevation is estimated at 30 to 40 m above sea level on the basis of the 1:50000 scale topographic map for the Tres Zapotes quad (E15A72) (INEGI 1984c) . Over the course of the 1995 season, a professional surveyor, Rodolfo A. García Morales, topographically mapped the central 4 km of the site with a Topcon digital theodolite (figure 2.1).

The surface collection strategy employed by RATZ took into account three overriding concerns. First, coverage had to be sufficiently intensive to identify and obtain samples from household-scale features. Second, the data recovered had to be comparable to those obtained from other surveys of large sites in the southern Gulf Coast region, particularly Matacapan in the Tuxtla Mountains (Santley et al. 1984, 1987; Santley and Ortiz 1985) and Cerro de las Mesas in the Mixtequilla (Stark 1991). Comparability with Santley's and Stark's surveys was deemed particularly important, not only because they constitute the extant database for large-site surveys in the regions adjacent to Tres Zapotes but also because they provided specific models of economic and settlement organization, which we intended to test. Third, the collection strategy had to be appropriate to the specific characteristics of the archaeological record and the existing field conditions at Tres Zapotes.

Settlement in the Mixtequilla region is characterized by nucleated mound centers interspersed within a relatively even distribution of low house mounds, which measure 41.9 x 33.6 m on average (Stark 1991:45). Stark's survey therefore focused on the identification and collection of surface materials from archaeological features, including house mounds and artifact concentrations (Stark 1991; Stark and Heller 1991a). Beyond the intensively mapped central zone of Cerro de las Mesas, modern field boundaries constituted sampling strata that were surveyed in transects spaced 20 m apart to ensure the identification of small house mounds and non-mound artifact concentrations, visibility permitting. The goal of the collection program was to acquire representative collections of sufficient size for chronological, social, and functional analysis (Stark and Heller 1991a:3). Collections were therefore made of rim sherds, decorated sherds, and other materials over measured areas of variable size, depending on the density of remains (Stark and Heller 1991a:6; Stark 1991:47).

In contrast to the Mixtequilla, settlement in the vicinity of Matacapan appears to be more nucleated. Although low house mounds do occur, they are much less common than in the Mixtequilla, and habitation areas are generally demarcated by variation in artifact densities (Santley et al. 1984; Santley, Ceballos, and Pool 1987; Santley and Ortiz 1985). Most of the site of Matacapan is cultivated in tobacco, maize, and beans, providing excellent visibility. The principal goals of the Matacapan survey were to provide information on settlement size, configuration, and history and on socioeconomic organization. The surface collection program employed stratified systematic interval transect sampling, using each modern agricultural field as a sampling stratum (see Redman 1973). Collection units measuring 3 x 3 m were spaced at 13 m intervals along transects 50 to 100 m apart. Within each collection unit, vegetation was removed and all cultural materials were collected (Santley et al. 1984:10–13; Santley, Ortiz, and Pool 1987:41–42; Santley, Arnold, and Pool 1989:112; Santley and Ortiz 1985:12–14).

Each of these collection strategies has advantages and disadvantages. The Mixtequilla procedure ensures the identification of all visible habitation sites and the collection of sufficient artifacts to ensure the applicability of statistically based chronological assessment, but because only decorated and rim sherds are collected and areas of low ceramic density are not sampled, it is difficult to assess variations in ceramic density over the site as a whole. (Stark [1991:44] did, however, attempt to alleviate this problem by counting sherds with handheld "clickers" over some measured transects.) The interval transect sampling employed by the Matacapan project and the removal of vegetation from collection units provides greater control over variations in artifact density and permits site definition by trend surface analysis, but the spacing between transects is too great to ensure detection of all artifact concentrations, and individual collections are too small (at

about thirty sherds per collection) to ensure statistically valid chronological control. It is also somewhat more labor intensive than the Mixtequilla method.

Field conditions at Tres Zapotes differ significantly from both the Mixtequilla and Matacapan. Like Matacapan, most of the site is currently under cultivation, but most of the cultivated land is planted in sugarcane, with small maize and bean plots taking up the remainder. Pastureland is largely confined to the less productive upland soils, although some pastures are located on the alluvial flood plain, particularly to the east of the Arroyo Hueyapan. Mapping and surface collection in a mature sugarcane field is virtually impossible, owing to the high, dense foliage. It is therefore essential to conduct surveys in sugarcane fields shortly after cane has been cut. The local harvest season for sugarcane is December through May. During the field season in June and July, cane plants generally ranged from 20 to 150 cm in height, foliage was moderate to sparse, and ground visibility in most fields was good to excellent between rows. Still, it proved prudent to work fields with higher cane first, before growth accelerated with the coming of the rains, which began in mid-June. Only a few fields could not be surveyed because of the maturity of the cane. This seed cane had been allowed to grow through the preceding season to provide cuttings for future plantings.

Taking the field conditions and the project's objectives into consideration, the Tres Zapotes surface collection program employed a two-tiered sampling strategy designed to detect household-scale features and to provide baseline data on artifact distributions. The first level of the surface collection program comprised a systematic interval transect strategy modeled on the Matacapan survey. Transects were laid out at 100 m intervals across modern agricultural fields, and all surface materials were collected from 3 x 3 m collection units spaced at 20 m intervals along the transect. In fields characterized by a continuous, high-density distribution of artifacts, the systematic transect interval was reduced to 40 m. This modification proved necessar y because treating these fields as extensive concentrations under the more intensive surface collection strategy described below would have required impractical expenditures of time and labor. Collection units were assigned coordinates in the Tres Zapotes site grid by reference to control stakes placed at 100 m intervals across the field. Transects were normally oriented to cardinal directions, but where mature cane hindered the measurement of distances, transects were laid out between cane rows. Where surface visibility was poor, as in pasture, covering vegetation was removed. The data from the systematic transect sample aid in site definition through trend surface analysis and provide a baseline against which to assess surface densities obtained from artifact concentrations in the second level of surface collection.

The second level of the surface collection program targeted architectural features and artifact concentrations in a manner comparable to the Mixtequilla survey. Field crews walked transects laid out with tape and compass at 20 m intervals between the systematic survey transects. When a crew encountered a discrete artifact concentration or architectural construction, its limits were determined in the field and marked with pin flags for surface collection. Within each demarcated feature, all surface materials were collected from 3 x 3 m collection units spaced at 20 m intervals along each transect, with covering vegetation removed from collection units having poor visibility. This strategy permitted rapid collection of surface materials from measured areas on small archaeological features, thereby providing household scale data comparable to those obtained by the Mixtequilla survey.

As the 1995 field season neared its close, it became obvious that the site was more extensive than had been expected and that the intensive surface collection program would not reach the limits of the site. To assess the overall extent of the site, one field crew was assigned the task of conducting a less intensive reconnaissance in four 700 to 900 m wide swaths extending between 1 and 1.3 km beyond the intensive survey boundaries toward the cardinal points of the compass (figure 2.2). This extensive survey identified areas of concentrated domestic occupation and small mound groups to the north, east, and south of the survey area, which we surveyed intensively in 1996. Small, dispersed artifact concentrations to the west of the survey area are interpreted as rural settlement lying beyond the boundary of the site proper.

The surface collection program sampled an area of 489 ha (figure 2.3). Within this area, the systematic transect sample produced collections from 2650 squares, each measuring 9 m², for a sampling intensity of 0.49%, which corresponds closely to the sampling intensity of 0.46% obtained by the Matacapan survey (Santley, Arnold, and Pool 1989:112). The full-coverage survey produced an additional 1531 collections from mounds and artifact concentrations, for a total of 4181. The average collection contained 117 sherds, nearly four times the amount we had expected based on previous experience in the Sierra de los Tuxtlas.

Survey Strategies and Feature Visibility

Using both full-coverage prospecting and systematic interval transect sampling in the RATZ survey allows us to identify biases of the two methods in detecting archaeological features. The visibility of surface features varies with characteristics of the features themselves and characteristics of the landscape, such as ground cover. In this section we consider the effects of artifact density, extent, and height on feature visibility, using data from the 1995 survey.

ARTIFACT DENSITY

For the purposes of the full coverage survey, we initially defined concentrations as areas having five sherds or more per square meter (forty-five sherds/collection). This figure proved to equal the 65th percentile for collections in the systematic transect sample. The full-coverage survey identified sixty-two separate concentrations, including the extensive area of high sherd density in the center of the site, where crews made collections along 40 m transects.

Figure 2.4 compares the results of the full-coverage and systematic transect strategies. Areas with ceramic densities exceeding forty-five sherds per collection in systematic transect collections are delimited with a bold line; concentrations defined by field crews in the full-coverage survey are shaded. Although the two strategies produced broadly similar impressions of settlement distribution, some significant differences bear comment. First, we defined mounds separately from concentrations; including mounds with high surface artifact densities among the concentrations would provide a closer fit with the systematic survey contours. Nevertheless, in the northern and southern parts of the survey it appears that off-mound concentrations escaped notice by the field crews. Second, some concentrations defined in the full-coverage survey are more extensive than the corresponding areas identified by systematic transect collections. This observation primarily pertains to cases where crews defined an entire field as a concentration and collected it using transects at 40 m spacing. In such cases, detailed analysis of sherd frequencies within collections corrects the overly generous field definition of the concentration. The third discrepancy consists of small, discrete concentrations in areas of generally low sherd density. The 100 m spacing of the transects was simply too coarse to consistently detect such concentrations.

Our analysis suggests that in full-coverage surveys, an element of subjectivity may enter into the definition of artifact concentrations, even when field crews are instructed to employ a specific limit, such as 5 sherds per square meter. A continuous background scatter of sherds tends to interfere with density estimates and masks concentrations with densities approaching the defined limit. Identification of concentrations improves in areas where background ceramic densities are very low.

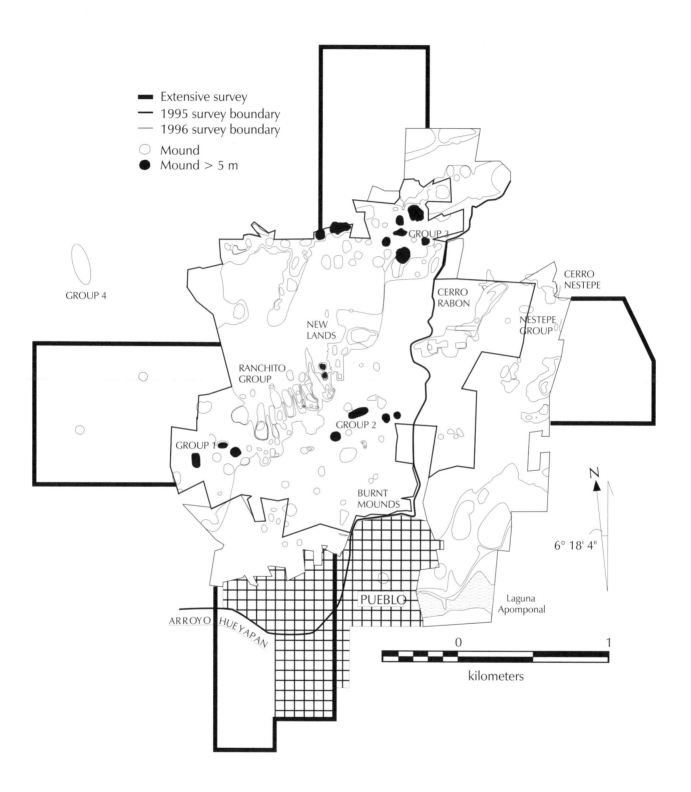

Figure 2.2 Map of Tres Zapotes, showing limits of intensive and extensive surveys. *Illustration prepared by Christopher A. Pool*

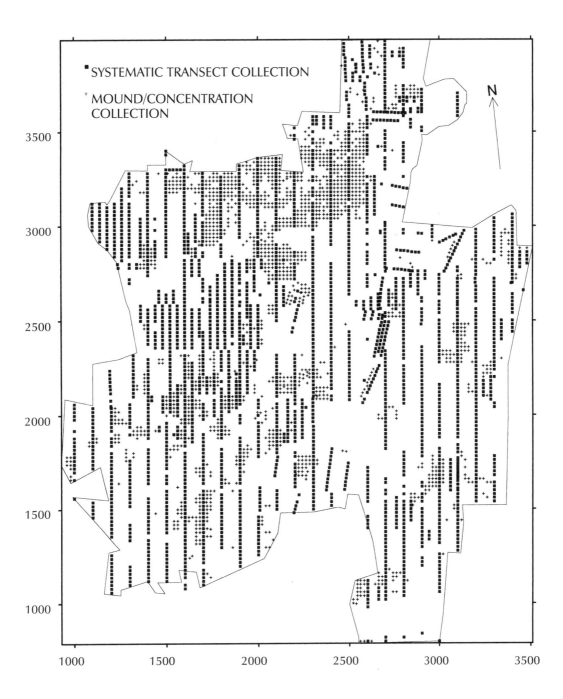

Figure 2.3 RATZ surface collection locations at Tres Zapotes. *Illustration prepared by Christopher A. Pool*

Table 2.1 Percentage of features in different size classes (by (perpendicular length) detected by systematic transects

LENGTH	MOUNDS		CONCENTRATIONS		ALL FEATURES	
	N	%	N	%	N	%
0–19	2	0.00	12	8.33	14	7.14
20–39	41	41.46	16	25.00	57	36.84
40–59	50	52.00	17	41.18	67	49.25
60–79	19	68.42	6	33.33	25	60.00
80–99	9	100.00	3	100.00	12	100.00
>100	10	100.00	8	100.00	18	100.00
Total	131	57.25	62	40.32	193	51.81

= percentage detected

Table 2.2 Percentage of features crossed by systematic transects, stratified by visibility class

		DETECTED		NOT DETECTED	
VISIBILITY	N	f	%	f	&
Low	93	35	37.63	58	62.36
Moderate	36	13	36.11	23	63.89
High	61	50	81.97	11	18.03
Total	190	98	51.58	92	48.42

EXTENT

In a survey that employs parallel transects, the detectability of a feature is related to its orientation relative to the transects. The measure of feature extent that is most relevant to detection is the length perpendicular to transects. The perpendicular length of mounds ranged from 15 to 200 m, with a prominent mode at 40 to 59 m (figure 2.5). Concentrations exhibited a greater range, from 5 to 1390 m for the continuous, high–density distribution of sherds in the center of the site (figure 2.5). The frequency distribution of concentration lengths is also multimodal, with modes at 10 to 19 m, 40 to 49 m, and 120 to 129 m. Concentrations appear to represent a broader range of features than mounds and may include small household middens as well as extensive areas of continuous occupation. Nevertheless, the broadly similar frequency distributions of the mounds and artifact concentrations suggest that many concentrations are the remains of destroyed residential platforms.

Systematic transects at 100 m intervals crossed 52% of all features, but the size of features strongly affected their chance of being intersected by transects (table 2.1). Systematic transects crossed all thirty features greater than 80 m in perpendicular length but the percentage drops sharply to 60% for features 60 to 79 m in perpendicular length, and continues to decline for progressively smaller classes of features. The systematic survey detected only one (7.1%) of the fourteen features smaller than the 20 m spacing of the full-coverage survey. We do not know, however, how many similarly small features were missed by the full-coverage survey.

Detection using a systematic interval transect strategy is particularly problematic for non-mound artifact concentrations. Systematic transects crossed only 40.3% of the sixty-two concentrations defined in the 1995 survey (table 2.1). Surprisingly, more concentrations between 40 and 59 m in perpendicular length were detected than in the 60 to 79 m range, but this probably reflects nothing more than the low frequency of the larger concentrations (n=6). Figure 2.6 illustrates the effects of the 100 m transect interval on the sampling of concentrations by the systematic survey. Very large concentrations were easily detected, of course, but smaller discrete concentrations on the valley plain and in the northern portion of the site escaped detection.

Mounds (including probably natural features that supported occupation) comprise 131 of the features identified in the 1995 survey. Systematic transects crossed 57% of these (table 2.1). Figure 2.7 illustrates the effects of mound orientation and size on the impression of settlement pattern provided by the systematic survey alone. Small mounds and mounds oriented north-south, parallel to most transects, are clearly underrepresented. As a result, exclusive reliance on the transect survey would have missed mounded occupation on the southerly trending ridge in the north part of the site, as well as small mounds in the Ranchito and New Lands group and on the southern portion of the valley plain.

HEIGHT

To assess fully the sensitivity of our systematic transect strategy, we must also consider the heights of features, since taller features would have been visible from the transects, even if they lay between them. Mounds ranged from less than 1 to 20 m in height for the modified hill, Cerro Rabon (figure 2.8). The distribution of mound heights is strongly skewed toward the low end of the range, with 65% of mounds 2 m or less in height. A small mode at 7 m represents the typical height of mounds in formal groups. Even under good conditions, mounds less than 1 m tall may be missed at a distance of 50 m, but in the sugarcane fields that cover much of Tres Zapotes, even 2 m high mounds may be difficult to detect using a systematic strategy.

The foregoing consideration of mound height and extent suggests a stratification of features into "visibility classes." High visibility features consist of all features with a perpendicular length greater than 80 m and mounds taller than 2 m. Moderate visibility features include mounds between 1 and 2 m tall and less than 80 m long. The low visibility class comprises concentrations and mounds with heights 1 m or less

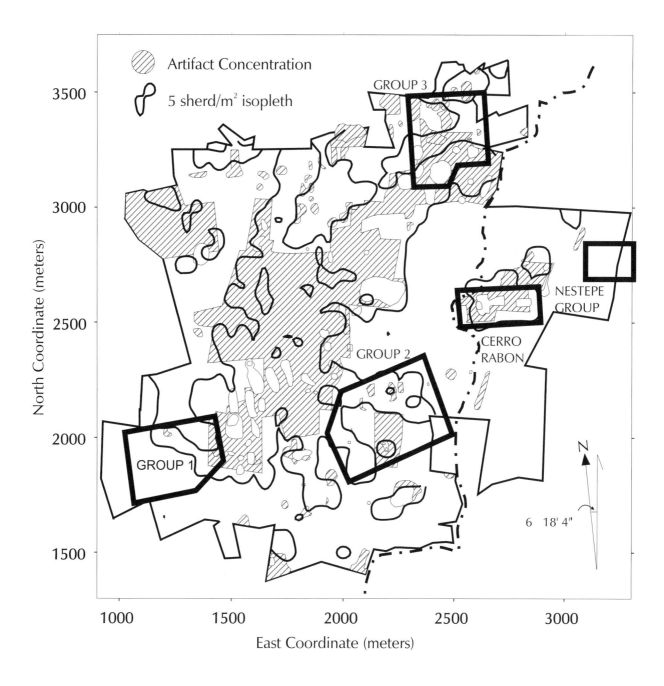

Figure 2.4 Comparison of ceramic concentrations identified by full-coverage survey (shaded) and systematic transect sample (bold contour line bounding areas containing 45 sherds/collection [5 sherds/m²]) in the 1995 survey. *Illustration prepared by Michael A. Ohnersorgen and Christopher A. Pool*

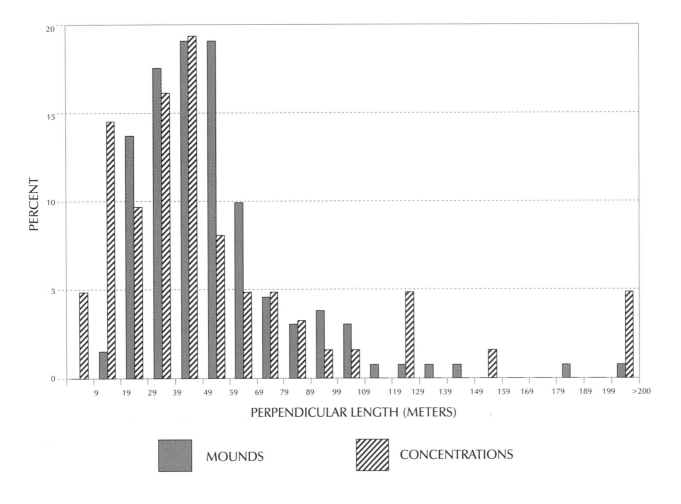

Figure 2.5 Frequency distribution of lengths perpendicular to systematic transects for mounds and artifact concentrations detected in 1995 survey. *Illustration prepared by Christopher A. Pool*

and perpendicular lengths less than 80 m. We exclude from this analysis three mounds for which heights were not recorded.

The sixty-one high-visibility features represent 32% of the 190 features for which heights were estimated. Systematic transects at 100 m spacing crossed 82% of the high visibility features (table 2.2), and we assume that the remaining high visibility features, all mounds greater than 2 m tall, would have been seen and collected by survey crews. In contrast, systematic transects crossed only thirteen (36%) of the thirty-six moderate visibility features and 35 (38%) of the 93 low visibility features. The remaining 81 low-to-moderate visibility features, constituting 43% of all features, probably would have been missed by the systematic survey crews.

The use of a dual survey strategy at Tres Zapotes provides detailed data on mounded and non-mound occupation

and permits us to identify and correct for distortions of the settlement pattern inherent in each strategy. Furthermore, we believe that our analysis has significant implications for the interpretation of settlement patterns derived from surveys that have employed one or the other of the strategies in the Gulf lowlands of southern Veracruz. As this study confirms, the use of a systematic interval transect strategy may severely underrepresent low mounds and small concentrations. In the systematic survey at Matacapan, the proportion of features not sampled was probably smaller than in the Tres Zapotes systematic survey. There, spacing between transect lines varied from 50 to 100 m, and peripheral areas of the site were crossed by transects running both north-south and east-west. In addition, features observed between systematic transects were sampled with secondary transects. On the other hand, the element of subjectivity in defining con-

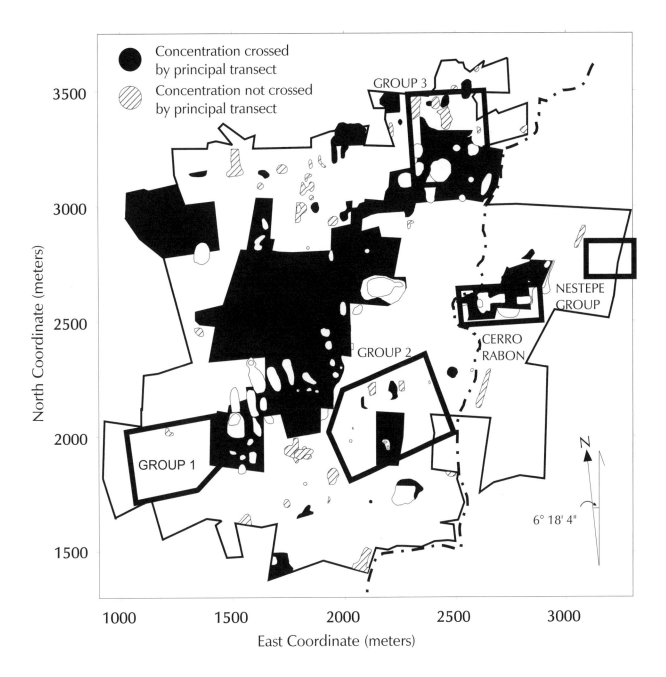

Figure 2.6 Artifact concentrations intersected by systematic transects at 80 to 100 m in 1995 survey. *Illustration prepared by Christopher A. Pool*

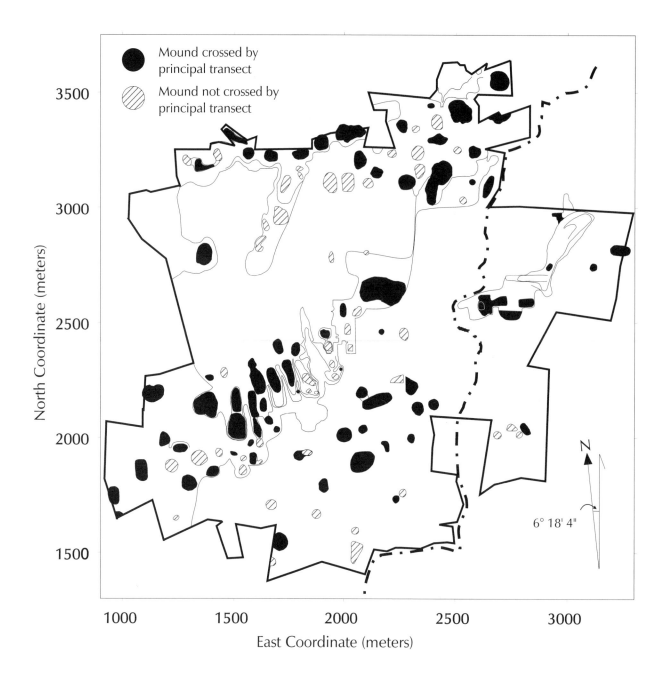

Figure 2.7 Mounds intersected by systematic transects at 80 to 100 m in 1995 survey. *Illustration prepared by Michael A. Ohnersorgen*

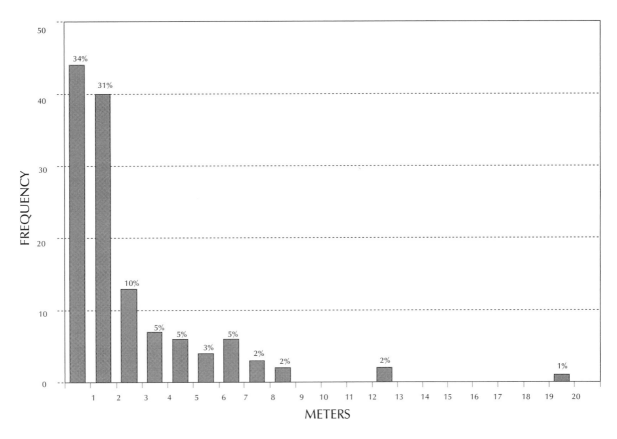

Figure 2.8 Frequency distribution of mound heights recorded in 1995 survey. *Illustration prepared by Christopher A. Pool*

centrations in full-coverage surveys like the one employed in La Mixtequilla may tend to underestimate the extent of non-mound artifact distributions. Roler and Stark (1992) suggest that smaller mounds and non-mound features in the Mixtequilla may represent poor households. Consequently, the biases in both kinds of surveys may create a social bias in archaeological interpretations as well, albeit in different ways and to different degrees.

Our results underscore the complementary nature of high-intensity, full-coverage survey and less intensive, systematic surveys. In general, however, the biases of systematic transect surveys against detection of low-visibility residential features appear to be more serious (for example, Cowgill 1990; Kintigh 1990; Parsons 1990). Other Gulf lowland survey projects, such as that of the Cotaxtla basin, which employed 400 m transect spacing (Daneels 1997), have undoubtedly sacrificed household-scale data to obtain greater areal coverage. Because household data are crucial to population estimates and socioeconomic reconstructions, it is important to carefully weigh survey and collection strategies against data requirements when developing research plans. When systematic interval transect methods are used, it is important to recognize that they are sampling methods as opposed to prospecting methods and that although they may sample *areas* in a reasonably representative fashion, it does not mean their sampling of *features* is similarly representative.

Surface Distributions

Although Stirling (1943:8–11), Drucker (1943a:5–9), and Weiant (1943:1–6) each described the overall layout of Tres Zapotes, the RATZ project has yielded a much more accurate and detailed picture of the site's natural features and ancient settlement (figure 2.9). Much of the site is occupied by the floodplain of the Arroyo Hueyapan. Entering the archaeological zone at its northeastern extreme, the arroyo makes a sharp bend to the south. About 2 km downstream the arroyo enters the modern village of Tres Zapotes, where it makes another sharp turn to the west. The straightness of the arroyo between these two points and the sharpness of the bends suggests that an underlying geological structure controls the course of this section of the arroyo. Evidence from auger testing (chapter 3) indicates that the course has

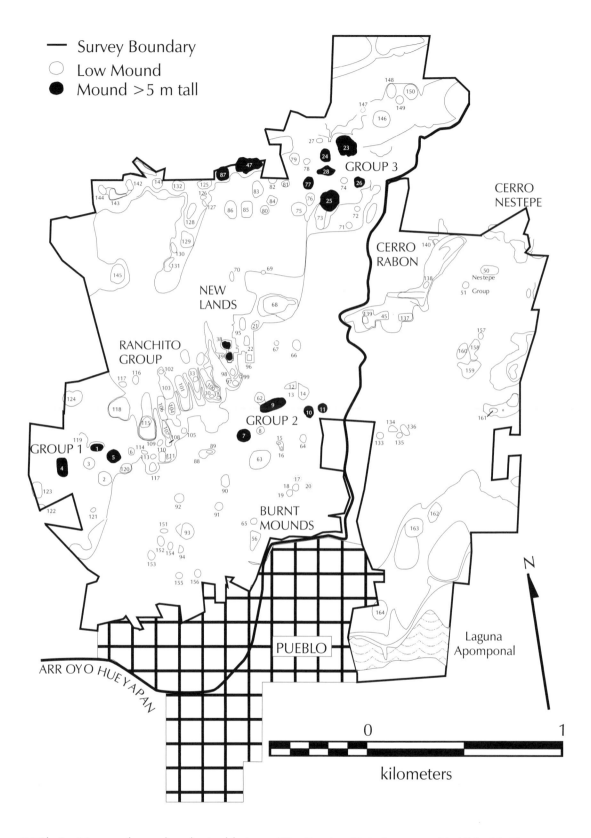

Figure 2.9 Planimetric map of mounds and natural features at Tres Zapotes. *Illustration prepared by Michael A. Ohnersorgen, Christopher A. Pool, and Kurt Rademaker*

changed little since the abandonment of the site. To either side of the arroyo is a flat alluvial plain subject to periodic inundation. Natural terraces bound the plain to the east and west. A consolidated volcanic ash, or *laja,* underlies the lower terrace, which rests upon earlier, and apparently sterile, clays and gravels. Cerro Rabon, an isolated hill formed by the same laja, rises above the plain on the east bank of the arroyo. A second eminence, Cerro Nestepe, lies to the northeast of Cerro Rabon. A range of low hills extending southward from Cerro Nestepe bounds the site on its eastern margin.

DISTRIBUTION OF ARCHITECTURE

The survey detected 160 mounds, artificial terraces, and modified natural features, more than tripling the number of features previously identified. The largest mounds are concentrated in three major mound groups to the west of the arroyo (figure 2.9). The most westerly of these, group 1, consists of six prominent mounds on the lower stream terrace. Four mounds measuring 3 to 6 m tall define a plaza measuring 200 x 100 m, which is oriented in its longest dimension on a bearing of 84° east of true north. A low mound (mound 3) in the center of the plaza divides it into eastern and western halves of nearly equal size. Mound 6, which rises about 3 m above the terrace, flanks the eastern end of the group. Weiant (1943:2-3) called group 1 the "Cabeza Group" for the "Cabeza Colosal de Hueyapan" (monument A), which was discovered to the north of mound 2 (Weiant's mound B).

Group 2 contains four prominent mounds grouped around a large plaza on the alluvial plain about 1 km to the east of group 1. Mound 7, known locally as "Loma Camila" for a previous owner of the property, is the tallest mound at Tres Zapotes. It rises to 12 m on the western end of the plaza. Located about 300 m away on a bearing 80° east of true north, mounds 10 and 11 are about half the height of mound 7. A low mound on the plaza directly in front of mound 7 lies along the same bearing. Mound 8 is currently less than 1 m in height, but Weiant (1943:13) indicates that the original plaza surface lies below about 2 m of alluvium. The "Long Mound" (mound 9) stretches for 135 m along the northern edge of the plaza and rises to a height of 7 m. The southern edge of the plaza is defined by three to four low, irregularly placed mounds, including mounds 15 and 16, which appear to correspond to Weiant's mounds I and J. Originally, three mounds (12, 13, and 14) occupied the northeast corner of the group. Mound 13 was extensively excavated by Stirling and is no longer visible, except as a concentration of artifacts. It corresponds to Weiant's (1943:13) mound G, which contained a stone platform, the only example of stone architecture known from the site.

Group 3 occupies a commanding view on the upper terrace, about 1200 m northeast of group 2. Its plan diverges from those of groups 1 and 2 in that the principal mound is on the northern edge of the plaza and the plaza is oriented to an axis running approximately 9° east of true north. Four prominent mounds are clustered tightly around a small plaza, which measures about 100 m on a side and is delimited on the east by the edge of the terrace. Mound 23 is about 12 m tall and lies at the north edge of the plaza. Behind it to the north the terrace drops off steeply into a broad gully. The other three mounds enclosing the plaza (mounds 24, 26, and 28) measure between 3 and 7 m in height. Eight smaller mounds (29, 71, 72, 75, 76, 77, 78, and 79) cluster around the southern and eastern edges of the group, and two broad platforms (25 and 73) with heavy concentrations of material are located on the southern edge of the terrace.

Group 3 contained several other features of interest. The lower portion of stela C was discovered by Stirling directly south of mound 23. It was set on its side next to a circular altar. The upper half of the stela was found nearby thirty years later. In 1997 RATZ excavated a plain stela (monument 44) located about 10 m south of Stirling's excavation of stela C. Made of similar basalt, monument 44 was accompanied by offerings of obsidian and Terminal Formative pottery. A broken basalt column rests on the summit of mound 27 (Weiant's mound E), a small mound on the northern edge of the terrace. Two irregular rows of boulders extend down the southern face of the mound and appear to have functioned as a crude balustrade. Three other basalt columns are set in a small projection of the terrace that juts eastward from mound 26.

Three imposing mounds measuring 5 to 6 m tall are located on the east-west ridge to the west of group 3 (mounds 47, 87, and 132). The most easterly of these (47) has an irregular shape and very little cultural material, suggesting that it may be a natural feature. Mounds 38 and 39 to the northeast of the Ranchito group correspond to Weiant's Ranchito group mounds J and K. Their respective heights of 6 and 4 m are enhanced by their location on the edge of the upper terrace. To the northeast of these two mounds an isolated mesa (67) juts eastward from the upper terrace. This natural feature, which corresponds to Drucker's (1943a: Fig. 6) "steepto bluff" in the New Lands locality, is formed by a resistant laja cap. It contains high densities of cultural material, and its surface appears to have been heavily modified.

About 700 m to the west of the northwest corner of the survey area is a small mound group in which stela D was discovered. Although Stirling (1943:14) designated it Mound Group 4, artifact densities are very low between

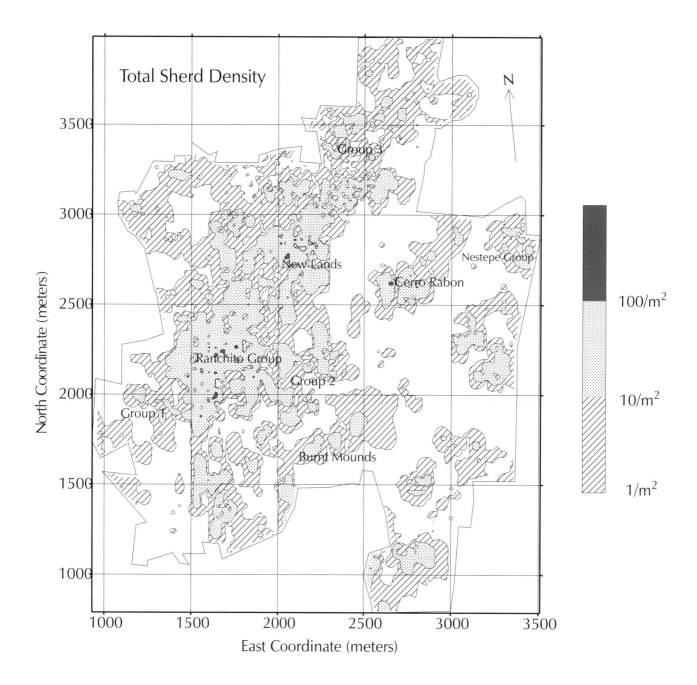

Figure 2.10 Map showing distribution of ceramic sherd frequencies in surface collections at Tres Zapotes. *Illustration prepared by Christopher A. Pool*

it and the survey area, and it should be considered an outlying settlement.

The most prominent feature to the east of the arroyo is Cerro Rabon. The southern end, which is lower than the northern end, was extensively filled and leveled to form a series of platforms on which low mounds were constructed. On the valley floor to the east of Cerro Rabon, the Nestepe group consists of a conical mound and an elongated mound on the western and northern sides of a small plaza, respectively. In this respect it repeats the layout of groups 1 and 2.

In addition to formal mound groups, RATZ detected over 100 low, presumably residential, mounds less than 2 m in height. Their residential function is supported by high frequencies of utilitarian ceramics in surface collections, as well as their relative abundance. The lengths and breadths of the 85 low mounds detected in the 1995 season average 55 m (± 28 m) and 38 m (± 18 m). By comparison, mounds less than 3.4 m high in the Mixtequilla average 41.9 (± 15.6 m) x 33.6 m (± 12.5 m), and individual house mounds at the lowland Maya site of Barton Ramie average about 21 x 20 m (Stark 1991:45). As in the Mixtequilla, low residential mounds at Tres Zapotes probably supported multiple structures, and they may have grown by horizontal as well as vertical accretion.

Low residential mounds are distributed in two broad zones. The northern zone comprises a series of residential terraces and platforms scattered along the ridge that extends westward from group 3. The southern zone encompasses the Ranchito, New Lands, and Burnt Mounds groups reported by Drucker but is more extensive, continuing to the south on the valley plain. Mounds in the Ranchito group are situated on five north-south trending ridges. Porter's (1989) map suggests that the ridges are artificial constructions, but Drucker (1943a:7) is probably correct that they were formed naturally by the erosion of shallow gullies between them. Their surfaces, however, were extensively modified for residential occupation.

DISTRIBUTION OF CERAMICS AND NON-MOUNDED RESIDENTIAL OCCUPATION

The distribution of visible architecture gives only a partial picture of settlement at Tres Zapotes. Heavy concentrations of ceramic artifacts occur on the alluvial terraces, particularly in the Ranchito group, and on Cerro Rabon (figure 2.10). A very heavy concentration of ceramics also occurs on the alluvial terrace between the Ranchito Group and Mound Group 3, in an area devoid of residential mounds. Moreover, moderate ceramic densities of 10 to 100 sherds per collection occurred over an extensive area of the upper terrace between the northern and southern zones of residential con-

struction, suggesting that large portions of the site were occupied by non-mounded architecture. On the alluvial plain, high ceramic densities tend to occur on house mounds or in discrete circular concentrations, which may represent mounds flattened by decades of plowing in sugarcane fields. In this respect it is worth noting that five of the seven mounds identified by Drucker (1943: Fig. 9) in the Burnt Mounds group no longer exist as anything more than artifact concentrations. Furthermore, low artifact densities on the alluvial plain should not be taken as conclusive evidence of less intensive occupation; Drucker's (1943:29-34) excavations in the Burnt Mounds group revealed deep sherd-bearing deposits below 3 to 4 m of sterile alluvium and volcanic ash.

As Hoag (chapter 4) discusses, the spatial pattern of residential occupation suggested by house mounds and ceramics is generally supported by surface frequencies of daub (see also Hoag 1997: Fig. 5.1, 5.2). Daub is found in highest frequencies in areas with moderate to high ceramic frequencies and is strongly associated with low mounds. Significantly, daub is not found in high frequencies on tall mounds that appear to have functioned as temple platforms.

Ceramic Chronology

Our reconstruction of settlement history at Tres Zapotes relies on changing distributions of temporally diagnostic ceramic categories. Previous research at Tres Zapotes has produced three ceramic chronologies, each based on different data sets and different ceramic classifications (Drucker 1943a; Weiant 1943; Ortiz 1975), as well as an important revision of Drucker and Weiant's chronologies by Coe (1965a) (figure 2.11). Each of these chronologies presents its own set of problems as a basis for reconstructing settlement history.

PREVIOUS CHRONOLOGIES

Weiant's (1943) sequence utilized collections from nonstratigraphic excavations and was based on typological comparisons with then-better-known sequences in the Maya lowlands, Central Mexico, Oaxaca, and central and northern Veracruz. Weiant divided his sequence into Middle Tres Zapotes A, Middle Tres Zapotes B (both Protoclassic), and Upper Tres Zapotes (Classic), naming his phases in deference to Drucker's (1943a) analysis, which was proceeding at the same time.

Drucker's (1943a) sequence utilized materials from five stratigraphic excavations. He identified a Lower Tres Zapotes phase sealed below a volcanic ash deposit that preceded Middle Tres Zapotes, and he distinguished a Postclassic Soncautla Complex, which had been lumped with Upper Tres Zapotes in

Chronological chart for the southern Gulf lowlands

Period (dates)	Weiant 1943	Drucker 1943	Coe 1965	This Study, Ortiz 1975	San Lorenzo (Coe and Diehl 1980, Symonds et al. 2002)	La Venta (Lowe 1989)	Central Tuxtlas (Pool and Britt 2000)	Mixtequilla (Stark 1998)
Early Postclassic (1000)		Soncautla	V	Soncautla				
Late Classic	Upper	Upper	IV	Quemado	Late Villa Alta		Late Classic	Late Classic
Early Classic (600)			III	Ranchito	Early Villa Alta / Ortices		Middle Classic / Early Classic	Early Classic
Terminal Formative (300, 100)	Middle B / Middle A	Middle	II	Nextepetl	Early to Middle Classic		Late Bezuapan	Terminal Preclassic
A.D. / B.C. — Late Formative (400, 500)		Lower	I	Hueyapan	Remplas	IV	Early Bezuapan	Late Preclassic (Pozas)
Middle Formative				Tres Zapotes	Palangana / Nacaste	III / II / I	Middle Formative	Middle Preclassic
Early Formative (900)				"Ocos"	San Lorenzo / Chicharras / Bajio / Ojochi		Early Formative	

Figure 2.11 Chronological chart for the southern Gulf lowlands. *Illustration prepared by Christopher A. Pool*

Weiant's sequence. He was unable, however, to differentiate phases within the Formative Lower Tres Zapotes phase.

The simultaneous publication of Drucker's and Weiant's sequences in 1943 produced considerable confusion (Ekholm 1945; Wauchope 1950) that ended in a rancorous debate between the principals (Drucker 1952; Weiant 1952). In 1965, Coe modified Drucker's sequence on the basis of typological correlations with more recently established sequences, subdividing Upper Tres Zapotes into Early and Late Classic phases. These became Tres Zapotes III and IV in his revised five-phase scheme. Despite the importance of Coe's revision, he unfortunately introduced some confusion by mistakenly replacing Drucker's (1943a) Tres Zapotes phases with his Cerro de las Mesas phases (Drucker 1943b) in a key table (Coe 1965a:686). Coe's (1965a:703) statement that the Early Classic period was never very important at Tres Zapotes appears to be the result of misinterpreting Drucker's "Polychrome" ware, which includes all untempered pottery regardless of their decoration, including several types that subsequent excavation in the region have shown to be Early Classic.

In order to refine the Formative chronology of the site, Ponciano Ortiz excavated a single test pit next to Drucker's trench 26, which had produced the Lower Tres Zapotes materials. In his 1975 thesis, Ortiz succeeded in dividing Lower Tres Zapotes into a Middle Formative Tres Zapotes phase and a Late Formative Hueyapan phase. He also identified a Protoclassic Nextepetl phase, broadly equivalent to Middle Tres Zapotes of both Weiant (1943) and Drucker (1943a). Ortiz further subdivided his phases into A and B subphases.

Two other small studies of Tres Zapotes chronology from the early 1980s deserve mention. Chase's 1981 article argued that the eruption evidenced by the volcanic ash that overlay Drucker's Lower Tres Zapotes occurred about 600 BC and caused a substantial hiatus at the site. Our research indicates that Chase was incorrect on both counts. In 1982, Ann Cyphers reinterpreted Drucker's material from trench 1 in the light of Ortiz's chronology at Tres Zapotes and her own ceramic analysis at Chalcatzingo. She confirmed Ortiz's relative stratigraphy and concluded that his Tres Zapotes A phase corresponded to the Cantera phase at Chalcatzingo (700–500 BC) and the Palangana phase at San Lorenzo and so overlapped with the La Venta sequence. Later Cyphers (1987:249) suggested that Tres Zapotes A and B corresponded to the San Lorenzo phase at San Lorenzo because of the presence of Calzadas Carved and Limon Carved-Incised sherds. These types are exceedingly rare at Tres Zapotes, though, and while they may indicate a sparse Early Formative occupation, they may also be reflecting the persistence of earlier decorative techniques, as in the "miscellaneous carved" sherds of the

Nacaste phase at San Lorenzo (see Coe and Diehl 1980a:198–199).

Most recently, Lowe (1989:57, Table 4.1) reassigned Ortiz's Hueyapan and Nextepetl phases to 600 to 300 BC and after 300 BC, respectively, on the basis of the reported association of polished orange ware with the Hueyapan phase (Ortiz 1975:80–81; 107–112; 117). Pool (2000a) adopted Lowe's chronology in a recent publication, but evidence from the auger tests discussed by Wendt in the next chapter suggests that Ortiz's original dates for his phases were closer to the mark.

RATZ CERAMIC CLASSIFICATION AND CHRONOLOGY

The RATZ ceramic classification is based on that developed for the nearby site of Matacapan by Ponciano Ortiz and Robert S. Santley (1988). The advantages of this classification over previous ones developed for Tres Zapotes include its finer typological divisions, its long temporal span, and its association with radiocarbon-dated stratigraphic levels at Matacapan and Bezuapan (Pool and Britt 2000). Moreover, comparisons with Ortiz's Formative sequence at Tres Zapotes are facilitated by his participation in developing the Matacapan classification.

Our division of the temporal sequence at Tres Zapotes into phases is based on quantitative analyses of ware, type, and variety frequencies in our surface collections and auger tests and typological comparisons with published sequences from Tres Zapotes (principally Ortiz 1975), Matacapan (Ortiz and Santley 1988), Bezuapan (Pool and Britt 2000), San Lorenzo (Coe and Diehl 1980a), and the Mixtequilla (Stark 2000). The analysis of ceramic frequencies in the surface collections utilized multidimensional scaling (Pool and Wendt 2000). Wendt describes his K-means cluster analysis of stratigraphic units in the auger tests in chapter 3. Because of the considerable continuity between phases in ceramic categories and the locations of settlement, few index types are identifiable at Tres Zapotes. Consequently, our evaluation of changing settlement patterns relies on distributions of ceramic categories that show strong, but not exclusive, associations with specific time spans.

For the Formative sequence we utilize Ortiz's (1975) phase designations with the following time spans: Tres Zapotes (Middle Formative, 900–400 BC), Hueyapan (Late Formative, 400 BC–AD 100), and Nextepetl (Terminal Formative or Protoclassic, AD 100–300) (figure 2.11, compare Pool 2000a:Table 1). Currently, the most problematic part of the sequence concerns the Hueyapan-Nextepetl phase transition. Although we would not be surprised to find that the transition occurred as early as 100 BC, we do not at present have strong evidence that would refute Ortiz's AD 100 estimate. To avoid confusion between Ortiz's Middle Formative period Tres Zapotes phase and Coe's Classic period Tres Zapotes III and Tres Zapotes IV phases, we propose two new designations: Ranchito (Early Classic, AD 300–600) and Quemado (Late Classic, AD 600–900). We also retain Drucker's original designation of the "Soncautla Complex" for an ephemeral Early Postclassic occupation (circa AD 1200), represented primarily in shallow cremation burials.

Settlement History

The following reconstruction of settlement history at Tres Zapotes considers variable frequencies of rim sherds belonging to temporally diagnostic categories in surface collections together with deposits belonging to each phase as determined in auger tests (figures 2.12 through 2.16). This discussion anticipates Wendt's detailed discussion of auger test stratigraphy in this volume. We map rim sherd frequencies rather than total sherd frequencies in order to include data from systematic transect collections, the body sherds from which detailed classification awaits. The resulting contour maps of surface sherd densities should not be interpreted as snapshots of settlement at precise points in time. Rather, they represent the current surface distribution of diagnostic sherds, most of which accumulated during the phase indicated in each map. Variations in surface sherd densities probably reflect real differences in the intensity of occupation within phases on elevated terrain. On the alluvial plain, however, the depth of overlying deposits and the incorporation of earlier material in mound fill strongly influences differences in sherd densities. Care should also be taken in comparing absolute sherd densities between phases, because the percentage of diagnostic sherds, even in unmixed assemblages, varies from one phase to another. As a result, the overall distribution of materials is more significant than differences in sherd density in interphase comparisons. Nonetheless, significant changes in settlement patterns may be discerned through a judicious evaluation of surface and subsurface artifact distributions.

The earliest evidence for occupation in our survey area dates to the Early Formative period (1500–900 BC). Surface collections yielded a very few sherds with decoration resembling Chaya Punctate, a diagnostic type of the Ojochi and Bajío phases at San Lorenzo (1500–1250 BC) (Coe and Diehl 1980a:138, 144, Figs. 101, 111). This corroborates Ortiz's (1975:132) recovery of a few redeposited sherds he assigned to a generalized Ocós or Ojochi horizon. Evidence for a ceramic component comparable to the Chicharras and San

Lorenzo phases (1250–900 BC) is similarly scarce at Tres Zapotes, consisting of a handful of sherds corresponding to the types Calzadas Carved, Limon Carved-Incised, and Tatagapa Red at San Lorenzo (Coe and Diehl 1980a:162–175, Figs. 132, 138–145). Moreover, neither Drucker (1943a) nor Weiant (1943) illustrates any clearly Early Formative pottery from Stirling's excavations. It appears, then, that any Early Formative occupation at Tres Zapotes must be deeply buried, and it is probably very small.

The Middle Formative period (900–400 BC) saw the first substantial settlement at Tres Zapotes. The largest concentration of Tres Zapotes phase ceramics lies on the alluvial terraces of the Ranchito group and extends eastward under the modern floodplain (figure 2.12). Evidence from the auger tests and our revised definition of Tres Zapotes phase diagnostics increases the estimated extent of this center to 80 ha, doubling our previous estimate (compare Pool 2000a:145). Several concentrations of Tres Zapotes phase pottery surrounding the center suggest the existence of rural homesteads and villages. The largest of these, revealed only by auger tests, covered about 15 ha on the opposite bank of the Arroyo Hueyapan. The remaining concentrations cover less than 5 ha.

Direct evidence for monumental mound construction during the Tres Zapotes phase is currently lacking. Of the fourteen mounds excavated by Stirling, only mound 5 in group 1 contained a possible Middle Formative construction stage, and its dating is uncertain (Pool 2000a:145; Weiant 1943:6–7). Nevertheless, some leveling and filling of the upper terrace in the Ranchito group may have begun in the Tres Zapotes phase. If correct, this emphasis on landscape modification instead of formal mound construction would parallel the case of the Early Formative Olmec center at San Lorenzo, as recently presented by Cyphers (1997:98, 102–106).

The stylistically Olmec sculpture from Tres Zapotes probably corresponds to this Middle Formative occupation. These sculptures include two colossal heads (monuments A and Q) and four full-round statue fragments (monuments H, I, J, and M). Most scholars now concur that the colossal heads constituted portraits of rulers who commissioned them as symbols of their authority (Grove 1981; Lowe 1989:45). Although many regard all Olmec colossal heads as an Early Formative sculptural type (for example, Lowe 1989:43; Clewlow 1974:28, Table 5), prior to the Middle Formative period there is simply no evidence of a center at Tres Zapotes large enough to have been the seat of a ruler or of a population numerous enough to have provided the labor necessary to transport these massive monuments. Stela A bears close thematic and iconographic resemblances to La Venta stelae 2 and 3 (Pool 2000a:149). This 5 m tall monument depicts a central figure flanked by two smaller figures in a niche with late Olmec-style "monster" masks above and below (see Pool 2000: Fig. 11). Although Pool (2000a:149) has previously discussed it as a Late Formative monument, stela A, which Stirling found to the north of group 2, may date to late in the Tres Zapotes phase, as may a basalt column enclosure in group 2, excavated by Millet (1979), which resembles tombs in La Venta Complex A.

Considering the presence of such massive stone monuments, the lack of conclusive evidence for investment in formal mound construction in Middle Formative Tres Zapotes is surprising. These interpretations, however, recall Cyphers's (1997:112) recent finding that formal mound complexes at San Lorenzo were constructed centuries after the fluorescence that produced the numerous colossal heads and other stone monuments at that site.

We defer detailed discussion of settlement organization during the site's Late to Terminal Formative apogee to the last chapter. In broad terms, during the Late Formative Hueyapan phase (400 BC–AD 100), the Tres Zapotes center and its rural satellites grew and coalesced to achieve a maximum extent of about 500 ha (figure 2.13). Auger tests and surface collections document heavy Hueyapan phase occupation of the floodplain and adjacent terrace margins, and surface collections with moderate frequencies of Hueyapan phase diagnostics extend westward over the terrace surfaces. The initial stages of mound construction in groups 1, 2, and 3 and in the Ranchito group, as well as four buried mounds detected by the auger tests, appear to date from the Hueyapan phase (Drucker 1943a:25–27, 144–145; Weiant 1943:6–7, 11–13; chapter 3). Most of the stone monuments at Tres Zapotes, including several tenoned monuments, stone boxes, stone cylinders, and stela D of the outlying group 4, were probably carved during the Hueyapan phase. If the AD 100 date for the end of Hueyapan phase is accepted, then stela C, with its 32 BC Long Count date, would also fall within this time span. Thematic and stylistic continuity with Olmec sculpture is found in the stylized monster mask and profile head on the reverse of stela C and in the placement of the human figures on stela D in a niche formed by the open maw of a feline (Pool 2000a:149–150).By the beginning of the Terminal Formative Nextepetl phase (circa AD 100–300), settlement had begun to withdraw from the banks of the Arroyo Hueyapan (figure 2.14). Large portions of the floodplain now lay abandoned, although occupation continued on elevated "cultural terraces," which had accumulated in the previous period and on the now-buried first terrace stair along the edges of the floodplain (see chapter 3). This reorganization of settlement caused a slight reduction in the total area of residential occupation, but the Ranchito group and group 2 continued to form the core of the site, and areas of concentrated residential settlement persisted in the Burnt Mounds group, the New Lands group, group 3, and Cerro Rabon.

The dispersed pattern of formal architectural groups begun in the Hueyapan phase persisted as mound construction continued in groups 1, 2, and 3, as well as at least one mound buried beneath alluvium on the floodplain (chapter 3). The only monument we can confidently associate with the Nextepetl phase is monument 44. This plain stela, excavated in 1997 in group 3, was associated with a differentially fired bowl covered by a plate of the same ware. The bowl contained charcoal dated at 1870± 50 BP (cal 2σ AD 55–250).

A volcanic eruption near the end of the Nextepetl phase accelerated the abandonment of the floodplain, such that no substantial deposits of the Early Classic Ranchito phase (AD 300–600) were present in our floodplain auger tests (see chapter 3) (figure 2.15). The distribution of Ranchito phase diagnostic sherds in surface collections further indicates that Early Classic residential settlement was reorganized into discontinuous zones along the natural terraces and on the southern floodplain separated by areas of sparser habitation. Intensification of residential occupation is particularly evident in the New Lands locality, and Drucker (1943a:12–19, 29–31, 98–100, 109–114) excavated substantial Early Classic contexts in the eponymous Ranchito group and in the Burnt Mounds group. Stirling's excavations in groups 1, 2 and 3 indicate continued massive construction in these formal complexes, suggesting that Tres Zapotes continued to serve as an important regional center in the Early Classic period (Weiant 1943:6–15). Monumental stone carving appears to have ceased by this time, although earlier monuments may have continued to be used and reset.

Tres Zapotes declined over the course of the three centuries following AD 600. Initially, Quemado phase occupation was concentrated in the same areas along terrace edges and on the southern floodplain to the west of the Arroyo Hueyapan as in the Ranchito phase (figure 2.16). Notably, Drucker (1943a:29–30, Plates 10,11) recovered a substantial cache of Late Classic Tuxtlas polychrome pottery in the Burnt Mounds group, and figurines of the Late Classic, hollow, mold-made San Marcos type are fairly common at the site. Occupation to the east of the arroyo was reduced, however, and by the end of the phase Tres Zapotes apparently lay abandoned.

Drucker (1943a:102–107) also isolated an Early

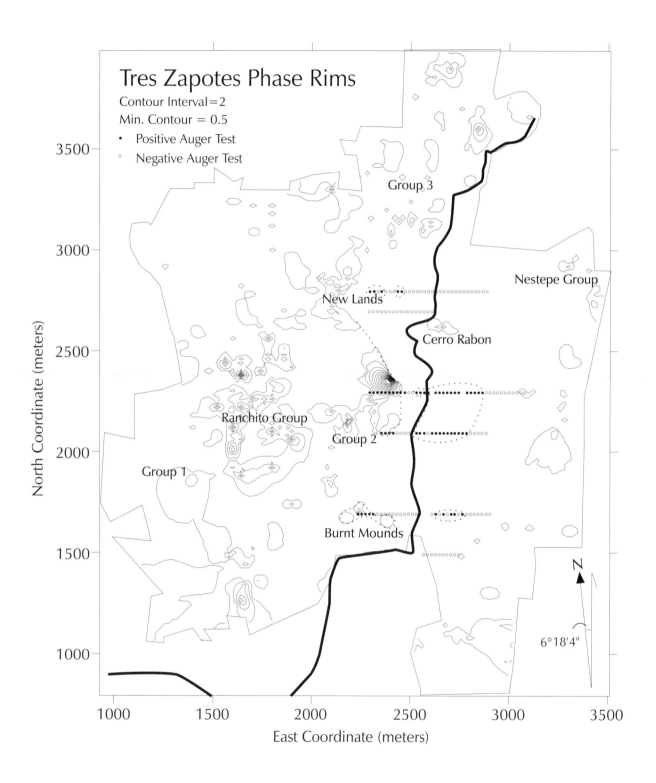

Figure 2.12 Map showing distribution of Tres Zapotes-phase ceramics in surface collections and auger tests containing Tres Zapotes-phase deposits. *Illustration prepared by Christopher A. Pool*

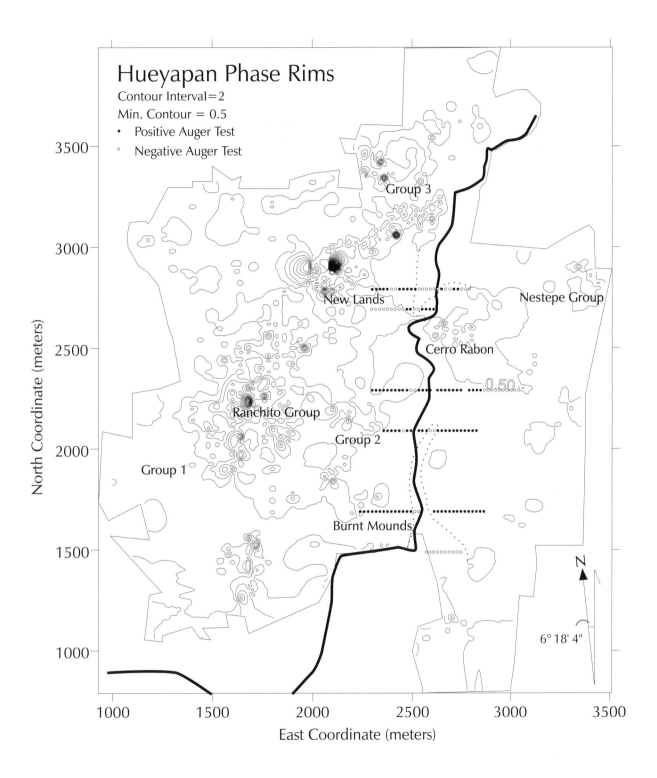

Figure 2.13 Map showing distribution of Hueyapan-phase ceramics in surface collections and auger tests containing Hueyapan-phase deposits. *Illustration prepared by Christopher A. Pool*

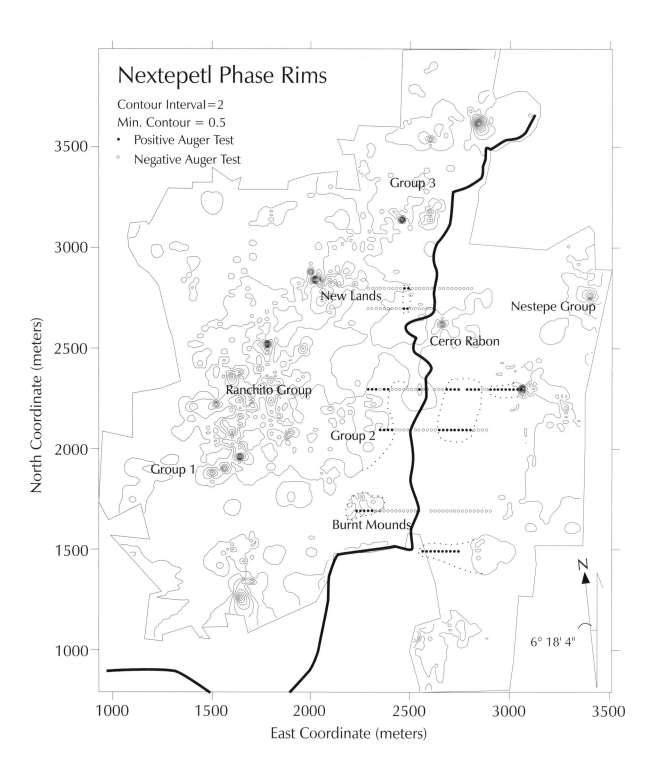

Figure 2.14 Map showing distribution of Nextepetl-phase ceramics in surface collections and auger tests containing Nextepetl-phase deposits. *Illustration prepared by Christopher A. Pool*

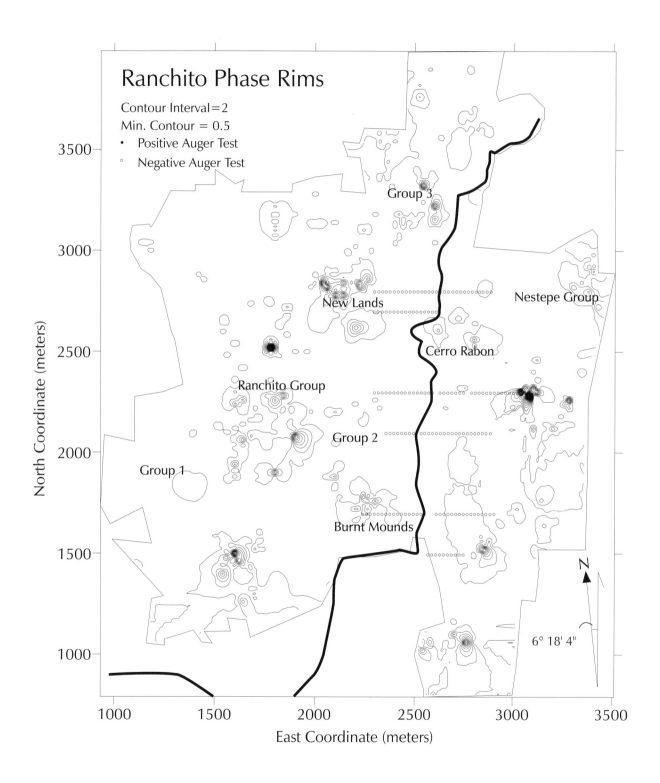

Figure 2.15 Map showing distribution of Ranchito-phase ceramics in surface. *Illustration prepared by Christopher A. Pool*

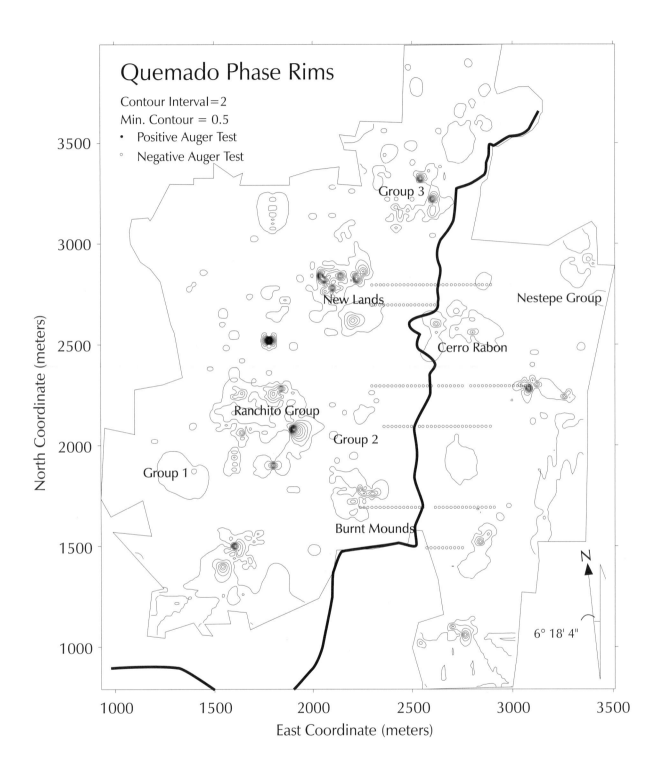

Figure 2.16 Map showing distribution of Quemado-phase ceramics in surface collections. *Illustration prepared by Christopher A. Pool*

Postclassic Soncautla Complex associated with shallow cremation burials that intruded into a humus-stained clayey surface layer, which overlay Classic period deposits. Extensive occupational deposits associated with the Soncautla Complex were not found by the National Geographic-Smithsonian project (Drucker 1943a:116). These observations, in combination with the distinctive forms and decorative motifs of the pottery, led Drucker to conclude that the Soncautla Complex represented a brief intrusion into the site following its abandonment in the Late Classic period. We have not yet been able to isolate the Soncautla Complex in our surface collections, a fact that tends to corroborate Drucker's characterization of the occupation. It is worth remarking that in general the identification of Postclassic occupation in the Tuxtlas region has proven very difficult, possibly owing to the continuation of Late Classic forms and wares in the domestic pottery assemblage (Pool 1995a).

Summary

The RATZ project employed a combination of full-coverage and systematic transect survey methods to obtain data on settlement patterns that could be compared to previous surveys in the southern Gulf lowlands in the Mixtequilla and at Matacapan. These two strategies have different advantages and disadvantages in terms of labor costs, data recovery, and interpretive possibilities. Empirical comparison of the effectiveness of the two strategies in detecting archaeological features at Tres Zapotes highlights their complementary nature. While full-coverage survey ensures the detection of household-scale features, subjective judgments of artifact density in the field may underestimate the extent of artifact concentrations. In contrast, surface collection employing systematic transect methods provides a quantitative baseline for judging artifact densities, which help define site boundaries through trend surface analysis. They substantially underrepresent, however, features smaller than the transect interval. These observations underscore the importance of carefully considering the effects of differential field methods in the initial design of surveys and the comparison of their results.

Substantively, the RATZ survey provides the first detailed picture of the history of settlement at Tres Zapotes. Located on the western frontier of the Olmec heartland, the area that would later become Tres Zapotes supported only a sparse Early Formative occupation. During the Middle Formative period, however, the Arroyo Hueyapan valley attracted Middle Formative Olmec settlers, who were likely drawn to the location by its abundance of fertile agricultural land and hard, volcanic stone for grinding implements. These people established a moderately sized, but politically important, Olmec center. We believe that it was the rulers of this Middle Formative center, rather than their less numerous and less powerful Early Formative predecessors, who commissioned the colossal heads and other Olmec monuments found at the site. As the eastern Olmec center of La Venta declined at the advent of the Late Formative period, Tres Zapotes prospered and grew to become the preeminent Epi-Olmec center east of the Río Papaloapan. Her rulers embarked on a program of mound building and intensified monument carving to express and legitimize their authority, drawing upon and modifying earlier Olmec themes. The persistence of many ceramic categories similarly suggests considerable cultural continuity from Olmec to Epi-Olmec times. Surviving a substantial Terminal Formative eruption, Tres Zapotes remained a center of administrative power, despite a reduction of population, into the Early Classic period. The Late Classic period, however, saw the diminishment and ultimate abandonment of Tres Zapotes.

BURIED OCCUPATIONAL DEPOSITS AT TRES ZAPOTES

The Results of an Auger Testing Program

Carl J. Wendt

In cases where natural and cultural deposits obscure earlier traces of occupation, some form of subsurface testing is necessary to acquire diachronic information on settlement organization. While such conditions occur throughout the world, they have recently received particular attention from archaeologists working in the neotropical lowlands, where extensive floodplains are a common feature of the landscape (Erickson 1995; Siegel 1995; Zeidler 1995). This chapter describes how a program of auger testing was used to elucidate settlement patterning in areas of Tres Zapotes where deep alluvium and volcanic ash cover earlier archaeological deposits. By combining these data with those of the larger Tres Zapotes data set, we arrived at a more complete representation of site organization during different occupational phases (see chapter 2). Thus the auger testing program provided valuable information on changing patterns of settlement at Tres Zapotes, the type of data that are often difficult to acquire through surface survey procedures alone.

Background

Analysis of distributional data from the first season of the RATZ project revealed large areas of the Arroyo Hueyapan floodplain in which surface artifact densities were low or nil (Pool 1997c, see chapter 2), corroborating observations of earlier researchers (Drucker 1943a:31–34, Figs. 9, 10; Weiant 1943:13). Philip Drucker (1943a:29–31), the first archaeologist to excavate stratigraphically at Tres Zapotes, identified Classic and Formative period deposits buried below sterile alluvium in the Burnt Mounds group, at the southern end of the floodplain (figure 3.1). Additionally, in separate cuts into the river bank on the adjacent valley plain, both Drucker (1943a:31–34) and Ponciano Ortiz (1975:35–36) located substantial deposits of ceramics dating to the Formative period

situated below 4 to 5 m of nearly sterile alluvium and volcanic ash. These data indicated that there was likely a significant buried prehistoric component at the site of Tres Zapotes which could not be identified by adhering to surface survey procedures. Consequently, during the second season of RATZ, Pool implemented an auger testing program to determine the extent of the buried occupational layers on the site's floodplain.

Auger Testing

Systematic subsurface testing to detect buried deposits is not common in Mesoamerican surveys. Nonetheless, some researchers in lowland Mesoamerica and other neotropical lowland regions have employed a variety of subsurface testing techniques, including shovel test pits (Zeidler 1995), postholing (Fry 1972; Scarborough 1983:736; Sheets et al. 1985), large vehicle-mounted mechanical augers (Siegel 1995), and hand-driven bucket augers (Erickson 1995:83, Fig. 3.8; Howell 1993). Owing to the great depth of the target deposits at Tres Zapotes and our desire to retain some control over vertical stratigraphy, we chose manual augering over other methods.

FLOODPLAIN TESTS

Pool designed the RATZ auger testing strategy to efficiently provide a statistically valid sample of subsurface deposits in the valley plain. Auger transects crossing the valley floor were chosen using a stratified random sampling strategy. The valley plain was divided into six east-west, 300 m wide bands, each containing three potential transects 100 m apart. One transect was then randomly selected from the three, and auger tests were positioned along it systematically at 20 m intervals. The transects were aligned with the site grid and are identified by their north coordinates (North-1500, North-1700, North-2100, North-2300 North-2700, and North-2800) (figure 3.2).

The length of each transect was predetermined by examining the 1995–1996 surface survey data in order to locate the areas on the floodplain which lacked visible mounds and where densities of surface material dropped off significantly. The transects ranged from 100 to 800 m long and contained from 10 to 39 tests. In all, 149 flood-plain tests were completed, 25 in the 1996 season and 124 in the 1997 season.

Auger tests were dug in 20 cm arbitrary levels using manually driven augers with bucket diameters of 10 cm. Early in the 1997 season we bent a section of the auger shaft in completing a test to 8 m. Subsequently, to prevent damage to the equipment and to conserve time, tests were completed to sterile deposits or a maximum depth of 6 m, except where impenetrable deposits, cave-ins, or groundwater prevented further boring. The depth of soil changes occurring within a single 20 cm bucket interval could be identified within about 10 cm. The soil extracted from each level was examined by hand for its color, composition, structure, and content of cultural material. The cultural material was then separated, bagged, and labeled in the field for later analysis. Soil samples were taken of every stratum encountered and at every meter within thick strata to test for the degree and nature of par-ticle size sorting. Documentation was completed by record-ing all pertinent stratigraphic, artifact, and soil information onto field forms.

It is important to note that the auger testing program was designed to determine the proportion of the floodplain occupied at different times, rather than the precise spatial distribution of ancient occupation on the valley plain. Nev-ertheless, the 20 m spacing of the auger tests allowed us to identify large-scale changes in subsurface topography, includ-ing possible buried mounds and other elevated features.

CONTROL TESTS
In addition to the auger tests on the alluvial plain, fifteen control tests were placed in three areas of known surface material density to obtain data on the relationship between surface and subsurface ceramic densities. Owing to the strong positive skew of ceramic frequencies in surface collections, the tercile distribution was used to define low, medium, and high surface density classes. Surface collections from heavily alluviated floodplain contexts, which generally had counts of fewer than 10 sherds per 3 x 3 unit, were omitted from these calculations. Low density collections were thereby defined as fewer than 41 sherds, medium density as 41 to 156 sherds,

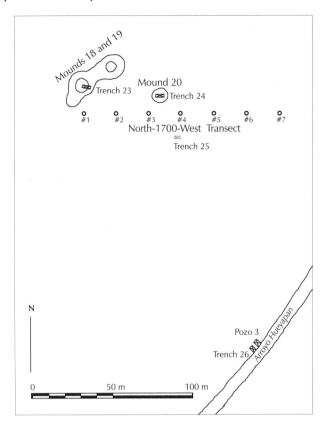

Figure 3.1 Burnt mounds locale showing Drucker's and Ortíz's trench locations and North-1700-West transect location.
Illustration prepared by Carl J. Wendt

and high density as greater than 156 sherds. As a result of this procedure, the low, medium, and high density areas se-lected for sampling were the group 1 plaza, the group 3 plaza, and the Ranchito group, respectively.

Five 3 x 3 m surface units were collected in each of these areas, and an auger test was placed in the southwest corner of each unit (figure 3.2). Since the density of artifacts in deep levels was irrelevant to the purpose of the control tests, we ceased boring at the arbitrary depth of 1 m in most of the tests. However, two of the tests in each group were com-pleted to sterile or impenetrable levels to examine the local stratigraphy. Comparison of ceramic densities in the control tests and their associated surface collections allowed us to estimate equivalent surface density figures for strata in the remaining auger tests. These data allowed us to infer relative occupational density on the floodplain in different phases.

Analytical Procedures
To infer changes in the extent and intensity of floodplain occupation at prehistoric Tres Zapotes, it was necessary to assign the strata encountered in the auger tests to phases. First we correlated strata between auger tests in each transect

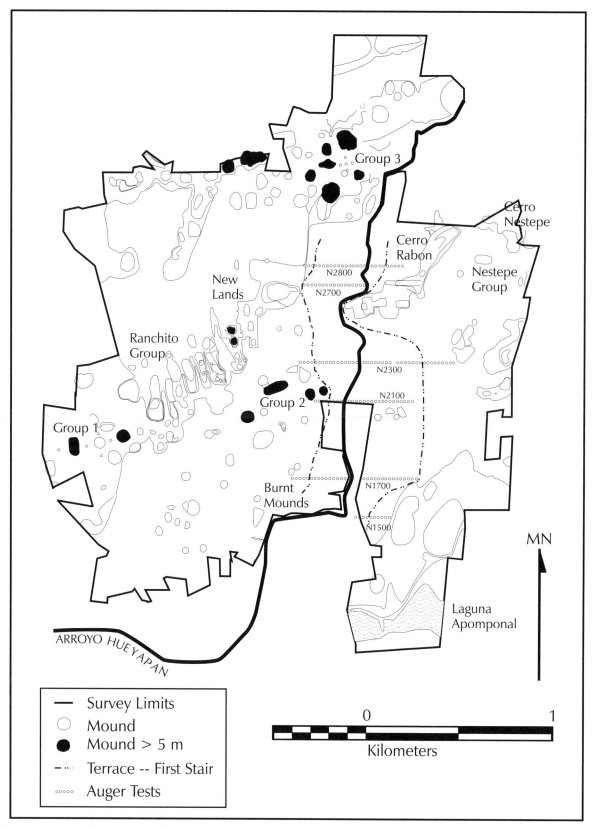

Figure 3.2. Map of Tres Zapotes showing auger test locations and extrapolated delineation of the terrace's first stair.
Illustration prepared by Michael A. Ohnersorgen, Christopher A. Pool, and Carl J. Wendt

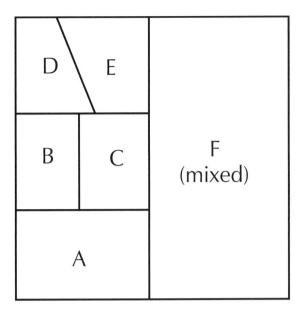

Figure 3.3 Schematic representation of stratigraphic relationships among K-means clusters. *Illustration prepared by Christopher A. Pool*

according to similarities in soil texture, color, composition, depth, thickness, and presence or absence of cultural material. In the field, as the tests were being dug, each supervisor attempted to correlate the strata as he or she drew each test's profile. Subsequently, all of the field forms and profiles were reanalyzed to refine the field correlations. In some areas, however, complex cultural stratigraphy frustrated attempts to establish detailed correlations between auger tests. Nevertheless, these problematic situations were relatively few, and it was possible to isolate many of these occurrences and treat them accordingly for the analyses.

The second procedure involved grouping ceramic counts from corresponding strata in the auger tests to increase sample size. This consisted of combining corresponding ceramic data in each transect with respect to each side of the river. The result was corresponding strata grouped in ten separate loci (North-1500, North-1700-West, North-1700-East, North-2100-West, North-2100-East, North-2300-West, North-2300-East, North-2700, North-2800-West, North-2800-East).

Strata were divided based on arbitrary levels in loci where correlations between strata could not be determined and in areas with deep sherd-bearing deposits where separate strata could not be identified. In both of these cases, the strata were divided in such a way as to maintain sufficiently high ceramic counts (> 95 sherds per division) so that they could be compared effectively with one another as well as to the remaining units. Additionally, ceramic data from separate

strata were combined where sample size was small (< 95 sherds per division) to increase sample size and provide effective comparisons to other divisions. These procedures resulted in 50 redefined stratigraphic units and allowed for temporal distinctions to be made with greater statistical confidence.

Once corresponding ceramic data were combined, they were subjected to a ceramic percentage frequency analysis and cluster analysis (Pool and Wendt 2000, Wendt 1998:68–70). First, the percent of each type was calculated for each stratigraphic unit. Very rare types and types that showed little variation between stratigraphic units were excluded from further analysis. The resulting data set, consisting of percentages for thirty-two ceramic types in fifty stratigraphic units, was subjected to a K-means cluster analysis using the SPSS statistical package (version 7.5, licensed to the University of Kentucky). The number of clusters varied between four and seven. The six-cluster solution was chosen because it conformed best to the depositional relationships of the strata. A separate hierarchical cluster analysis subsequently confirmed the validity of the six-cluster K-means solution. Using between-group average linkage and the Pearson's correlation distance matrix, the hierarchical cluster analysis reproduced the K-means clusters with seven exceptions (14% of the cases). Based on the hierarchical cluster analysis, two cases would be reassigned from the Middle Formative cluster A to the Late Formative cluster C, and four cases would be reassigned from the mixed cluster F to cluster C. (Phase assignments for clusters are discussed below.) Therefore, the K-means cluster analysis proved to be more conservative in assigning stratigraphic units to specific chronological phases.

Results from the ceramic percentage frequency analysis and cluster analysis, along with regional comparisons (mainly with the site of Bezuapan in the Sierra de los Tuxtlas) and three radiocarbon dates, allowed us to date roughly the floodplain strata and determine general patterns of settlement on Tres Zapotes's floodplain (Wendt 1998). The resulting clusters and their ceramic type associations are as follows (figure 3.3). For clarity I have changed my original nonsequential numeric designations to sequential alphabetic designations (compare Wendt 1998). Cluster A consistently contained units that occurred in the lowest stratigraphic position. Ceramics associated with this cluster consist of three types of coarse paste black ware, two differentially fired categories, and a white-slipped variety of Coarse Paste Black-and-Tan. Cluster A strata were usually overlain by strata falling into cluster B, which, based on ceramic frequencies and stratigraphic positioning, appears to be contemporaneous with strata grouping into cluster C. Strata grouping into clusters B and C are

North-1700-West

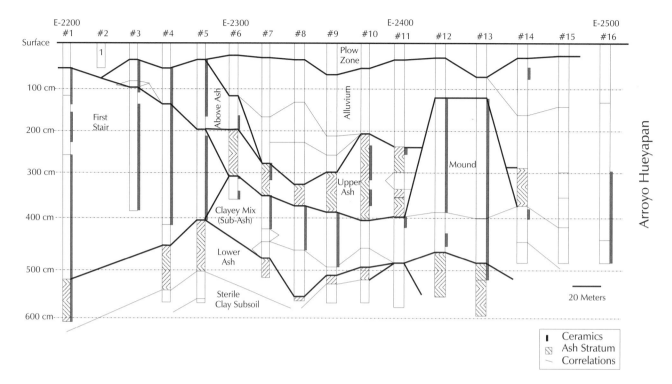

Figure 3.4 North-1700-West profile. *Illustration prepared by Carl J. Wendt*

strongly associated with Fine Paste Black-and-White, Fine Paste Black-and-Tan, unslipped varieties of Coarse Paste Black-and-Tan, Red on Coarse Brown, and White-slipped Coarse Red with Coarse White Temper ceramics. Clusters D and E contain stratigraphic units that appear to be generally contemporaneous with one another, although some strata grouping into Cluster E may be slightly younger. Cluster F appears to represent mixed deposits and is thus of little importance here.

Physical and Cultural Stratigraphy

The physical geography of Tres Zapotes comprises a series of floodplain terrace steps, natural eminences, various cultural modifications, and other alluvial and volcanic landforms. From the surface topography, previous scholars (Drucker 1943a:7; Stirling 1943:9; Weiant 1943:1) identified the terrace surrounding the Ranchito group and New Lands locale as the lowest terrace of the Arroyo Hueyapan. Our auger tests, however, revealed an additional terrace stair closer to the arroyo (figures 3.2, 3.4). This terrace stair, which is no longer visible owing to alluvial deposition on the valley plain, was surely important to those who lived in Tres Zapotes prior to the floodplain's more recent alluvial deposition. The edge of this first stair marks the point at which I delineate the

prehistoric boundary between the "floodplain" and the "elevated ground."

Six widespread strata comprise the generalized physical stratigraphy of the alluvial plain. From top to bottom, they are plow zone, alluvium, volcanic ash, a clayey mix deposited by cultural and natural processes, a lower volcanic ash, and sterile clay subsoil (figure 3.4). The sugarcane fields that cover much of the alluvial plain are plowed very deeply. Alternating plowing and alluviation created a disturbed layer that occasionally reached depths of 100 cm. This "plow zone" frequently overlay a 100 to 500 cm thick layer of brown silty clay and silty clay loam that contained few cultural materials. The structure and texture of this stratum suggests it was alluvially deposited, and some of the cultural material recovered from it seems to have been deposited by alluvial processes as well. In 52% of the auger tests, we encountered a black sandy volcanic ash stratum, which lay below the alluvial deposits. This layer ranged between 20 and 400 cm thick and at times contained cultural material. Its stratigraphic position indicates that it correlates with the volcanic ash found by Drucker (1943a) and Ortiz (1975) (figure 3.5). Where our equipment allowed us to penetrate below the ash layer (67% of the auger tests encountering ash or 35% of all tests), we often encountered a culturally rich clayey mix (clay, silty

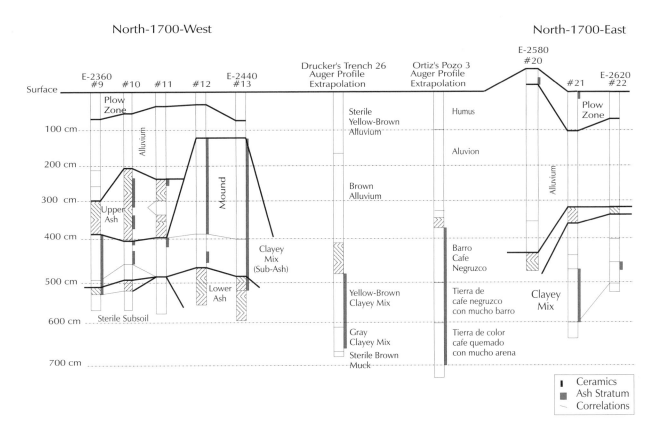

Figure 3.5 Correlation between Drucker's trench 26, Ortíz's pozo 3, and auger tests on the North-1700-West transect. *Illustration prepared by Carl J. Wendt*

clay, or clayey silt). A deeper ash layer, which was often hard, compacted, and generally devoid of cultural material, lay beneath the clayey mix. The seven tests that penetrated below this lower ash encountered sterile clay subsoil deposits.

In over one-third of the auger tests, it was not possible to reach a sterile stratum, and therefore we were not able to determine the maximum depth of the cultural deposits in those areas because of time constraints, concern for equipment damage, or strata too compact to penetrate or too loose to extract. Additionally, many tests reached the water table at depths between 4 and 6 m. This resulted in difficult augering conditions, including cave-ins of sandy ash and time-consuming cleaning of the equipment in clay deposits (see also Schuldenrein 1991; Stein 1986, 1991). Despite the difficulties, we were able to obtain valuable information on the stratigraphic and depositional characteristics of the areas tested.

The floodplain's stratigraphic signature indicates that both cultural occupation and natural processes played an active part in producing its subsurface stratigraphy. The distribution of cultural materials in auger tests indicates extensive occupation of the floodplain between the two volcanic ashfalls. We encountered cultural material in 89% of the au-

ger tests that penetrated below the upper ash (51% of all tests). The deepest cultural deposits on the valley plain, occurring between roughly 3 and 6 m in depth, often lay atop the lower ash. These early cultural deposits, which range between 1 and 3 m thick, represent remains of the floodplain's initial occupation. They are evident over much of the floodplain but appear to be concentrated in its southern portion, particularly between intermittent waterways and tributaries leading into the Arroyo Hueyapan. Mound construction appears to have commenced towards the end of this initial occupation. Unlike the non-mounded initial deposits, however, these 3 to 5 m tall buried mounds do not appear to be concentrated in any one portion of the valley floor (figures 3.4, 3.6). Eleven of the 149 tests encountered buried mounds, suggesting that 7.4% of the floodplain held mounded occupation.

In addition to the buried mounds, we encountered an extensive (approximately 300 m wide) and intensively occupied buried cultural terrace above the lower ash in the eastern portion of the N-2100 and N-2300 transects (figures 3.6, 3.7). We use the term *cultural terrace* to describe elevated and expansive occupational deposits containing complex stratigraphy. These areas appear to have been formed by the accretion of natural and cultural materials0 in a manner similar to the large house mounds that Barbara Hall describes as "tells in miniature" (1994). The cultural terraces at Tres Zapotes, however, are much larger. Their size, stratigraphy, and the presence of house construction material all provide evidence that they accumulated as the result of extensive residential occupation. The cultural terrace in question first dips and then rises as it approaches the arroyo. Cultural material is continuous throughout the 4 m thickness of its complex stratigraphy. Taking into consideration its extent and the persistence of cultural material, it was likely formed early and was continuously occupied for much of the site's temporal span.

Following the primary construction of the floodplain mounds and initial formation of the cultural terrace, Tres Zapotes was covered by sandy black volcanic ash (figures 3.4, 3.7). This primary ash layer seems to have subsequently eroded from the floodplain's elevated areas (for example, mounds, cultural terrace, and the first terrace stair), collecting in its lowest zones (for example, arroyo tributaries) and capping early deposits in several locations (see also Drucker 1943:33–34). Because of the inferred erosion and redeposition, it is difficult to determine the original thickness of this ash layer, but evidence suggests that it was at least 50 cm thick.

After the second ash fall, deposition of alluvial deposits gradually continued to build up the floodplain to its present level (figures 3.4, 3.7). Evidence for occupation on the floodplain is much more sparse in deposits occurring stratigraphically above the upper ash layer. Cultural material in alluvial strata surrounding the arroyo is nearly absent, and the few, often eroded, artifacts recovered from these loci were probably redeposited by the arroyo during seasonal floods. Areas of occupation appear to be limited to rises formed by natural and cultural processes, including the first terrace stair, mounded features, and accretional cultural terrace.

The alluvial strata begin to thin as they approach the elevated first stair of the natural terrace (figure 3.4). This first stair appears to delineate the extent of the major prehistoric floodplain and the point at which severe effects of alluvial deposition diminish significantly. Judging from its stratigraphic positioning and the amount of cultural material in its composition, this elevated first terrace step developed from centuries of natural deposition, river cutting, and cultural occupation, both before and after the upper ash deposition. Additionally, there is no stratigraphic evidence to support a cessation in the occupation on this terrace. The apparent continuous occupation indicates that the ash deposit had little effect on those living on this elevated ground. Judging from the scarcity of cultural material in layers stratigraphically above the ash deposits, the volcanic event seems to have significantly disrupted settlement on the valley floor (see also Drucker 1943a:34).

Temporal Assignments for Buried Features

The combined results of the ceramic frequency analysis, cluster analysis, and radiocarbon dating indicate that the majority of the occupation on the central valley floor dates to the Formative period (Pool and Wendt 2000). Three AMS radiocarbon dates were obtained from carbon samples recovered in the floodplain auger tests (table 3.1). Calibrated intercepts for these assays range from 485 BC to 375 BC , with calibrated two-sigma ranges from 775-390 BC to 400-190 BC. Unfortunately, two of the dates from the same auger test (samples Beta-115431 and Beta 115432) were stratigraphically reversed. Nevertheless, the dates generally confirm the Middle to Late Formative ages of the deposits below the upper ash (compare Bernal 1969:109; Chase 1981).

Comparison among the results of the cluster analysis, the percentage frequency analysis, Ortiz's (1975) ceramic stratigraphy, and cross correlation with other sites in the region (Coe and Diehl 1980a; Ortiz and Santley 1988; Pool and Britt 2000) permits the assignment of stratigraphic units and buried features to finer temporal divisions (Pool and Wendt 2000; compare Wendt 1998). These analyses indicate that the floodplain was occupied from the Tres Zapotes phase (cluster A) (900–400 BC) through the Hueyapan phase (clusters B and C) (400 BC–AD 100) and into the Nextepetl phase (clusters D and E) (AD 100–300). The following discussion, based solely on results from analyses of floodplain ceramic material, addresses the temporal affiliation of the deposits on the terrace's first stair, the various elevated features on the floodplain, and deposits not associated with elevated features.

Transects North-1500, North-1700-West, North-2100-West, North-2300-East, North-2300-West, North-2800-East, and North-2800-West all provided evidence for occupation on the buried first stair of the terrace. The deepest levels of this occupation date to the Tres Zapotes and Hueyapan phases and focused mainly on the west side of the arroyo. The upper levels of this occupation, detected only in one area (North-2100-West, tests 1–4), date to the Nextepetl phase.

The occupation on non-mounded areas of the prehistoric valley floor was clearly a pre-upper ash, Tres Zapotes and Hueyapan phase phenomenon. Nextepetl phase material, occurring in very small percentages, is restricted to the upper levels of the floodplain's mounded features, cultural

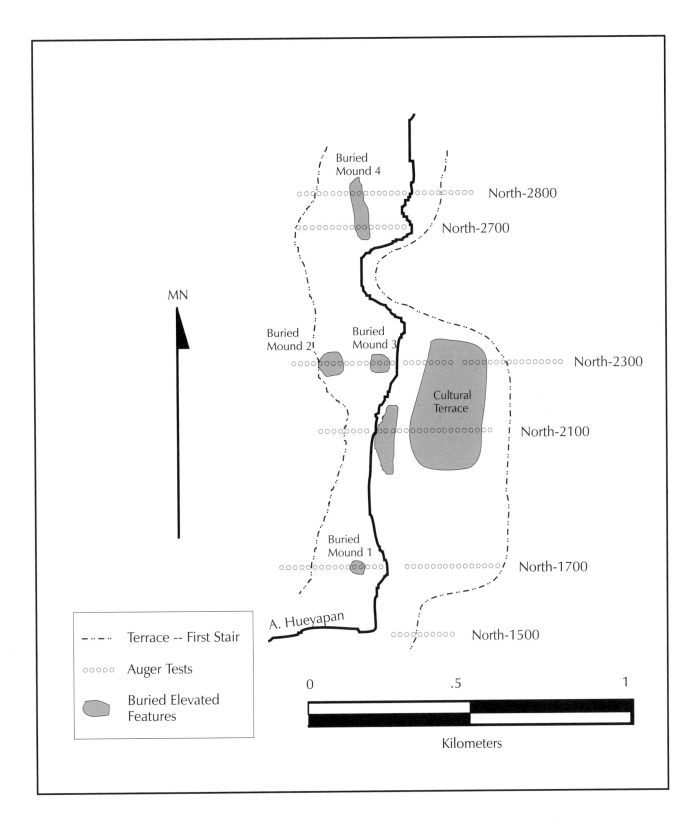

Figure 3.6 Extrapolated location of the buried floodplain mounded features. *Illustration prepared by Carl J. Wendt*

terrace, and first stair. All of the deposits that underlay the upper ash stratum contain only Tres Zapotes and Hueyapan phase material. This fact adds credence to the suggestions that the upper ash deposits predate the Classic period phases.

The following is a discussion of the suggested dates for the features and strata that lay on the prehistoric floodplain (figures 3.6, 3.8–3.10). Some of these features, which we label *mounds* and *cultural terraces*, may actually be the remains of one or more early occupied features that were delineated or perhaps cut by tributaries leading into the Arroyo Hueyapan.

Buried mound 1, detected in tests 12 and 13 of North-1700, contains material from the Hueyapan phase (figure 3.6). Dividing this mounded feature into three arbitrary levels did not produce evidence for a multiphase deposition. The remaining cultural deposits in this transect (all below the upper ash) date from the Tres Zapotes through the Hueyapan phase.

Moving north (North-2100), the second elevated feature detected on the valley floor was the southern portion of the expansive cultural terrace. Based upon ceramic material and one radiocarbon date, this feature dates from the Tres Zapotes phase through the Hueyapan phase and into the Nextepetl phase. Low ceramic frequencies prevent dating of the lowest deposits away from the first stair on the western portion of this transect. However, since these deposits lay below the upper ash, they probably date to the Tres Zapotes or Hueyapan phase.

Buried Mounds 2 and 3, which lay in the western portion of North-2300 (tests 5 through 8 and 13 through 15), are difficult to date because they are composed of stratigraphic units that grouped into cluster F and thus probably represent mixed deposits. The cultural terrace, located in the eastern portion of this transect (Cultural Terrace-North, likely the northern portion of the same cultural terrace located in North-2100), appears to have been occupied, and heavily built up, during the Hueyapan phase.

The last feature discovered on the floodplain was buried mound 4, encountered in tests on the North-2700 (tests 10 through 11) and North-2800 (tests 9 through 10) transects. Ceramic material recovered from deposits in the North-2700 tests provides evidence to suggest that this feature was constructed from Hueyapan phase (lowest deposits) and Nextepetl phase (uppermost deposits) materials. The northern portion of this mounded feature (mound 4b) exhibits only Hueyapan phase material. Therefore, the mound may have grown gradually toward the south through accretion.

Results of the auger testing program indicate the floodplain at Tres Zapotes was initially settled in the southern area sometime during the Tres Zapotes phase (figure 3.8).[1]

Between the Tres Zapotes phase and the Hueyapan phase occupation expanded northward. Occupation on the floodplain became most extensive during the Hueyapan phase (figure 3.9). By the Nextepetl phase, much of the floodplain was abandoned (figure 3.10). The only areas that remained occupied during the Nextepetl phase were the floodplain's highest areas (that is, the uppermost levels of the cultural terrace and mound 4). Additionally, it should be noted that daub and burnt earth were present in all the levels of the buried features, which suggests that these features were loci of residential occupation throughout their temporal spans.

Intensity of Floodplain Occupation

The density of ceramics for strata within the auger tests provides a relative measure of the intensity of occupation on the floodplain at different times in its history. Additionally, our control tests provide a basis for comparing ceramic densities for 20 cm levels within the auger tests with surface ceramic densities elsewhere in the site.

Before proceeding further, it is important to acknowledge some of the limitations of auger testing. First, sample sizes of cultural material in auger tests tend to be small. Out of the 164 auger tests we recovered around 7500 sherds (an average of 45 sherds per test). Second, utilizing the auger test method we were unable to distinguish with confidence house remains from midden debris in our samples. We noted the presence of daub and charcoal in our samples, but we were only able to associate these materials with large features such as mounds and cultural terraces, as opposed to individual house floors and middens. Finally, we encountered a small degree of mixing between 20 cm levels. However, this represented a very limited occurrence and, therefore, does not appear to have affected the overall results.

A series of potential problems must be discussed with regard to how auger testing methods may have affected the density results. Data recovered from the auger control tests in the "medium" density area (mound group 3) were found to be problematic. In this location, the areas exhibiting medium surface densities produced no subsurface material. It appears that the discrepancy between quantities of surface and subsurface material in this vicinity was the result of a superficial layer of slope wash originating from the mounds in this location. Since cultural material occurred only within the first few centimeters of soil, this area is not a reliable location for predicting subsurface densities from surface densities. Therefore, the data from these medium control tests were omitted from the linear regression.

In a study to determine the effectiveness of using auger testing to predict subsurface sherd density, Todd Howell

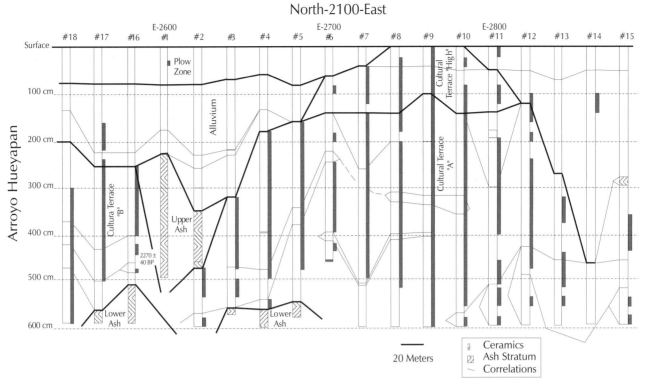

Figure 3.7 North-2100-East profile. *Illustration prepared by Carl J. Wendt*

Table 3.1 AMS radiocarbon dates

LAB #	C¹⁴ AGE*	CALIBRATED INTERCEPT	1-SIGMA RANGE	2-SIGMA RANGE	CONTEXT
Beta-115431	2430± 50 BP	485 BC & 465 BC & 425 BC	755-685 BC & 540-405 BC	775–390 BC	N-1700, Test 28, Stratum 3, 440-460 cm
Beta-115432	2270± 50 BP	375 BC	390-350 BC & 300-215 BC	400–190 BC	N-1700, Test 28, Stratum 4, 560-580 cm
Beta-115433	2270± 40 BP	375 BC	385-355 BC & 290-230 BC	395–200 BC	N-2100, Test 16, Stratum 6, 480-490 cm

* Conventional C¹⁴ age

(1993) highlighted several potential factors that may lead to inaccurate representations of subsurface material. Two of those factors apply here. First, Howell (1993:478–480) noted the propensity for the auger's bit to break sherds, thereby inflating ceramic counts. Second, he noted that the probability of acquiring an accurate indicator of subsurface density increases as the frequency of the sherds recovered in the auger bucket increases. This increased accuracy results from a reduction in sampling error.

We were able to reduce the possible effects of the increased ceramic counts by counting and weighing the sherds from each level. Therefore, the possibility of an accurate representation of the density of subsurface deposits was increased. However, ceramic counts turned out to be the more reliable measure for calculating surface density equivalents in the Tres Zapotes auger test data set. The fact that few sherds from the auger tests exhibited fresh fractures further suggests that breakage due to auguring did not inflate subsurface sherd frequencies.

With regard to Howell's second point, we noted that as surface sherd density increased, so did the probability that the first 20 cm of the auger test was able to reflect this change.

Table 3.2 Distribution of sherd densities by phase in positive auger tests

PHASE	LOW	LOW-MOD.	HIGH-MOD.	HIGH	MEAN	N
	1–5 (%)	5.01–10 (%)	10.01–15 (%)	>15(%)		
Nextepetl	57	14	21	7	6.37	14
Hueyapan	40	44	10	4	6.63	77
Tres Zapotes	59	32	5	5	4.98	22

Control tests having sherd counts of fewer than 10 sherds or ceramic weights less than 20 g per 20 cm level were not accurate indicators of surface sherd density. For example, a control test with 4 sherds in the first 20 cm had 573 sherds in its associated 3 x 3 surface collection unit, while a test with 9 sherds in the first 20 cm had only 2 sherds in its associated 3 x 3 surface collection unit. Nevertheless, we report these "low density" figures so as not to inflate our estimates of occupational intensity.

Despite these caveats, the linear regression analysis indicates a strong and significant relationship between subsurface and surface density levels ($r = 0.85$, $p < 0.004$). The regression formula is

$$y = -41 + 60x$$

where y is the surface sherd frequency and x is the sherd frequency in a 20 cm auger test level. Judging from the amount of ceramic material found in the floodplain strata, prehistoric occupation on the floodplain appears to have been quite intensive; 80% of the auger test levels assigned to temporal phases exhibited sherd densities equivalent to the upper tercile of surface sherd densities (>156 sherds per surface collection or >3.3 sherds per 20 cm auger test level). This relationship holds approximately for each phase identified in the auger tests. Seventy-nine percent of auger test levels assigned to the Tres Zapotes phase and about 84% of the levels assigned to the Hueyapan and Nextepetl phases have densities equivalent to the upper tercile of surface densities. Howell (1993) has pointed out that exceptionally high sherd densities are often associated with buried features. Howell's point is well taken and certainly applicable to portions of the cultural deposits we encountered, but it seems unlikely that 80% of the dated deposits we encountered were features. Nonetheless, we did encounter areas of extremely dense deposits within strata. For example, in a 20 cm level below the upper ash layer in North-2800, we collected 35 sherds, weighing 194 g. This is equivalent to a surface density of 2059 sherds in a 3 x 3 surface collection unit, which greatly exceeds the highest surface density of 1290 sherds encountered in the high-density Ranchito group area of the site.

Given the high densities overall in the dated auger test units, it was useful to create arbitrary divisions of auger test densities so as to assess relative intensities of occupation across the floodplain (figures 3.8 through 3.10). To do so, density figures were calculated for dated strata in each positive test. These figures, ranging from 1 to 28, represent the average number of sherds (given in a 20 cm level average) per test for each phase. Arbitrary cut points were established for low density (1 to 5 sherds), low-moderate density (5.01 to 10 sherds), high-moderate (10.01 to 15 sherds), and high density (more than 15 sherds).

Stratigraphic variations in sherd densities appear to reflect changing intensities of occupation on the floodplain (table 3.2). Mean sherd densities increased from the Tres Zapotes phase to the Hueyapan phase, then declined slightly in the Nextepetl phase. Similarly, the modal density of sherds shifted from low (59%) in the Tres Zapotes phase to low-moderate (44%) in the Hueyapan phase. In the Nextepetl phase, the modal sherd density shifted back to the low range (57%), but the Nextepetl phase also exhibits the highest proportion of cases in the high-moderate and high-density ranges. It is tempting to interpret this slightly bimodal distribution of sherd densities in the Nextepetl phase as reflecting more intensive maintenance of residential house lots with sherds being deposited in discrete dumps. However, it may be a consequence of the low sample size for the phase (N=14).

Distribution of Occupation

In addition to documenting overall changes in the proportion of the floodplain occupied and the relative intensities of occupation, the auger tests provide information on changes in the distribution of occupation on the Arroyo Hueyapan floodplain through time. These data complement the picture of changing settlement organization inferred from surface collections, as described in chapter 2.

Unfortunately, many of the auger tests did not reach levels deep enough to sample Tres Zapotes phase deposits. Nevertheless, based on analyses of the sample deposits, it is suggested that settlement on the floodplain during this phase was centered in the southern portion and was not as intense as in later phases (figure 3.8). The construction of the buried mounded features on the floodplain cannot be assigned to the Middle Formative period, because Tres Zapotes phase ceramics in these mounds are mixed with Hueyapan and Nextepetl phase materials, probably owing to the excavation of earlier deposits for mound fill. Although the results of the auger testing show that the total extent of Tres Zapotes phase occupation is greater than the surface collections alone suggest, overall they corroborate the surface data, indicating

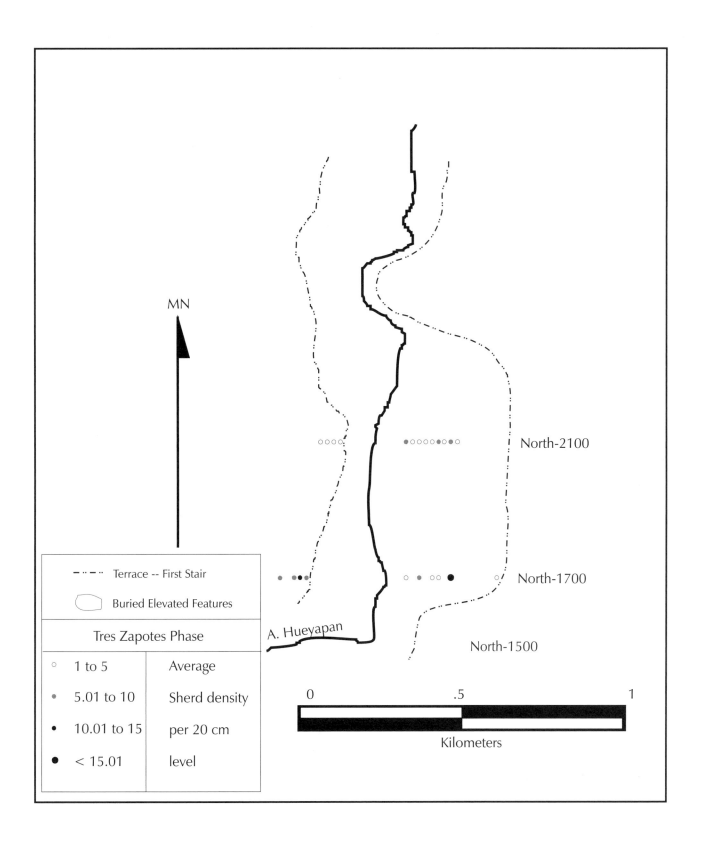

Figure 3.8. Distribution and densities of Tres Zapotes phase ceramic material. *Illustration prepared by Carl J. Wendt*

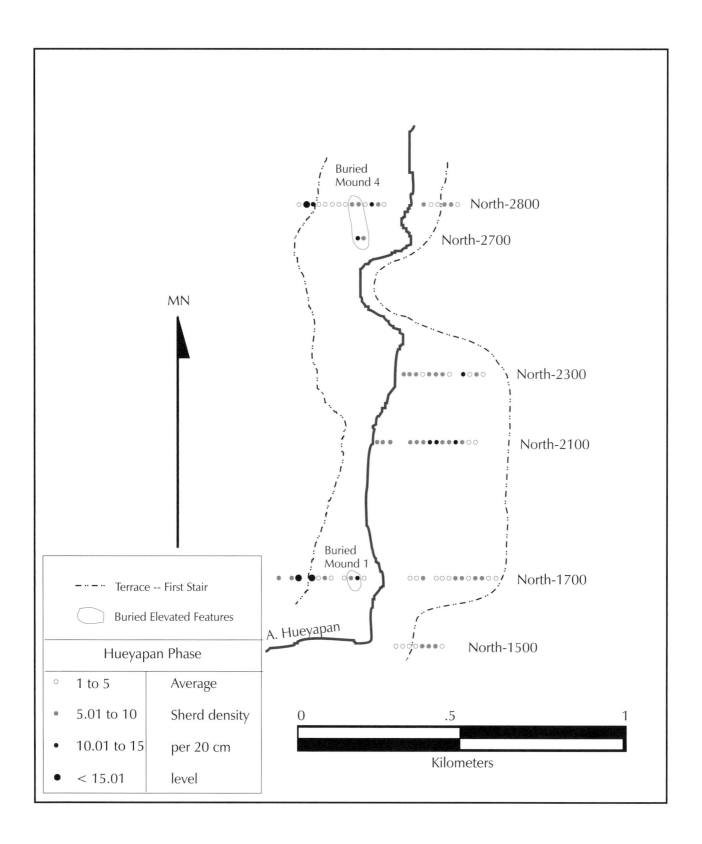

Figure 3.9 Distribution and densities of Hueyapan-phase ceramic material. *Illustration prepared by Carl J. Wendt*

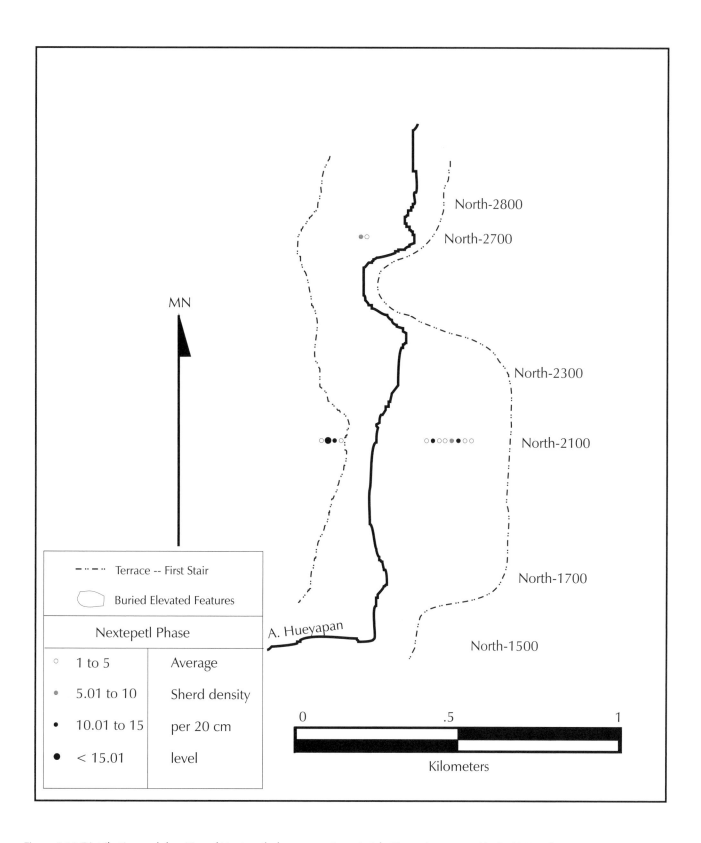

Figure 3.10 Distribution and densities of Nextepetl-phase ceramic material. *Illustration prepared by Carl J. Wendt*

widely dispersed, small settlements surrounding a moderate size center.

Surface data indicate that Tres Zapotes reached its apogee during the Late to Terminal Formative period. This conclusion is further supported by data recovered from the auger tests. Deposits dating to the Hueyapan phase are not only the most horizontally expansive when compared to other periods, they contain the densest amounts of ceramic material (figure 3.9). Major mound construction and cultural terrace formation on the floodplain appears to have occurred during this period as well. These data corroborate Pool's (1997c:20) suggestion that mound construction was initiated at Tres Zapotes in the Late Formative period.

Data obtained through the auger testing program, combined with surface survey data, paint a picture of a fairly continuous, densely occupied Late Formative Tres Zapotes. The continuity and density of occupation suggests a relatively nucleated settlement pattern at the site during this period. Auger data support Pool's (chapter 7) suggestion that Late Formative Tres Zapotes exhibited a residential core that extended onto the site's floodplain. Evidence indicates that this is the first period in which the site was organized into one contiguous settlement.

Auger tests encountered Nextepetl phase deposits only on cultural terraces, buried mounds, and the first terrace stair. Therefore, it appears that occupation had begun to withdraw from the lower parts of the floodplain by the beginning of the Terminal Formative period. The upper volcanic ash was absent from auger tests containing Nextepetl deposits, rendering the relationship between these strata ambiguous. Stratigraphic units assigned to the Nextepetl phase cluster E, however, lie above and below the contact between the upper and lower levels of cultural terrace A in transect North-2100-East (figure 3.7), and this contact correlates laterally with the base of the upper ash. Furthermore, Ortiz (1975: Perfil 1), found a Nextepetl phase midden deposit lying conformably on top of Hueyapan phase deposits and below the volcanic ash in his excavation in the bank of the arroyo. Together, the evidence from the auger tests and Ortiz's excavation suggest that the upper volcanic ash was deposited during the Nextepetl phase. In addition, the absence of the ash from buried elevated features and Stirling's excavations on the higher terraces implies that the ash was eroded from higher parts of the site, collecting on the lower floodplain and arroyo tributaries (see also Drucker 1943a:33–34). The overall effect of the upper ash fall appears to have been to accelerate significant restructuring of settlement, which had already begun by the beginning of the Nextepetl phase (figure 3.10) (compare Chase 1981).

Following the ash fall, alluvial processes dominated deposition on the floodplain, which may suggest an increase in the frequency of flooding. While such floods would have increased the fertility of the floodplain soils, they would also have made the floodplain less suitable for habitation. Perhaps for this reason, little evidence exists for Classic period occupation on the tested areas of the floodplain, being confined to the above-ash deposits on the first terrace stair in transect North-1700-West (figure 3.4) (Wendt 1998: Table 8). Surface data also indicate Classic period occupation on portions of the first stair not sampled by the auger tests. It appears that as the population of Tres Zapotes began to decline in the Classic period, the majority of the site's inhabitants were able to avoid floods by occupying the preferable raised areas, at the same time freeing up the prime agricultural land near the arroyo.

Conclusion

As Drucker (1943a) recognized long ago, the deep sub-ash deposits of the Arroyo Hueyapan floodplain hold the key to the early chronology of Tres Zapotes. Prior to the RATZ investigation, however, only three excavations, Drucker's trenches 24 and 26 and Ortiz's (1975) pozo (pit) 3, had tapped these vitally important strata. Moreover, all were located in the small area of the Burnt Mounds group and the nearby bank of the Arroyo Hueyapan. Sampling nearly 100 ha to depths generally ranging from 4 to 6 m, the RATZ auger testing program has greatly expanded our view of the floodplain stratigraphy, resulting in a much more complete understanding of changes in intra-site settlement patterns and their relationship to natural processes. Clearly test-pitting to these depths at this scale would have been a practical impossibility, and surface collection alone would have failed to reveal the remains of these deeply buried occupations. Therefore, the results of this auger-testing program argue strongly for similar subsurface testing methods to be implemented as a standard part of surveys at sites suspected to have deeply buried cultural deposits.

NOTE

1. Editor's note: Distributions of occupation in figures 3.8 to 3.10 are more conservative than in figures 2.12 to 2.14 because auger tests with average densities of less than 1 sherd per 20 cm level are not indicated.

4

INTERPRETING BURNED EARTHEN ARTIFACTS

A Spatial and Quantitative Analysis of
Daub and Kiln Debris from Tres Zapotes

Elizabeth A. Hoag

THE USE OF UNFIRED EARTH AS A CONSTRUCTION MATERIAL FOR dwellings and other facilities has an antiquity and geographic extent comparable to the use of clay for pottery and figurines. Indeed, the oldest known ceramic artifacts, figurines from the Upper Paleolithic site of Dolne Vestoniče in the Czech Republic, were associated with a clay oven (Klima 1965). Mud brick, adobe, or wattle-and-daub construction appears in early dwellings from China, South Asia, Southwest Asia, Egypt, Europe, and North, Central, and South America. In each of these areas, the recovery of earthen construction materials, often preserved by accidental firing, offers evidence for the presence and relative permanence of settlement.

In Mesoamerica, wattle-and-daub houses and occasional uses of adobe have been reported from sites dating back as far as the Early Formative period. In addition, recent field projects in southern and south-central Veracruz have documented the use of tempered mud for building ceramic kilns (for example, Diehl, Gonzales, and Zarate 1997; Hoag 1997; Pool 1997a; Santley, Arnold, and Pool 1989; Stark 1992). Nevertheless, earthen construction materials have received relatively little systematic study in Mesoamerica or elsewhere.

This chapter demonstrates the potential of earthen construction materials in archaeological inference, using specimens preserved by incidental and intentional burning at Tres Zapotes. The goal of my analysis here is twofold. First, I examine variation in attributes among artifact classes. Second, I investigate the spatial distributions of these artifacts to understand better the spatial distribution of residential structures and the locations of pottery manufacture at the site. Prior to the RATZ project, fieldwork at Tres Zapotes had not focused on craft production or residential distribution. Results from this study show that questions about economy and settlement organization can be aided by a systematic study of burned earthen materials

Material Identification

Ethnographic and archaeological examples of kilns and daub houses from throughout Mesoamerica offer useful information on the differential characteristics and origins of burned earthen materials. There are undoubtedly other activities that can create fired earthen materials that would survive in the archaeological record. The origins of two specific types of structures, kilns and daub houses, are considered here because they are the most readily identifiable and are the best documented in the ethnographic record.

DAUB STRUCTURES

Wattle-and-daub construction is a technique of applying mud to a framework of vertical or horizontal poles or of bundles of twigs and grass. Ethnographic accounts of this type of construction technique come from many parts of Mesoamerica, including Michoacan (Beals 1944), Sonora (Fay 1970:10–14), the Yucatan peninsula (Wauchope 1938:94–103), the Mexican highlands (Stenholm 1979:51–53, 77), and northern Veracruz (Kelly and Palerm 1952). The mud used for construction is often tempered with straw or grass, although other tempering agents such as pine needles or small rocks may be used (Stenholm 1979:134). There is also variation in the application of daub. Some Totonac houses from northern Veracruz are plastered on only one side or have areas free of daub to increase ventilation (Kelly and Palerm 1952:176, 184–185). These accounts can be used as analogies for construction materials and techniques seen in prehistoric daub structures.

The best archaeological example of wattle-and-daub construction in Mesoamerica comes from the site of Cerén in El

Figure 4.1 Ceramic kiln under construction, San Isidro Texcaltitan, Veracruz. *Photograph by Elizabeth A. Hoag*

Salvador. This Classic period site was completely buried under several meters of volcanic ash from a single eruption around AD 600 (Sheets et al. 1990:83; Sheets 1992). Nine intact structures were excavated and found to have fiber-tempered daub walls built on a framework of vertical poles (Kievit 1994; Sheets 1992:42; Sheets et al. 1990). The use of grasses in the daub matrix may have acted as a tempering agent to prevent the walls from cracking as they dried (Sheets 1992:42). Under less ideal conditions of preservation, rain and groundwater cause unprotected daub to disaggregate, making it difficult to identify. Consequently, those pieces of daub recorded archaeologically have usually been hardened by heat. Such fired pieces of daub additionally suggest that structures were either accidentally burned or purposely razed and burned down to make way for new construction (Flannery, Marcus, and Payne 1994:28; Hall 1994). This firing preserves impressions of organic materials as well as finished wall surfaces.

Large pieces of identifiable daub have been reported from a few other sites in Mesoamerica. At Barton Ramie, Belize, Willey et al. encountered what they referred to as "briquette materials" (1965:511). Many of these daub pieces exhibited pole impressions and fine impressions from the grass temper, vines, or twigs, as well as smooth surfaces, or "dressed corners," that correspond to finished edges of the daub walls (Willey et al. 1965:516). Lumps of "adobe" with stick and pole impressions were recorded from mound fill at the site of La Victoria, Guatemala (Coe 1961:27). Daub from the site of Cuello, Belize, retained impressions of "wall posts, poles, or canes infilling between them, vine binders, vegetable matter mixed in for stiffening, and...impressions of leaves used

for thatch" (Gerhardt and Hammond 1991:102). Household excavations from the Valley of Oaxaca yielded daub that exhibited impressions of canes or reeds, squared corners, whitewash, and in one example, impressions of the "canes in the wall and the cords used to lash them together" (Marcus and Flannery 1996:124, Fig. 129; Flannery 1976:18–19). The similarities in preparation and construction methods documented by these ethnographic and archaeological accounts of daub houses helped to define the characteristics that were used to identify daub pieces at Tres Zapotes. Fire-hardened daub may retain the impressions of the wattle or lath to which it was applied, along with smooth surfaces from the interior or exterior of the wall. It may also contain aplastic additives, such as fiber temper, used to strengthen the walls. Cook (1997) found that daub walls may also contain imprints from insect nests, such as those of mud-dauber wasps. A burned mud-dauber nest was encountered in excavations at Bezuapan, Veracruz, although no such nests occurred among the specimens recovered at Tres Zapotes. Daub also frequently contains sherds or other artifacts that were incorporated into the matrix of the wall. When earth is dug from previous occupation levels, artifacts often become mixed with wall materials and incorporated into the structure (see Holl 1987:133-134). This certainly occurred at Tres Zapotes, where some of the best examples of daub wall fragments had imbedded obsidian blades and ceramic sherds.

KILNS

Although kiln firings are not as common in Mesoamerica as simple open firings, their use has been well documented. Modern potters in many parts of Mexico use kilns of the updraft variety in which the ceramics being fired are separated from the fuel used to heat the kiln (see Rice 1987b:158; Rye 1981:100; Sinopoli 1991:32–33). In Oaxaca, for example, potters from the village of Atzompa use kilns that are built of mud and "reinforced with stones or bricks" (Hedry 1992:69). These kilns have adobe arches that separate the ceramics from the fuel. Similarly, potters in Tlacotalpan, Veracruz, build kilns out of bricks set in a clay mortar, with metal rods used to separate the fuel from the firing chamber above (Stark 1984). Kilns are also reported in use at Oteapan, Veracruz (Krotser 1980:138); Coyotepec, Oaxaca (Van de Velde and Van de Velde 1939); Cuauhtitlan, a village north of Mexico City (Rendon 1950); and in several other villages in central and southern Mexico (Foster 1955).

I observed several kilns on house lots in the pottery-producing village of San Isidro in the Tuxtla Mountains (see also Arnold 1991; Pool 1997a; Hoag and Pool 2000). Potters there build kilns of mud tempered with grasses that grow around the village and in outlying pastures. The walls of the kiln, which can be as high as 60 to 70 cm, are built up of alternating layers of clay and rocks (figure 4.1). According to local informants, these small rocks and grass temper help to give structural integrity to the kiln (see also Arnold 1991:54). Many of the kilns in San Isidro showed vitrified inner surfaces, especially in the fire-box area. The kiln walls often exhibited color zonation from the inside to outside corresponding to different levels of heat and oxidation during vessel firing (Hoag 1997:15–19; Pool 2000b).

In recent years, kilns have been uncovered in archaeological settings in Mesoamerica, demonstrating the pre-Hispanic origin of these features in the New World. Pit kilns have been identified at sites in the Ejutla Valley in Oaxaca (Balkansky, Feinman, and Nicholas 1997; Feinman and Balkansky 1997), Nayarit (Bordaz 1964), and Teotihuacan (Cabrera Castro 1988). These kilns did not separate the fuel from the vessels, but they still offered substantially more control than open firing procedures (Sinopoli 1991:33). Sites that have yielded true ceramic kilns include Monte Alban (Payne 1982; Winter and Payne 1976); La Sierra, Honduras (Urban et al. 1997); and several sites in Puebla (Abascal 1976). Evidence of kiln use has also been reported from sites of La Mojarra (Diehl et al. 1997), Matacapan (Pool 1990, 1997a; Santley, Arnold, and Pool 1989), and the Mixtequilla region (Stark 1992), all in Veracruz.

Of these, the best-documented site with kilns is Matacapan, located in the Tuxtla Mountains of southern Veracruz. In situ remains of at least forty double-chamber updraft kilns were identified at Matacapan, and fragments of kilns ("kiln debris") were recovered from numerous surface collections (Arnold et al. 1993; Arnold and Santley 1993; Pool 1990:202, Ortiz 1997b; Santley, Ortiz Ceballos, and Pool 1987, Santley, Arnold, and Pool 1989). These features were made of "puddled fiber-tempered adobe walls" (Pool 1997a:160), with adobe arches separating the oven chamber from the fire box (Pool 1997a:160; Arnold et al. 1993:183). Wall fragments of the ancient kilns "display a color gradation from interior wall surface to exterior" corresponding to the differential exposure to high heat (Arnold et al. 1993:183). At the nearby site of Bezuapan, kiln use has been inferred through the discovery of kiln debris, slag, and overfired sherds (Pool, Wright, and Brit 1993:6; Pool 1997b:58).

In the Naco Valley, Honduras, archaeologists have reported the existence of two pottery kilns from the site of La Sierra (Urban et al. 1997:173). Kiln debris from this site shows evidence of fiber tempering, and signs of "vitrification and melting" from frequent exposure to high temperatures (Urban, Wells, and Ausec 1997:187). Urban et al. (1997:187)

also report marks left in the daub from a "post and stick armature" used to construct the form of the kiln before the mud or clay application. Further, the larger pieces of kiln debris were slightly curved, indicating the round, domed form of the kiln. Finally, the bases of the two kilns at La Sierra are built of cobbles (Urban, Wells, and Ausec 1997:184). Although reminiscent of cobble use in modern San Isidro, the kilns from Naco contain many more cobbles.

From these examples, it is clear that there are similarities that can be used to identify pieces of kilns in the archaeological record. The repeated firing within the kiln causes the inner surfaces to become vitrified or melted, and the uneven oxidation of the walls of a kiln results in color zonation. These characteristics are consistent and can be used as defining attributes in archaeological analysis. More variable attributes of kiln construction include use of grass temper or other fibrous materials, aplastic mineral inclusions, and small stick impressions from the forming of the kiln.

Locating Daub Structures and Kilns

Daub is often encountered on or around house mounds in Mesoamerica, although it is not limited to these contexts. When found within mound deposits, daub may reflect the accretion over time of materials from perishable house construction (Hall 1994:31). Ethnoarchaeology carried out in West Africa demonstrated this point (McIntosh 1974). Once a wattle-and-daub structure had eroded to the point that it could no longer be repaired, it was torn down, and daub was left to weather and erode in situ (McIntosh 1974; Holl 1987). Daub from previous buildings contributed to the creation of low mounds on which new structures were built. When daub structures were burned down, the daub would become sintered and preserve any impressions or temper it once held. Experimental archaeology conducted on the collapse of wattle-and-daub buildings demonstrates that intentional razing of daub structures results in more fire-hardened daub than do accidental fires (Schaffer 1982:145, 1993). Thus, large quantities of daub encountered archaeologically suggest that such an action may have contributed to the growth of residential mounds (Hall 1994).

Large amounts of burned daub from both domestic and ritual contexts have been found in several Middle Formative Rosario phase villages in the Valley of Oaxaca (Marcus and Flannery 1996:124, 128–129). The authors believe that this is evidence of intentional, destructive burning related chiefly to warfare (Marcus and Flannery 1996:124). While daub found in archaeological contexts is likely the result of human actions, we cannot say definitively whether the structures were razed as an act of aggression or simply to make way for new building episodes.

If daub from razed structures was discarded with other house trash rather than left to erode in situ, it would likely be encountered in refuse areas situated behind or adjacent to these residential mounds. Ethnographic and archaeological research in the Tuxtla Mountains has demonstrated that refuse generated from residential areas is discarded in a similar, predictable manner (Arnold 1990; Killion 1990, 1992; Santley 1992; Pool 1997b; Pool et al. 1993). Killion (1992) formalizes this pattern as the Tuxtlas House Lot model. This model recognizes several distinct activity areas that are focused around the dwelling structure or living area (Killion 1990:202, 1992:126). On the periphery of the structural core are the intermediate and garden areas, where inorganic and organic refuse, respectively, are deposited (Killion 1992:126). Discarded daub that was removed from a razed structure may also end up in the intermediate area. Hall (1994:39–40) found daub in several trash pits associated with mounds from excavations in the Mixtequilla region of Veracruz.

In instances of kiln firings, archaeologists rarely encounter intact kiln walls or even their remains. Areas of pottery production typically are spatially limited to begin with, and they are often difficult to detect in archaeological settings (Arnold and Santley 1993:228, 230; Stark 1985; Feinman and Balkansky 1997). Other indicators of ceramic production aid in the location of pottery production when the kiln evidence is fragmentary. These can be grouped into three basic categories: technology such as firing facilities and other tools used in production; by-products such as overfired sherds, ash, slag, and fire-cracked rock; and assemblage characteristics of production results, including high sherd densities, skewed ceramic inventories, and evidence of vessel standardization (after Pool 1990:101; Santley, Arnold, and Pool 1989:110; see also Stark 1985). Using only one of these indicators can give a false indication of pottery production (Stark 1992:189). Kiln fragments alone cannot always be used to adequately identify ceramic production because kiln structures can be used for other purposes, such as lime plaster production (Pike 1980; Abrams 1996; Abrams and Freter 1995). Other ceramic production evidence must be used with kiln fragments to strengthen the argument for kiln use.

Further, the spatial distribution of these indicators can aid in the identification of ceramic production loci (Smyth 1998; Santley, Arnold, and Pool 1989). Often, the indicators of production are encountered in proximity to one another, suggesting that ceramic production took place at a specific location. The co-occurrence of indica-tors of technology, by-products, and production results, in conjunction with their context within a site, strengthens arguments for the identification of ceramic production loci. This strategy has been successfully employed at many sites in the Gulf Coast region and elsewhere (Arnold and Santley 1993; Balkansky, Feimann, and Nicholas 1997; Canto 1986; Curet 1993; Hayashida 1999; Pool 1990; Stark 1985, 1992; Sullivan 1988) and is the method that I adopt to locate evidence of kiln use and ceramic production at Tres Zapotes (Hoag 1997).

Classification and Analysis

In its 1995 season, RATZ collected 10,736 pieces of burned earthen material. These specimens were classified into three categories—daub, kiln debris, and burned earth—based on conservative criteria derived from ethnographic and archaeological examples like those discussed above. Pieces classified as daub (n=1116) had pole impressions or smoothed surfaces indicative of a prepared wall. Initially, inclusion of artifacts, such as obsidian or sherds, was also considered an indicator of daub, but I discarded this criterion after I observed sherds embedded in the walls of ethnographic kilns at San Isidro Texcaltitan, Veracruz. Pieces classified as kiln debris (n=205) exhibited color zoning or a vitrified surface, or they possessed the form of a recognizable part of a kiln, such as the grate or its supporting adobe post.

Any specimen that did not exhibit one of these defining attributes was classified as burned earth (n=9415), indicating that its origin was indeterminate. The burned-earth class may include unrecognized pieces of daub and kiln debris, as well as fired earth from hearths, bonfires, or other features. In excavated contexts, it may be possible to classify burned earth based on context alone. In excavations of residential architecture at Kaminaljuyu, Guatemala, pieces of burned clay that did not have pole impressions or "surfacing" indicative of wall fragments were classified as "floor tempering," referring to their use in prepared floor surfaces (Reynolds 1979:241, Table 2). Such a classification as floor tempering was not possible with fragments of burned earth from Tres Zapotes surface collections because their exact contexts are unknown. Another possibility we considered was that many indeterminate specimens of burned earth in surface collections might have been produced by contemporary burning of agricultural fields, especially the extensive sugar cane fields, which are burned annually prior to harvest. To test this possibility we collected samples of burned earth from around the stalks of recently burned cane. These specimens proved to be only lightly fired, and they disaggregated readily in water. Thus, if such recently formed pieces of burned earth were collected in the survey, it is doubtful they would have survived washing in the laboratory and so would not have entered the data set.

ATTRIBUTE ANALYSIS

A more detailed analysis was conducted on a sample of daub, kiln debris, and burned earth to examine covariation in a broader set of attributes. For each artifact class, a minimum of 100 surface collections containing that class were selected using different sampling proportions. This procedure resulted in 138 collection units (100%) containing kiln debris (175 pieces), 100 collection units (20.8%) containing daub (164 pieces), and 138 collection units (10%) containing burned earth (728 pieces). Attributes recorded for each piece included fiber temper impressions, mineral inclusions (sand and gravel), vitrification, color (including single colors and zoned color patterns), pole impressions, and discernible form (as of a wall surface or kiln part). One aim of this analysis was to establish sets of attributes, such as temper categories, which might permit the identification of kiln debris and daub in the large indeterminate category of burned earth.

Table 4.1 presents the frequencies of specimens classified as daub and kiln debris exhibiting the presence of each recorded attribute. Recognizable forms were less common among fragments of kiln debris than daub, probably because of the more careful finishing of daub wall surfaces and the destructive effects of thermal stresses in kilns. About one-third of the pieces classified as kiln debris exhibited vitrification. As a defining attribute of kiln debris, vitrification was absent from pieces classified as daub. Color zoning was the most prevalent diagnostic attribute of kiln debris, but this attribute also occurred infrequently in pieces identified as daub by their preserved wall surfaces or pole impressions, evidently because of differential burning on the interior and exterior of the structure. More than half of the daub pieces exhibited pole impressions. Seven pieces recorded as having pole impressions also exhibited vitrification and so were classified as kiln debris. It is possible that these latter pieces derived from burned structures in which temperatures were locally high enough to vitrify daub. The impressions in these pieces are less than 0.5 cm in diameter, though, and so do not represent true poles; they are better described as stick impressions. They may represent the impressions of an armature like that inferred for the Naco Valley kilns reported by Urban et al. (1997:173) (Hoag 1997:47). Cultural inclusions are generally scarce, but they appear to be somewhat more prevalent in daub than kilns, perhaps reflecting differences in the areas of the house lot from which mud was obtained. The less common occurrence of sherds in kiln debris is somewhat surprising, since sherds resulting from the breakage of vessels during firing are typically common around kilns, but these sherds tend to be larger than those deposited and trampled around houses; so, they may be more easily excluded from the mud matrix. No single class of aplastic inclusion (fiber, sand, or gravel) is exclusive to kiln debris or daub. The presence of sand in all specimens suggests that it occurs naturally in the earth used for construction at Tres Zapotes, and fiber temper appears to have been added with similar frequency to daub and kiln debris. Only gravel is markedly more common in one class of burned-earthen material (daub) than the other.

Cluster analysis was conducted on the daub and kiln debris artifact classes to investigate whether particular sets of co-occurring attributes provided additional possibilities for distinguishing daub from kiln debris. A cluster analysis starts with undifferentiated groups and then attempts to "create subgroups which differ on selected variables" (Kachigan 1991:262). The identified daub and kiln debris were pooled and tested together in an attempt to replicate their defined artifact classes. Using the SYSTAT statistical software package, I performed two clustering procedures: a hierarchical cluster analysis using the percentage distance measure and a K-means cluster analysis using the Goodman-Kruskal gamma correlation coefficient. Neither procedure identified groups of variables, other than the defining criteria, that could distinguish all daub from kiln debris.

Logistic regression was also used to analyze the data for covariance of attributes and to evaluate the effectiveness of particular combinations of attributes for classifying the specimens. This technique groups the attributes independently of the classes to which they are assigned and compares the findings to the class designation. Table 4.2 shows the percentage of daub and kiln debris correctly classified for each of several combinations of attributes, as well as the overall percentage of specimens correctly classified. The most useful set of attributes for classification were fiber impressions, gravel inclusions, pole impressions, color zoning, and vitrification. These attributes account for 95% of the daub and 97% of the kiln debris. Table 4.3 gives the correlation matrix for the logistic regression. Some of the original defining characteristics were included in this test to see how other attributes correlated with them. Gravel and pole impressions exhibit weak to moderate negative correlations with the color zonation and vitrification taken as indicators of kiln debris, while color zonation shows a moderate positive correlation with vitrification.

This information was used to attempt a discrimination of daub and kiln debris in the large body of burned earth.

Table 4.1 Frequencies of attribute presence in daub and kiln debris

ATTRIBUTE	KILN DEBRIS		DAUB	
	N	%	N	%
Form	41	23	67	41
Vitrification	57	32	0	0
Color zoning	159	91	6	4
Pole impression	7	4	96	58
Cultural Inclusion	3	1	12	7
Fiber impression	88	50	109	55
Sand	175	100	164	100
Gravel	57	32	90	55
	175		164	

Table 4.2 Logistic regression results

TEST	ATTRIBUTE						% KD	% DAUB	%OVERALL
	G	F	PI	V	CZ	CI			
1	X	X	X				96	58	78
2	X	X	X	X			87	77	82
3	X	X		X			50	79	64
4	X	X	X	X		X	87	79	83
5	X	X	X	X	X		95	97	96

G = gravel; F= fiber; PI=pole impression; V=vitrification; CZ=color zoning; CI=cultural inclusion; KD = kiln debris

Table 4.3 Correlation matrix for logistic regression

	FIBER	GRAVEL	POLE	CZ	V
Fiber	1				
Gravel	-0.01091	1			
Pole	0.03065	0.28821	1		
Color Zone	-0.26696	-0.55498	-0.5040	1	
Vitrification	-0.04056	-0.37379	-0.6288	0.41978	1

CZ=color zone; V=vitrification

However, reexamination of burned earth for the presence and absence of pole impressions, gravel, fiber impressions, vitrification, and color zoning yielded very few pieces that could be successfully identified. This is likely owing to the nature of the burned-earth artifact class. Most of the pieces in this class were small and lacked any sign of the attributes I was studying. Therefore, while this analysis was useful in confirming attributes already present in kiln debris and daub, it was not useful in further classifying other pieces of burned earth.

SPATIAL ANALYSIS

In the analysis of the spatial distribution of daub and kiln debris, several interesting trends become apparent. When the locations of collections yielding daub are mapped with mound locations, there is a general correspondence between the two. Knight (1999:127) reported a similar finding in his survey of the hinterland center of Palo Errado. There, Knight (1999: Fig. 5.1) encountered daub on or near all but two of the fourteen mounds in his survey area. Eighty of the 127 mounds within the 1995 survey boundaries at Tres Zapotes had daub on them, and many mounds had daub located near them (figure 4.2). Further, several of the areas with the most daub also contained heavy ceramic densities. If ceramics were discarded near the house lots where they were used or produced, then it is likely that these areas of high ceramic densities and daub are remnants of residential areas (figure 4.3).

Because areas of heavy artifact concentrations at the site were sampled more intensely, the above observation needs to be further evaluated. Transect collections made at systematic intervals across the site offer an unbiased control sample that can be used to validate trends observed in mound and concentration collections. Therefore, systematic transect collections that contained both daub and ceramic artifacts (n=240 collections) were analyzed to evaluate the potential correspondence between daub and ceramic refuse weights. A Pearson correlation shows that daub and ceramic weight are weakly but significantly correlated ($r=0.23$, $r_{crit} =0.19$, $\alpha=0.05$), supporting the observed trends in the data. It is reasonable to say that in areas of mounds and concentrations, the co-occurrence of daub and ceramic refuse is not due to a more intensive collection strategy but to human activities.

As previously mentioned, the combined occurrence of ceramic firing technology, products, and by-products can serve as a good indicator that ceramic production with kilns was taking place in certain localities at Tres Zapotes. Plotting kiln debris, overfired sherds, and ceramic densities suggests that ceramic production was widespread at Tres Zapotes but with a tendency to cluster in specific parts of the site (figure 4.4). Systematic transect collections were again used to assess the visual clusters of ceramic producing areas. A Pearson correlation of kiln debris and ceramic densities from line collections (n=80 collections) yielded a positive but statistically insignificant correlation ($r=0.12$, $r_{crit}=0.21$, $a=0.05$). As Pool (chapter 5) observes, many of the sherds classified as wasters exhibit vitrified edges that suggest postbreakage refiring. Inclusion of these "overfired" sherds in the present analysis may exaggerate the overall extent of ceramic production. However, the fact that sherds identified as wasters tend to occur in areas of high ceramic density and near collections containing kiln debris suggests that the exaggeration is not great. At the nearby site of Matacapan, production areas were identified by using a more stringent "polythetic

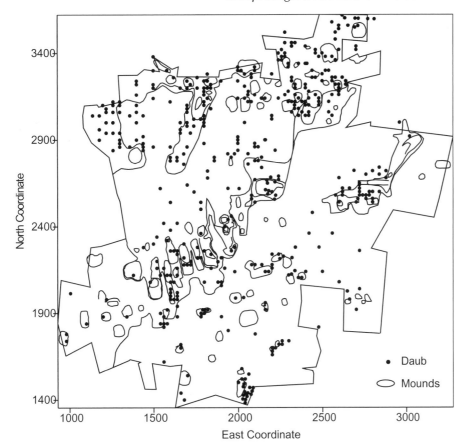

Figure 4.2 Map showing location of mounds and daub in 1995 survey. *Illustration prepared by Elizabeth A. Hoag, Michael J. Ohnersorgen, and Christopher A. Pool*

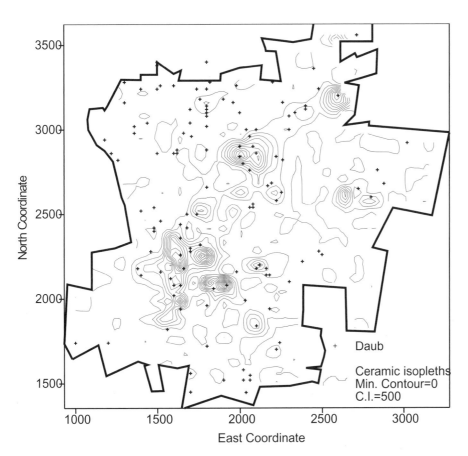

Figure 4.3 Location of daub with ceramic densities in 1995 survey. *Illustration prepared by Elizabeth A. Hoag*

Figure 4.4 Map showing location of ceramic production indicators in 1995 survey. *Illustration prepared by Elizabeth A. Hoag*

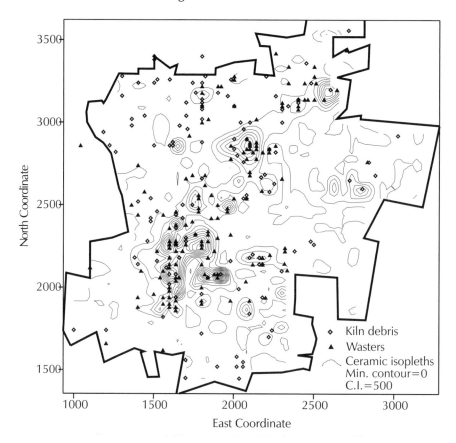

set of criteria" (Arnold and Santley 1993:235; Santley, Arnold, and Pool 1989:112–113). Surface collections at this site that had both high densities of ceramics and misfired sherds or the presence of kiln fragments were classified as production squares. By applying similar criteria, 126 collections have been identified from line collections at Tres Zapotes (chapter 5; Pool 1997c: 23), most of which cluster into several production areas across the site. Pool's more restrictively defined production areas probably represent loci of specialized ceramic production, while the broader distribution of kiln debris and wasters discussed in this chapter may include areas of less intensive production.

DISCUSSION

Overall, locations of daub from survey collections at the site conform to expected locations of recovery, based on mound formation processes (Hall 1994) and refuse disposal (Killion 1992). It is interesting to note that there are areas in the site where daub is located away from mounds, especially in the northwest corner of the site. The daub there may derive from mounds that have been obliterated in modern times as a result of agricultural practices. It is also possible that ancient daub structures were not built on mounds there at all because of the natural elevation of that part of the site. Additionally, perishable materials, such as pole and thatch, could

easily have been used for house construction. Ethnographic research suggests that perishable structures would have little or no archaeological visibility, therefore skewing our assessment of prehistoric habitation in favor of structures built of less perishable materials (Moore and Gasco 1990).

Ceramic Production and the Political Economy

As demonstrated above, artifacts associated with ceramic production were encountered together at the site. The locations of these production areas cluster around several different contexts that suggest different levels of production organization. Many of these production areas are also areas where house daub was recovered, suggesting that ceramic production was mainly organized at the household level. There are many ethnographic examples of pottery production taking place within the house lot (for example, P. Arnold 1991; Deal 1998; Foster 1955; Lackey 1982). In these cases, kilns were often present on the house lots of specialized potters who produced wares for themselves as well as for use within a community or expanded region.

Some elite sponsorship of ceramic production is suggested by the occurrence of kiln debris and waster sherds in two civic-ceremonial mound groups (Groups 2 and 3), and an elite residential complex (Cerro Rabon) (figure 4.4) (see chapter 5 for further discussion). The pottery production carried out in these contexts may indicate production by attached specialists for elite patrons (see Costin 1991:9, Costin and Hagstrum 1995:623; Brumfiel and Earle 1987). Similar findings have been reported from Matacapan, where it is argued that a ceramic kiln and associated ceramic refuse area located near an elite mound reflects attached, or tethered, specialist production (Santley, Arnold, and Pool 1989).

Although there is some evidence for political sponsorship of ceramic production in these areas, the general pattern that emerges here is one of a more decentralized political economy. The fact that production areas are not centrally located at the site suggests that there was generally not much elite/political involvement in the ceramic production cycle. This has several implications for the political organization and its ties to the economy. Control over the production and exchange of goods can be a basis for political power in some societies (Earle 1997:7). At Tres Zapotes, ceramic production may not have played a large part in the economic base for the ruling class nor been an important source of political power because of its dispersed nature.

Other aspects of the settlement pattern at Tres Zapotes tend to reinforce this picture of a decentralized political economy. Formal mound groups are widely distributed through the site. Furthermore, although Group 2 is centrally located, it is rivaled in the size of its constructions by Group 3 (chapter 7). Although the building sequences and degree of contemporaneity among the mound groups are less clear than we would like, this dispersed pattern of mound groups and less centralized ceramic industry suggests that perhaps the nature of the political economy at Tres Zapotes was less unitary and more decentralized. This does not mean that there was not a concentration of power at the site but that "power was shared across different groups and sectors of society" (Blanton et al. 1996:2). Power may still have been centralized and hierarchical, but no *one* person or group of people was in control of power (Blanton 1998:151).

Conclusion

We have seen in ethnographic and archaeological examples how kilns and daub houses are built and how they appear once they enter the archaeological record. This information was used to create models that were employed to provide a better understanding of residential patterns and ceramic production at Tres Zapotes. The results of this application were the identification of several areas of residential occupation and pottery production. Further, from the co-occurrence of

daub and kiln debris within specific locales, it is possible to make inferences about the nature of ceramic production organization. It appears that pottery production often took place in domestic contexts at Tres Zapotes and more rarely in elite contexts. In the future, studies of daub and kiln debris will be greatly enhanced at Tres Zapotes by excavation. Ceramic production zones that have been inferred from the surface finds can be confirmed or refuted, allowing us to refine the models we use to identify such activities from survey data. Although surface distributions of artifacts can act as reliable indicators of subsurface phenomena (Downum and Brown 1998), the relationship between surface and subsurface remains to be addressed. Finally, the conclusions about the nature of political control over ceramic production need to be evaluated with respect to the regional economy of the area. We currently have little settlement data to determine the role that Tres Zapotes played in the region. It is possible that if we change the scale of our investigations from site to regional level, we may see that Tres Zapotes actually played a larger role in ceramic production and that production may have been more centralized at a regional scale than it currently appears.

The attribute analysis of burned-earth materials also yielded results that will be helpful in the future analysis of daub and kiln debris. There are certain groups of traits that characterize both artifact types. The presence of pole and fiber impressions along with gravel is indicative of daub, while the absence of those attributes combined with the presence of color zoning and vitrification distinguishes kiln debris. While the attribute analysis better defined attributes of the two classes, it was not able to aid in the classification of the large corpus of unidentified burned earth. Although this portion of my study was not as conclusive as hoped, there is room for more work. With good contexts from excavated daub walls and kilns, this attribute analysis can be further refined. Flannery (1976:19), for example, reported that daub from excavated contexts exhibited signs of surface treatment, including burnishing, smoothing, and whitewashing. The surface-collected daub analyzed here was too eroded to discern any such finishing treatment. Further, chemical and compositional analyses of daub and kiln debris may yield important and useful differences between the two groups. Identification of the species of plants used to temper daub and kiln debris may lead to yet another way to distinguish these artifact classes. Lastly, a systematic classification scheme implemented at other sites will allow us to create a more descriptive characterization of these burned earthen materials.

5

CERAMIC PRODUCTION AT TERMINAL FORMATIVE AND CLASSIC PERIOD TRES ZAPOTES

Christopher A. Pool

IN THE PAST TWO DECADES, RESEARCH IN SOUTHERN VERACRUZ, Mexico has begun to reveal significant variability in the organization of ceramic production systems pertaining mainly to the Classic period. In the lower Papaloapan basin, studies by Stark (1985, 1989, 1992) at Patarata and in the Mixtequilla region (figure 1.1) suggest that specialized ceramic production was generally carried out in domestic contexts at low intensities, although Postclassic production of *comales* in the Mixtequilla appears to have been conducted in more intensive domestic workshops (Curet 1993). In addition, Diehl's (1997:201–203) excavation of possible ceramic kilns in the plaza of a civic-ceremonial mound group at La Mojarra may indicate some attached specialist production for elite patrons, although their temporal relationship to the mounds is unclear, and the suggested Early Postclassic date of the kilns is much later than the famous Terminal Formative stela from this site. At the Classic period center of Matacapan in the Tuxtla Mountains, Santley, I, and our colleagues have proposed the existence of a more diversified ceramic production system that included intensive, large-scale production entities in addition to smaller workshops and household industries (Arnold et al. 1993; Pool 1990; Santley, Arnold, and Pool 1989).

The data obtained by RATZ on distributions of ceramic production residues, including Hoag's detailed analysis of kiln debris in chapter 4, offer additional information relevant to variability in the organization of production within and among sites in southern Veracruz. In this chapter, I characterize ceramic production systems of the Terminal Formative Nextepetl phase (100 BC–AD 300) and Early Classic Ranchito phase (AD 300–600) at Tres Zapotes, compare them with the Matacapan system using comparable data sets, and discuss potential causes for the differences.

Assessing the Organization of Ceramic Production

Recent studies of variability in preindustrial ceramic production have employed one of two approaches, which can be distinguished as typological and characterizational. The typological approach, exemplified by van der Leeuw (1976) and Peacock (1982), assigns archaeological production areas to one or more production modes derived from ethnographic or ethnohistorical analogs. Typological approaches often distinguish production modes with respect to the degree of elite control or sponsorship, as in Earle's (1981) distinction between attached production, in which specialists produce pottery for elite clients, and independent production (see also Costin 1991:5–7; compare Sinopoli 1988; Peacock 1982). Independent production modes are typically ranked according to degree of specialization, as in van der Leeuw's scale from household production to large-scale industry.

The characterizational approach attempts to capture the multivariate quality of the organization of production by assigning archaeological production areas to points along multiple dimensions of variation. These dimensions of variation may include the context or location of production entities and their relative concentration, scale, intensity, efficiency, degree of activity segregation, and variability of products. Costin (1991) and Pool (1992) provide detailed discussions of the characterizational approach to production organization.

In practice, purveyors of typological and characterizational approaches use similar kinds of data to assess production organization, such as size of production entities, density of materials, diversity of assemblages, and standardization of products. The major differences in the approaches lie in their theoretical aims and their views of specialization. The typological approach seeks to assign production entities to universal modes, which typically are seen as responding to factors of political control and economic efficiency. Their heavy reliance on contemporary and historically documented modes of production and formalist economic principles, however, potentially obscures variability in production modes and undermines their implied claims to universality. Characterizational approaches remain closer to the archaeological data and permit recognition of organizational arrangements and factors not documented in the ethnographic and historical literature. Variation in field and analytical methods, however, may complicate intersite and interregional comparisons.

Santley, Arnold, and Pool's (1989) analysis of the ceramic production system at Matacapan, which constitutes the main comparative base for this chapter, employed both characterizational and typological analysis. Variation in production organization was initially assessed with regard to variables related to the size, intensity, context, and activity segregation of production areas. Based on this characterizational analysis and additional considerations, Santley, Arnold, and Pool (1989) then assigned production areas to modes derived from van der Leeuw (1976) and Peacock (1982). Recent criticisms of the Santley, Arnold, and Pool (1989) article and related works (Arnold et al. 1993; Pool 1990) by Costin (1991:29), Balkansky et al. (1997:156), and Feinman (1999:97–98) question the typological assignment of the production areas and the characterizaton of activity segregation, particularly with regard to the nucleated industry or manufactory identified at the outlying site of Comoapan. Although activity segregation is not addressed in this chapter, comparison with the production system at Tres Zapotes along other dimensions of variation provides a broader context for understanding the organization of production at Matacapan and avoids the problems of attempting to assign production areas to a priori modes, such as "nucleated industry" or "manufactory."

Ceramic Production at Tres Zapotes

The data on ceramic production examined in this chapter derive from the 1995 season of RATZ. To ensure comparability with the results of the Matacapan project, I examine only data obtained by the systematic transect survey. This data set comprises 1837 3 x 3 m collections from an area of 320 ha, for a sampling intensity of 0.52%, slightly greater than the 0.46% sampling intensity at Matacapan (Santley, Arnold, and Pool 1989:112).

IDENTIFICATION OF CERAMIC PRODUCTION

Identification of ceramic production areas at Tres Zapotes uses criteria established by Santley and his colleagues (Arnold and Santley 1993:235–236; Pool 1990:202; Pool and Santley 1992:212; Santley et al. 1989:110–111, 112;) at Matacapan. Production indicators include deformed wasters (cracked, warped, and vitrified sherds) and high surface sherd densities. High sherd densities are expected to result from the accumulation of "de facto wasters," that is, vessels broken in the manufacturing process but which do not exhibit the characteristics of deformed wasters (Stark 1992:191). A third production indicator that is useful in the Tuxtlas region is kiln debris. Pre-Hispanic ceramic kilns excavated at Matacapan were formed from mud mixed with vegetable fibers. Repeated firings hardened the mud, vitrified the interior surface, and produced a characteristic color zonation from interior to exterior (Pool 1997a; Santley et al. 1989). Elizabeth Hoag's (1997; chapter 4) detailed attribute study distinguished kiln debris at Tres Zapotes from fired daub resulting from the burning of residential structures. She found that fiber tempering was often present in daub as well as in kiln debris, reducing the utility of this attribute as a defining characteristic, although vitrification, color zonation, lack of wattle impressions, and the characteristic forms of some kiln parts still distinguish kiln debris from daub.

As Hoag observes, both deformed wasters and kiln debris are widely distributed at Tres Zapotes (see figure 4.4), particularly in areas with domestic artifact assemblages, which suggests that ceramic production frequently occurred in domestic contexts. Many of the sherds classified as wasters, however, exhibit vitrified edges that suggest postbreakage refiring. The vitrified edges on these sherds render them ambiguous as production indicators, because refiring could reflect reuse as kiln furniture accidental refiring unrelated to pottery production. Therefore, I use a more stringent definition of ceramic production areas, requiring that deformed wasters or kiln debris be associated with high ceramic densities. Following Pool and Santley (1992), I define "high density" as the upper tercile of sherd frequencies, excluding collections from the heavily alluviated floodplain (see chapter 3). This figure equals 156 or more sherds per collection, or more than 17 sherds per square meter. A total of 126 surface collections meet this more stringent definition.

At Matacapan, production areas were defined initially as containing either waster sherds or kiln debris associated with a high density of sherds, with high density being defined as the mean plus one standard deviation (Santley et al. 1989:112). Later, due to the positive skew of the distribution, we redefined high density by the upper tercile criterion used here, and we required the co-occurrence of at least two of the three criteria (Arnold and Santley 1993:235–236; Pool 1990:202; Pool and Santley 1992). Altering the definition in this way did not change the number of production areas identified (41) but did increase their areal extent (Pool 1990:202). By this definition, co-occurrence of wasters and kiln debris could define a production area, whereas at Tres Zapotes, either or both must be associated with high ceramic densities. This difference in defining criteria has little impact in the comparison of these two sites, however, because review of the data from Matacapan shows that, in fact, ceramic densities in the upper tercile were characteristic of all production areas.

DEFINITION AND TEMPORAL ASSIGNMENT OF PRODUCTION AREAS

Except in densely settled urban centers and some industrial contexts, by-products of ceramic firing are likely to be deposited near firing facilities. Such is typically the case in contemporary Mesoamerican contexts (for example, Arnold 1991) and is true for all excavated ceramic production contexts at Matacapan (Pool 1990). Because the identification of collections with evidence for ceramic production at Tres Zapotes relied on the facilities and by-products associated with firing, these collections probably represent the loci of firing activities; I therefore refer to them as *firing squares*.

Clusters of firing squares define broader *production areas,* which frequently include collections containing no firing residues. Non-firing activities conducted within these production areas would probably have included paste preparation, vessel forming, vessel drying, and, in household contexts, domestic activities unrelated to ceramic production. Following Santley et al. (1989:112–113), I also include under the term *production area* isolated firing squares and their immediately adjacent collections, located 20 m away in our survey transects.

Because of the long history of occupation at Tres Zapotes and frequent reoccupation of large areas of the site, most of our collections are multicomponent, and production areas defined by spatial proximity of firing squares alone are especially likely to contain residues from several chronological periods. To better discriminate production areas whose main output was from particular periods, I calculated the ratio of Classic to Formative wares and compared the results to ratios from excavated contexts at Tres Zapotes (Ortiz 1975), Bezuapan (Pool and Britt 2000), and Matacapan (Ortiz and Santley 1988). Collections with no Classic wares were assigned to the Middle Formative Tres Zapotes phase and Late Formative Hueyapan phase. Terminal Formative Nextepetl phase collections contain Classic and Formative wares in a ratio of greater than 0 and less than 1. Classic period squares have a Classic to Formative ratio of greater than 2. Squares with values between 1 and 2 were initially regarded as tempo-

rally mixed. Consistent spatial association of squares in this last category with Classic squares justifies attributing their major output to the Classic period, however. "Undetermined" squares lack diagnostic sherds. Considering the spatial and temporal associations of firing squares together permits the definition of forty-one separate production areas, of which six are purely Middle to Late Formative, twenty-one are Terminal Formative, and fourteen date to the Classic.

CHARACTERIZATION OF CERAMIC PRODUCTION AREAS

My analysis of variation in ceramic production at Tres Zapotes focuses on four dimensions chosen for comparability with the Matacapan data set. These dimensions are production area context, production area size, production intensity, and product specialization. Product specialization refers to emphasis on the manufacture of specific classes of products, which in this study are defined as wares in the ceramic classification. The measurement of product specialization independent of context, size, and intensity is discussed in a later section. A fifth dimension of variability used at Matacapan, activity segregation, is not considered here. Activity segregation may be assessed within production areas or at the site scale in terms of the segregation of workshops from domestic contexts. Evidence on the segregation of activities within production areas is ambiguous in the survey data, however, and segregation of workshops away from domestic or elite contexts has not been identified at Tres Zapotes.

Context. Production area context is assessed as a dichotomous variable: attached or independent. As defined by Brumfiel and Earle,

> *Independent specialists* produce goods or services for an unspecified demand crowd that varies according to economic, social, and political conditions. In contrast, *attached specialists* produce goods or provide services to a patron, typically either a social elite or governing institution. (1987:5, emphasis in original)

Operationally, I distinguish attached from independent contexts based on their architectural associations. As defined by Costin (1991:25), attached contexts are those associated with elite domestic structures or government facilities (in this case civic-ceremonial mound groups). All of the production areas identified at Tres Zapotes contain off-mound firing squares and so are unlikely to represent fill from mound construction.

Independent specialists generally produce utilitarian or "subsistence" goods, and attached specialists usually produce high-value, high-status "wealth" goods or weaponry (Brumfiel and Earle 1987:4–5; Costin 1991:7, 11; Stein and

Blackman 1993:30). This observation assumes theoretical importance because it links the development of attached specialization to elite efforts to control the distribution and consumption of wealth goods and weaponry as a means of strengthening and maintaining their political control (Brumfiel and Earle 1987:5; Costin 1991:7). Consequently, some authors (for example, Lewis 1996:358) would make the nature of the products a necessary criterion for distinguishing attached from independent specialization. In accord with the characterizational approach advocated in this study, however, I monitor product specialization as a separate variable. Empirical, methodological, and theoretical considerations justify treating context and products separately.

Empirically, none of the ceramic wares discussed here appear to have been restricted exclusively to elite consumption. For Tres Zapotes, this observation is supported by surface distributions and excavated assemblages reported by Drucker (1943a:Appendix A; Ortiz 1975), and it is paralleled in excavations at Matacapan (Santley et al. 1987) and Bezuapan (Pool and Britt 2000) in the Tuxtla Mountains. In addition, the one production area in an elite precinct at Matacapan, which Costin (1991:6) identifies as a case of attached specialization, concentrated on the production of Coarse Orange storage jars as well as burnished Brown-slipped Fine Orange serving vessels (Pool 1990:221). Although rank or class distinctions are evident in access to exotic goods, architectural patterns, and, at Tres Zapotes, stone monuments, they are not as strongly expressed in ceramic inventories. Rather, differences in the proportional representation of more finely crafted and decorated wares would appear to reflect functional variation and wealth distinctions within ranks or classes (Pool and Britt 2000).

Methodologically, identifying the production of high-status goods outside of elite precincts helps to identify cases of dispersed corvée (Costin 1991) or "noncentralized attached specialization" (Lewis 1996:375). On the other hand, a rigid insistence that independent specialists produce only utilitarian goods and attached specialists produce only wealth goods conflates product specialization with context and fails to address a number of ethnographically and historically documented relationships between elites and producers. Among these are production of wealth items by independent specialists (Brumfiel and Earle 1987:5), specialization in utilitarian wares in response to state demands for surplus production (Earle 1981:230; Rice 1981:223), the production of utilitarian items for non–elites by part-time attached specialists to supplement their employment (Clark and Perry 1990:302; Lewis 1996:367), and the duplication of subsistence and utilitarian craft activities by attached specialists for

the internal consumption and quotidian maintenance of elite households and state institutions (Stein and Blackman 1993:50). Stein and Blackman argue from textual evidence that the latter situation occurred in ancient Mesopotamia, where

> These 'duplicated' professions...apparently included farmers, herders, fisherman, woodcutters, bakers, and possibly even potters as well – this last group producing small volumes of utilitarian pottery for the internal consumption of the temple or palace. (1993:50)

Similar cases of duplicated professions attached to elite households appear to include production of bricks and amphorae on Roman estates (Peacock 1982:223) and pottery production for the king of the Baganda (Roscoe 1965:399–403). This variant of attached specialization, which appears to have particular relevance to the Tres Zapotes case, might best be labeled *elite household production*. It is of theoretical interest because in some historical trajectories, it may have provided a model for the development of attached specialization in wealth goods exclusively used by elites.

Size and intensity. Production area size and intensity are evaluated with respect to continuous variables. At Matacapan, the number of collection squares contained within a production area was used as a proxy measure of size (Santley et al. 1989). Because sampling intensity varied more at Tres Zapotes than at Matacapan, I measure size as the total area, in hectares, covered by the production area. I use two variables to assess production intensity. The first is sherd density in sherds per square meter. Because sherd density is likely to be strongly affected by practices of household and workshop maintenance, discard, and breakage rates, in addition to the number of vessels produced, I also use the proportion of firing squares to non-firing squares as a measure of the proportion of the area devoted to firing activities, including discard of firing errors.

SIZE, INTENSITY, AND CONTEXT AT TRES ZAPOTES
As table 5.1 illustrates, summary statistics reveal little difference between Terminal Formative and Classic period production areas with regard to the size of production areas or the proportion of their areas devoted to firing activities. Mean and median sherd densities are higher in the Terminal Formative production areas, although the range of sherd densities is nearly identical to the Classic period production areas.

Considering these dimensions of variability and the contexts of the production areas in concert, however, highlights differences in the earlier and later production systems (table

Table 5.1 Descriptive statistics for Tres Zapotes ceramic production areas

CLASSIC PERIOD					TERMINAL FORMATIVE PERIOD				
AREA	CONTEXT	SIZE (HA)	FIRING PROPERTY	DENSITY (SHERDS/M²)	AREA	CONTEXT	SIZE (HA)	FIRING PROPERTY	DENSITY (SHERDS/M²)
A22b	Attached	0.24	0.40	35.3	B30a	Attached	0.46	0.40	42.3
B32	Attached	0.04	0.33	40.6	A22a	Attached	0.24	0.60	42.5
C31	Attached	0.04	0.33	38.4	C39	Attached	0.04	0.33	112.6
A29b	Independent	1.12	0.50	114.9	A03	Attached	0.04	0.33	55.9
C07	Independent	1.08	0.50	74.0	B03	Attached	0.04	0.33	69.7
C11	Independent	1.60	0.56	36.7	A12	Attached	0.04	0.33	20.6
C15a	Independent	0.80	0.33	58.7	C17	Independent	0.64	0.42	64.0
B29	Independent	0.24	0.43	161.9	C15b	Independent	0.40	0.56	58.7
C13	Independent	0.04	0.50	47.0	A29a	Independent	1.00	0.43	78.0
C37	Independent	0.04	0.33	18.4	B07	Independent	1.20	0.29	102.6
A31b	Independent	0.04	0.33	21.3	A31a	Independent	0.72	0.38	84.0
C05	Independent	0.04	0.33	21.4	C14	Independent	0.48	0.38	83.7
A37	Independent	0.04	0.33	26.6	B30c	Independent	0.92	0.33	58.0
B30b	Independent	0.04	0.33	22.3	A21	Independent	1.00	0.25	35.4
					C19	Independent	0.32	0.40	161.9
					A29c	Independent	0.16	0.50	62.5
					B31	Independent	0.16	0.50	49.1
					A30	Independent	0.04	0.33	43.6
					A26	Independent	0.04	0.33	18.0
					C22	Independent	0.32	0.33	46.8
					A52	Independent	0.04	0.33	21.2
Mean		0.39	0.40	51.26	Mean		0.40	0.39	62.43
Std		0.51	0.08	39.58	Std		0.37	0.09	33.14
Median		0.04	0.33	37.56	Median		0.32	0.33	58
Min		0.04	0.33	18.44	Min		0.04	0.25	18.00
Max		1.60	0.56	161.85	Max		1.20	0.60	161.94

5.2). In this stage of the analysis I dichotomize the continuous variables into large and small production area sizes, high and low firing proportions, and high and low sherd densities with respect to values above and below the means for each variable, following Santley et al.'s (1989:116) procedure at Matacapan. Permutations of the resulting categories for firing proportion and sherd density create a quadripartite ranking of intensity into categories of low (low firing proportion and low sherd density), low-moderate (low firing proportion and high sherd density), high-moderate (high firing proportion and low sherd density), and high (high firing proportion and high sherd density). Inspection of tables 5.1 and 5.2 reveals two interesting differences in ceramic production organization in the Terminal Formative and Classic period at Tres Zapotes. First, the Terminal Formative production system included at least one large attached specialist, at area B30a[1], whereas all Classic period attached production areas were small. This may suggest a decline in reliance on attached specialization in the Classic, although the ratio of

independent to attached specialist production areas remained nearly constant at about 3:1. Second, the Classic period production system included a greater proportion of small, low-intensity areas and a smaller proportion of large, and low to low-moderate intensity production areas than the Terminal Formative period, suggesting less spatial aggregation of lower intensity production.

Comparison of the spatial distribution of production areas in the two periods supports the inference that low-intensity production areas were more widely separated in the Classic period (figures 5.1 and 5.2). Even more remarkable, however, is the much greater separation among the three large, independent areas with high and high-moderate production intensities. By comparison, the three large, independent, and high–intensity areas of the Terminal Formative period lie adjacent to one another in the central and western portions of the house mound concentration known as the Ranchito group. Together these three production areas encompass an area of some 5.25 ha, which is larger than the

Table 5.2 Context, size, and intensity classes for Tres Zapotes and Matacapan ceramic production areas

CONTEXT	SIZE	INTENSITY	TRES ZAPOTES		MATACAPAN
			TERMINAL FORMATIVE	CLASSIC	CLASSIC*
Attached	Large	High	0	0	0
Attached	Large	High-moderate	1	0	0
Attached	Large	Low-moderate	0	0	0
Attached	Large	Low	0	0	0
Attached	Small	High	0	0	0
Attached	Small	High-moderate	1	1	0
Attached	Small	Low-moderate	3	0	0
Attached	Small	Low	1	2	0
Independent	Large	High	3	2	2
Independent	Large	High-moderate	0	1	1
Independent	Large	Low-moderate	4	1	1
Independent	Large	Low	1	0	8
Independent	Small	High	2	1	5
Independent	Small	High-moderate	1	1	7
Independent	Small	Low-moderate	0	0	4
Independent	Small	Low	4	5	13

* excludes one attached production area found in excavation

large-scale production loci at area 199 (2.2 ha) and Comoapan (area 411, 4 ha) in Matacapan (Pool 1990:241; Santley et al. 1989:119).

PRODUCT SPECIALIZATION AT TRES ZAPOTES

The last dimension of variability I consider in the Tres Zapotes ceramic production system is product specialization. At Matacapan, the relative frequency of the most common wares was used to identify the principal product of production areas (Santley et al. 1989:121–126). Application of this measure assumes that all or most of the types represented in production areas were made there. While this assumption is probably warranted for the most intensive forms of specialization, it may mischaracterize the output of household producers who produce "a little extra" of one ware for exchange, or who manufacture only certain wares for their own use and acquire the remainder of their household ceramic inventory through exchange, thereby diminishing the proportion of their own products in the assemblage. An alternative procedure better able to capture this kind of low-level product specialization is to seek elevated frequencies of specific wares relative to average frequencies of that ware (compare Stark 1992:193).

Here I employ both measures but place greater weight on the latter one. For the purposes of this chapter, I define "elevated frequency" of a ware as greater than or equal to the 90th percentile of the frequency of rim sherds of that ware in all collections at Tres Zapotes. I use a more stringent criterion of the 95th percentile for Fine Gray ware (W1100)

because it is so rare that over 90% of collections with Fine Gray contain only a single sherd of this ware. I also exclude from consideration two very rare, mainly Middle Formative wares. In addition, production areas with samples of fewer than thirty rims are excluded from the analysis, leaving eight Classic period production areas and sixteen Terminal Formative production areas. As a result, all but one of the small, low density areas with low firing proportions are eliminated, but all other production area classes are represented. Table 5.3 presents the results of the analysis.

As a group, Terminal Formative production areas exhibit elevated frequencies in six of the nine wares considered, including three coarse utilitarian wares. Significantly, the most common ware rarely coincides with a ware having an elevated frequency as defined above, and four production areas exhibit elevated frequencies for more than one ware. There is little consistency in the most prevalent wares or wares with elevated frequencies within classes of production areas, except that independent large, high-intensity production areas tend to have differentially fired vessels (W2200) as their most prevalent ware. However, no ware constitutes more than 33% of the rims from a single production area. In general, then, product specialization in the Terminal Formative production system appears to have been low, although individual production areas produced particular wares in elevated amounts.

In contrast, Classic period specialized production appears to have emphasized Fine Orange vessels (W1200). This untempered serving ware exhibits elevated frequencies in

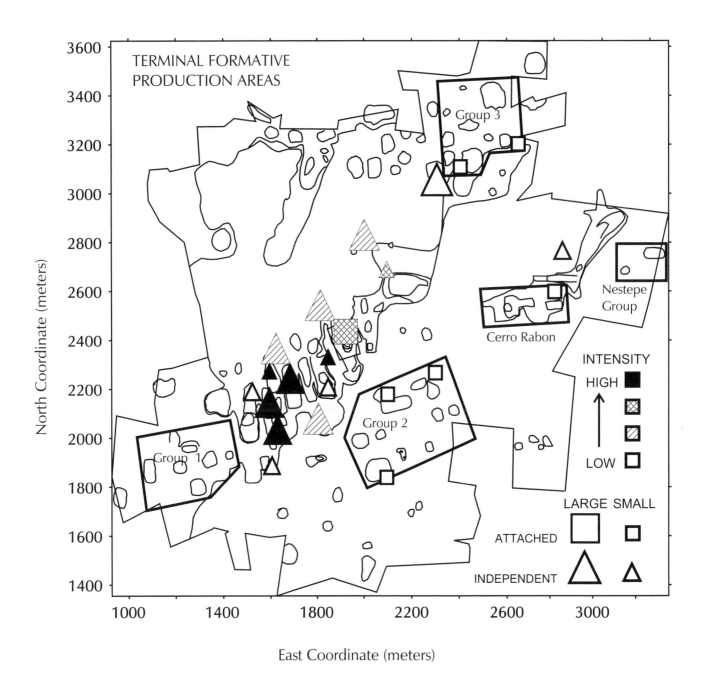

Figure 5.1 Terminal Formative (Nextepetl phase) production areas at Tres Zapotes. Principal mound groups are outlined. Scale of symbol indicates small or large production area. Shading of symbols indicates intensity of production as follows: open, low intensity; hatched, low-moderate intensity; cross-hatched, high-moderate intensity; solid, high intensity. *Illustration prepared by Christopher A. Pool*

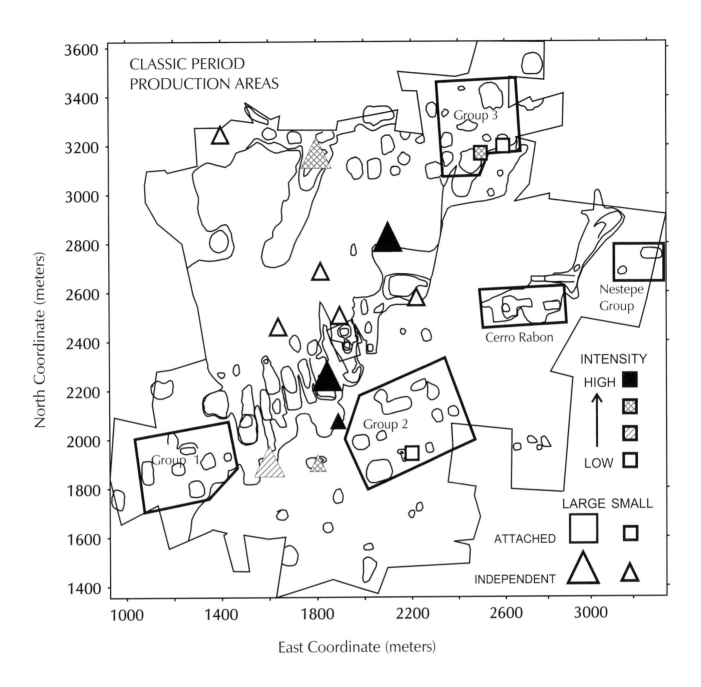

Figure 5.2 Classic-period production areas at Tres Zapotes. Principal mound groups are outlined. Shading of symbols indicates intensity of production as follows: open, low intensity; hatched, low-moderate intensity; cross-hatched, high-moderate intensity; solid, high intensity. *Illustration prepared by Christopher A. Pool*

seven of the eight production areas retained for analysis, and it is the most prevalent ware in each of these seven areas. Two of the seven Fine Orange producers also produced elevated frequencies of Fine Gray ware (W1100) (at the 95th percentile). Interestingly, the one attached production area with a high firing proportion yielded elevated frequencies of two utilitarian wares (Burnished Coarse Brown [W2500] and Coarse Brown with Fine Quartz Temper [W2600]), and the quartz tempered ware was also the most prevalent in the production area. Three other production areas exhibit elevated frequencies in two wares; in two cases the wares are Fine Orange and Fine Gray, but in one the elevated frequencies occurred in Fine Orange and Coarse Brown with Fine Quartz Temper. Nevertheless, overall there appears to be a notable increase in product specialization among specialized Classic period producers, despite a tendency for less spatial concentration of production areas.

Comparison with Matacapan

Because survey methods and the variables used to characterize production areas are similar at Tres Zapotes and Matacapan, it is possible to compare directly the ceramic production systems at these two sites (table 5.2). This comparison indicates several marked differences between the Classic period production systems at Matacapan and Tres Zapotes.

First, attached specialist production appears to have been less prevalent at Matacapan than in either period at Tres Zapotes. Only one attached production area has been identified at Matacapan (Santley et al. 1989; Pool 1990). It was detected in the excavation of a single 3 x 3 m pit rather than in surface collections; so, its extent and proportion devoted to firing activities cannot be assessed, and it is excluded from table 5.2. Sherd densities near the kiln were low compared to other excavated production loci (Pool 1990: Table 5); so, it probably represents relatively nonintensive production comparable to most of the attached production areas at Tres Zapotes.

Greater dispersal of civic-ceremonial groups at Tres Zapotes could contribute to the appearance of more attached specialization there, as this creates a greater probability that a non–elite production area might be located near a civic-ceremonial or elite residential structure. There is a tendency for production areas identified as attached to be located near low mounds in elite precincts; however, the formal arrangement of these low mounds with respect to plazas and other buildings suggest that they are integral components of the elite precincts and probably housed members of the elites' retinues. The attached production area at the northeast corner of Group 2 (area A12), near the low mounds 12, 13, and 14, would appear to be an especially good example of ceramic production by a retainer household. Stirling excavated mound 13 (Weiant's [1943:13, Maps 9 and 10] mound G), finding that it contained a rare example of a stone platform. The unusual quality of construction in this Terminal Formative house mound and its location near a range structure in a civic-ceremonial precinct suggests elevated status and/or elite sponsorship of its inhabitants.

Second, independent ceramic production at intermediate levels of size and intensity is more prevalent at Matacapan than at Classic period Tres Zapotes, particularly with respect to large, low-intensity production areas and small production areas with low-moderate to high production intensities. Twenty-six (63%) of the forty-one independent production areas identified at Matacapan fall between the extremes of small, low intensity and large, high intensity areas. At Tres Zapotes, only eight of twenty-one (38%) Terminal Formative production areas and four of fourteen (29%) Classic Period production areas are independent production areas in the same range of size and intensity. Third, large, high–intensity production areas constitute a smaller proportion of the production areas at Matacapan than in either period at Tres Zapotes. Notably, however, none of the large, high–intensity production areas at Tres Zapotes approaches the size of the two largest production areas at Matacapan (areas 199 and 411), which cover about 2.2 and 4 ha, respectively. Product specialization is also much higher in the large-scale production areas at Matacapan, where Coarse Orange jar sherds represent 55 to 58% of the total sherd assemblage and 84% of all excavated rims in the Comoapan locality (area 411) (Santley et al. 1989:122–123). At Tres Zapotes, no single ware constitutes more than 32% of the assemblage in any large, high-intensity production area. This picture of larger, more highly specialized production areas at Matacapan is modified if the three adjacent large, high-intensity Terminal Formative areas at Tres Zapotes are considered as one 5.25 ha area, but product specialization in the combined production area would still be much lower than in Matacapan area 199 or Comoapan (area 411).

Differences in the Classic period political economies of Tres Zapotes and Matacapan offer the most comprehensive explanation for differences in the organization of their ceramic production systems. Differences in the political sphere are best reflected in the distributions of formal civic-ceremonial architecture at the two sites. At Matacapan, civic-ceremonial architecture is highly concentrated in a 1.2 km^2 area at the center of the site, suggesting a high degree of centralized political control (Santley et al. 1987). In contrast,

Table 5.3 Percentages of wares in ceramic production area assemblages at Tres Zapotes

| | | | | | WARES | | | | | | | | | |
AREA	CONTEXT	SIZE	F. PROP.	DENSITY	W1100	W1200	W2100	W2200	W2500	W2600	W2650	W2700	W2800	TOTAL
CLASSIC														
A22b	Attached	Small	High	Low	0.00	19.05	7.14	9.52	_11.90_	**28.57**	11.90	9.52	2.38	42
B32	Attached	Small	Low	Low	_9.09_	**45.45**	3.03	18.18	3.03	12.12	0.00	6.06	3.03	33
A29b	Independent	Large	High	High	5.59	**31.12**	8.39	11.19	3.85	15.73	9.79	9.79	3.85	286
C07	Independent	Large	High	High	3.79	**31.82**	6.82	9.85	3.79	12.12	6.82	16.67	3.79	132
C11	Independent	Large	High	Low	6.67	**28.57**	2.86	7.62	3.81	_27.62_	9.52	9.52	1.90	105
C15a	Independent	Large	Low	High	4.00	**36.00**	8.00	12.00	6.00	14.00	2.00	14.00	2.00	50
B29	Independent	Small	High	High	5.05	**35.86**	7.07	5.56	5.05	16.16	4.55	18.18	1.52	198
C13	Independent	Small	High	Low	_5.97_	**40.30**	5.97	8.96	4.48	16.42	8.96	2.99	2.99	67
TERMINAL FORMATIVE														
B30a	Attached	Large	High	Low	0.00	11.11	5.56	**22.22**	4.44	11.11	8.89	**22.22**	_12.22_	90
A22a	Attached	Small	High	Low	2.67	6.67	9.33	20.00	_9.33_	14.67	10.67	**21.33**	5.33	75
C39	Attached	Small	Low	High	_6.25_	18.75	12.50	**21.88**	3.13	18.75	3.13	12.50	3.13	32
A03	Attached	Small	Low	High	2.04	2.04	_20.41_	14.29	_8.16_	8.16	10.20	22.45	_12.24_	49
B03	Attached	Small	Low	High	0.00	14.29	11.90	16.67	7.14	4.76	11.90	**23.81**	7.14	42
C17	Independent	Large	High	High	1.85	6.17	_16.05_	**21.60**	7.41	16.05	12.96	12.35	4.32	162
C15b	Independent	Large	High	High	1.53	11.45	10.69	**22.90**	_12.98_	15.27	2.29	16.03	3.05	131
A29a	Independent	Large	High	High	3.41	3.41	13.64	**25.00**	3.41	10.23	13.64	17.05	9.09	88
B07	Independent	Large	Low	High	2.75	2.75	8.26	21.10	4.59	14.68	9.17	**28.44**	7.34	109
A31a	Independent	Large	Low	High	1.50	1.50	12.78	**22.56**	_15.04_	15.04	6.02	20.30	5.26	133
C14	Independent	Large	Low	High	2.13	3.19	7.45	21.28	0.00	10.64	7.45	**32.98**	_10.64_	94
B30c	Independent	Large	Low	High	0.00	13.56	13.56	19.49	_9.32_	**20.34**	10.17	7.63	4.24	118
C19	Independent	Small	High	High	2.83	**19.81**	13.21	17.92	5.66	10.38	12.26	11.32	5.66	106
A29c	Independent	Small	High	High	0.00	2.00	_24.00_	22.00	_10.00_	8.00	4.00	**26.00**	2.00	50
B31	Independent	Small	High	Low	3.45	8.62	3.45	**25.86**	_10.34_	6.90	6.90	**25.86**	_8.62_	58
C22	Independent	Small	Low	Low	1.52	9.09	9.09	**30.30**	_15.15_	1.52	9.09	16.67	7.58	66

Note: F. Prop.= Firing property. Total = Total rims. <u>Underlining</u> indicates elevated frequencies above the 95th percentile for W1100 (Fine Gray) or 90th percentile for all other wares. **Bold** text indicates most prevalent ware.

formal mound groups are more widely dispersed at Tres Zapotes, and the total volume of architecture appears to be much less. This is despite the fact that all of the excavated temple mounds and elite residential platforms contain Late to Terminal Formative construction phases and thus do not vary markedly among themselves in their general temporal assignments (Drucker 1943a:25–27, 144–145; Weiant 1943:6–7, 11–14; see also chapter 7). Sociopolitical hierarchy appears, therefore, to have been less strongly developed at Tres Zapotes. Consequently, the elites of Tres Zapotes may have had to rely more heavily on attached specialists within their household retinues for utilitarian and serving vessels, while the elites of Matacapan could have met their ceramic needs more effectively through duties collected from the site as a whole. The need to meet these demands at Matacapan could also have encouraged intensification at intermediate levels by independent specialists, while elite administration of production for regional distribution or export would ex-

plain the establishment of a small number of very large, intensive, and nucleated production areas highly specialized in the manufacture of specific products, as seen at Comoapan and area 199. In contrast, the greater tendency of Classic period specialists at Tres Zapotes to emphasize Fine Orange pottery than their contemporaries at Matacapan is more readily explained by differences in the availability of the kaolinitic clays used in their manufacture. These clays are readily available from massive exposures in the vicinity of Matacapan, but exposures appear to be smaller and more distant in the Tres Zapotes region (Pool and Santley 1992:Fig. 1). Specialists at Tres Zapotes may therefore have geared much of their production to meet the widespread demand for ceramics produced from these more difficult to obtain materials, leaving much of the production of utilitarian wares to less intensive household producers.

Despite the marked differences in the Classic period ceramic production systems at Matacapan and Tres Zapotes, these sites share several characteristics. They exhibit an internally differentiated ceramic production system that included both independent and attached specialists, as well as independent specialists organized at varying scales and intensities. Moreover, independent production in both sites was most frequently carried out in domestic contexts, despite the possible presence of a non-household workshop complex at Comoapan in the Matacapan suburbs (Santley et al. 1989; Arnold et al. 1993; compare Feinman 1999:97).

Comparison with the western Papaloapan basin

The adjacent region of the western lower Papaloapan basin offers contrasts to the Matacapan and Tres Zapotes cases. In the swamps of the lower basin, Stark (1985, 1989) found evidence for ceramic production in a domestic context at Patarata 52, and Diehl (1997) excavated pit kilns in a civic-ceremonial plaza at La Mojarra, which, depending on their as-yet-unknown temporal relationship to surrounding mounds, might suggest the possibility of attached specialization for elite patrons. In the Mixtequilla region, located on higher ground on the western margin of the basin, Stark (1992) identified several pottery production locations from surface data. The Mixtequilla production locations were all associated with residential features; thus, no cases of production locations in elite civic-ceremonial contexts have been identified. Moreover, in only one case, that of Postclassic *comal* production, did ceramic surface densities or elevated proportions of a specific ware approach the values for the larger, more intensive production localities at Matacapan or Tres Zapotes (Curet 1993; Stark 2000). Thus, given current evidence, ceramic production at Matacapan and Tres Zapotes appears to have been more differentiated and to have included more intensive production modes than in the Mixtequilla and other sites of the Papaloapan lowlands.

In a recent summary, Stark (2000) called attention to the effects of the different analytical methods used in these studies. In the Mixtequilla, analyses considered co-occurrences of unusually high frequencies of a particular pottery type with primary production indicators as well as co-occurrence of primary production indicators with high surface density. High surface density was defined more stringently than at Matacapan (or in this chapter at Tres Zapotes), as the upper decile of densities. High frequency of a particular pottery type was also defined stringently as the top five percentages for that type (as opposed to a fixed quantile). The aim in the Mixtequilla analyses was to evaluate the clearest cases of specialized production, at the expense of failing to identify less specialized cases. In contrast, the tercile criterion for defining high density at Matacapan and Tres Zapotes may

inflate the number of small-scale, low-intensity production areas, because primary production indicators have a 33% chance of being associated with the upper tercile of collections by chance alone (Stark 2000). As Stark notes, this risk is reduced in those cases where there is a spatial association of squares, because it is less likely that adventitious spatial associations would occur. Nevertheless, it is true that isolated squares identified as production localities may represent "false positives." Stark aptly sums up the situation: "we have one subregion where judgments were stingy and another where they were generous in designating production locations." (2000)

I am not yet prepared to conduct a direct comparison of data relating to scale and intensity of production between Tres Zapotes and the Mixtequilla, although such a comparison may be possible in the future using the data from the full-coverage stage of the RATZ survey. Nevertheless, we may productively ask what picture would emerge if the situation were reversed using less stringent criteria for identifying production localities in the Mixtequilla? Stark (1992) provides some published data that permit such a comparison. Within a 40 km² block of the Mixtequilla surveyed using full-coverage methods, Stark (1992:Fig. 8.5, Table 8.1) recovered fifty-eight overt indicators of pottery production distributed among forty-nine surface collections, of which thirty-nine had ceramic frequencies greater than the median for all collections. If all thirty-nine of these collections represent actual cases of pottery production (and Stark does not claim they do), then the density of production areas would be 0.98 per km². Restricting consideration to all collections with production indicators within a 2 km radius around the geographic center of Cerro de las Mesas yields a similar figure of 1.03 possible production areas per km² (thirteen collections in 12.6 km²). By comparison, a more stringent definition requiring occurrence of production indicators in collections in the upper tercile of ceramic densities at Matacapan identified forty-one possible production areas in an area of 7 km² (5.9/km²) surveyed using systematic transect methods. At Tres Zapotes, methods and criteria similar to those at Matacapan yielded forty-one possible production areas in 3.2 km² (12.8/km²).

The picture of more concentrated ceramic production areas in Matacapan and Tres Zapotes holds even when differences in the temporal span of the sites are considered. The Mixtequilla production areas relate to the Classic and Postclassic periods (AD 300–1500, or a maximum of 1200 years), the Matacapan collections are confined to the 600 years of the Classic period (AD 300–900), and the Tres Zapotes production areas to the Terminal Formative and Classic (100 BC–AD 900, 1000 years). Dividing the densities of identified possible production areas by these generously defined temporal spans yields figures of one production area per century at Matacapan and 1.3 at Tres Zapotes, but only about 0.1 production area per century at Cerro de las Mesas and the Mixtequilla in general. Clearly, many more production areas must have existed in each of these sites to fulfill the demand for ceramics. Nevertheless, comparing the areas using very generous standards for the Mixtequilla and more restrictive criteria for the sites to the east of the Papaloapan still supports the inference of a heavier concentration of specialized ceramic production in the latter sites.

Conclusion

The characterizational approach to analyzing variation in ceramic production systems utilized in this chapter offers the advantages over a typological approach of remaining closer to the archaeological data and allowing us to identify organizational arrangements not documented in ethnographic and historical studies. Use of the characterizational approach, however, requires careful consideration of field and analytical methods. It will be most effective within sites and regions investigated under a single research design or between regions in which sampling procedures have been designed to collect commensurate data, as illustrated in this chapter by my comparison of Tres Zapotes and Matacapan. The data collected in the full-coverage stage of the RATZ survey may allow a similarly direct comparison with the Mixtequilla. At present, however, Stark's (2000) review and the comparison to the Mixtequilla offered in this study highlight the difficulty of making interregional comparisons when different field and analytical methods are employed.

Despite this caveat, some general observations may be offered about the organization of ceramic production in the lower Papaloapan basin and Tuxtla Mountains of south-central and southern Veracruz. Throughout this broad region, specialized ceramic production appears to have been carried out most frequently in domestic contexts. Moreover, isolated finds of production indicators unassociated with markedly high ceramic densities, as in the Mixtequilla and at Tres Zapotes, raise the possibility of widespread production at intensities too low to be securely confirmed archaeologically. From La Mojarra on the Acula River to Matacapan in the western Tuxtlas Mountains, however, the existence of some ceramic production loci in civic-ceremonial contexts suggests that elites at least occasionally supplied their needs through patronage of attached producers, particularly at Tres Zapotes. Current evidence also suggests some instances of the development of more intensive forms of production and more highly concentrated patterns of specialized production

Nucleated	(Tres Zapotes)	(Matacapan)
	↑ intensive ↑ concentrated ↑ attached	↑ intensive ↑ concentrated ↓ attached
SETTLEMENT Dispersed	(Mixtequilla) ↓ intensive ↓ concentrated ↓ attached	↓ intensive ↓ concentrated ↑ attached
	Factional	Centralized
	POLITICAL ORGANIZATION	

Figure 5.3 Effect of settlement and political factors on the organization of ceramic production in the southern Gulf lowlands. *Illustration prepared by Christopher A. Pool*

at Tres Zapotes and especially at Matacapan.

Based on these admittedly few cases, a general model of factors affecting variation in the organization of ceramic production in the Gulf coastal lowlands may be offered as a hypothesis for future testing (figure 5.3). The boundary conditions for this model, which emphasizes demographic and political variables, are a tropical lowland setting, hierarchical sociopolitical organization, and production of a commodity widely used by elites and commoners alike. Centralization is considered here as an organizational phenomenon in which power, authority, and responsibility are concentrated in a relatively few persons, groups, or institutions. It is distinguished from the spatial phenomenon of nucleation, which concerns the geographical clustering of activities, populations, and their physical manifestations (chapter 7). Under this model, dispersal of population favors low scales and intensities of ceramic production, carried out in domestic contexts with relatively few, widely dispersed specialists producing for highly localized sets of consumers. Such a pattern corresponds to the Mixtequilla case, as described by Stark (1992:204). As population becomes more nucleated, as appears to be the case at Matacapan and Tres Zapotes, closer proximity to larger sets of consumers encourages the development of larger, more intensive independent production areas, though in the Gulf lowlands setting they continue to be situated primarily in household contexts, and they do not completely replace lower scales and intensities of production. Centralization of political authority, as appears to be evident at Matacapan, may further encourage the development of larger, more nucleated, and more intensive modes of nominally independent production, if elites employ taxation or tribute to extract some portion of that production for their own use or for regional distribution or export.

Political factors may have played a much different role in the development of attached specialization as it relates to ceramic production in the Gulf lowlands. First, it should be recalled that none of the wares produced at Tres Zapotes or Matacapan were restricted to elites. This contrasts with the (perhaps more common) cases in which attached specialists produced luxury or wealth items or weaponry (Costin 1991:11). Nevertheless, elite households do require a supply of cooking, storage, and service vessels for their own use. Furthermore, elites have available to them various strategies for acquiring goods (Hirth 1996). Direct and exclusive control of the output of attached producers is only one of these. Elites may also demand some portion of the productive capacity of independent producers through taxation, tribute, or patronage, either in kind or in labor (the latter as in the case of dispersed corvée [Costin 1991:8]). These latter strategies will be more effective under conditions of more centralized political authority, as suggested above for Matacapan, while higher degrees of factionalism, such as are inferred for Tres Zapotes, may favor the support of attached specialists as a means of ensuring a regular supply of products.

The case of the Mixtequilla represents an apparent challenge to this portion of the model, because attached specialization has not been identified in a setting in which civic-ceremonial mound complexes are closely spaced, and, as Stark observes, "No single formal complex dominates the surrounding landscape as thoroughly as, for example, central Tikal" (1999:219). The formal mound complex at Cerro de las Mesas, however, which covers 1.46 km², including its northern and southern extensions of Ojochal and Cerro del Chivo, is much larger than any one of the formal complexes at Tres Zapotes, and it contrasts much more with the next largest center at Los Azuzules (0.16 km²) (Stark 1999:213, 215; see also the discussion in chapter 7). Classic period sculpture is also highly concentrated at Cerro de las Mesas. Stirling found twenty-three monuments there, while only one each has been reported from the next largest centers at Los Azuzules and Zapotal (Stark 1999:219, Stirling 1943:31–47). By contrast, stone sculpture at Tres Zapotes, mainly dating to the Late and Terminal Formative periods, is much more evenly distributed. Thus, despite suggestions of factionalism in the Mixtequilla region, political power appears to have been more highly centralized in the formal architectural complex at Cerro de las Mesas than in any complex at Tres Zapotes, which would support the general outlines of the model presented here.

NOTES

1. Production area designations are based on alphanumeric field codes for modern agricultural fields in which they are located. Where more than one production area was identified within an agricultural field, they are distinguished by lowercase letters appended to the end of the field designation (for example, areas A22a and A22b). Production areas may extend into adjacent fields.

OBSIDIAN PRODUCTION, CONSUMPTION, AND DISTRIBUTION AT TRES ZAPOTES

Piecing Together Political Economy

Charles Knight

Aɴ ɪᴍᴘᴏʀᴛᴀɴᴛ ᴄᴏᴍᴘᴏɴᴇɴᴛ ɪɴ ᴏᴜʀ ᴜɴᴅᴇʀsᴛᴀɴᴅɪɴɢ ᴏꜰ ᴛʜᴇ development and maintenance of sociopolitical inequality in Mesoamerica has been identifying the nature of the production, distribution, and consumption systems of local and non-local resources (for example, Charlton 1984; Clark 1987; Clark and Parry 1990; Hirth 1996; Rathje 1971, 1972; Santley 1983, 1984). One resource widely exchanged in pre-Hispanic Mesoamerica was obsidian, a volcanic glass used for an array of purposes, both utilitarian and prestige. The inhabitants of the southern Gulf lowlands of Veracruz (figure 6.1) relied heavily on imported obsidian throughout the Formative and Classic periods, because locally available, fine-grained stone was exceedingly scarce. Source variation in the southern Gulf lowlands suggests the participation in numerous long-distance exchange networks throughout Mesoamerica, but especially with the central Mexican highlands. As a result, the acquisition of obsidian and control over its production, distribution, and consumption may have played an important role in the development and maintenance of social, political, and economic differences in the southern Gulf lowlands. In this chapter, I investigate the obsidian assemblage from surface collections at Tres Zapotes, Veracruz, Mexico, to shed light on the role obsidian may have had in the local political economy.

Models

Archaeologists have developed numerous models of ancient economic strategies, focusing either on the production, distribution, or service sectors of prehistoric economies. Recently Hirth (1996) has stated that these unitary strategy models fall short in understanding the role of resource mobilization in political economies, because individually they

do not consider the full array of resource mobilization strategies available to aspiring elites. Instead, it is important that we recognize the multitude of strategies available to elites, which crosscut these various sectors of the economy. Hirth identifies four key principles that underlie the structure of political economies: accumulation, context, matrix-control, and ideology. These principles recognize the mix of production, distribution, and payment strategies used in the mobilization of resources as being fundamental to the development and maintenance of sociopolitical inequality (Hirth 1996:221).

According to Hirth (1996:221–226), the accumulation principle pertains to the reasons why elites, or aspiring elites, accumulate strategic resources and the corollary effects of such accumulation. Implementing resource-accumulation strategies benefits such individuals by affording them the wherewithal to improve their ability to attract supporters and enhance their own power (Hirth 1996:221). The context principle is based on how and where resources are accumulated, that is, the level at which accumulation takes place, such as in the individual household or in more special-purpose contexts controlled by the elite. Individual-oriented accumulation occurs in multiple general-purpose contexts and predominates where centralized economic leadership is weakly developed (Hirth 1996:223). Conversely, context-oriented accumulation occurs in special social contexts of production or accumulation under the direction of elites. By defining these contexts at higher levels than individual production units, elites increase the number of potential contributors to the system (Hirth 1996:224). The matrix-control principle concerns the placement of individuals in centrally advantageous positions, which provide those individuals with greater influence, direct or indirect, over produc-

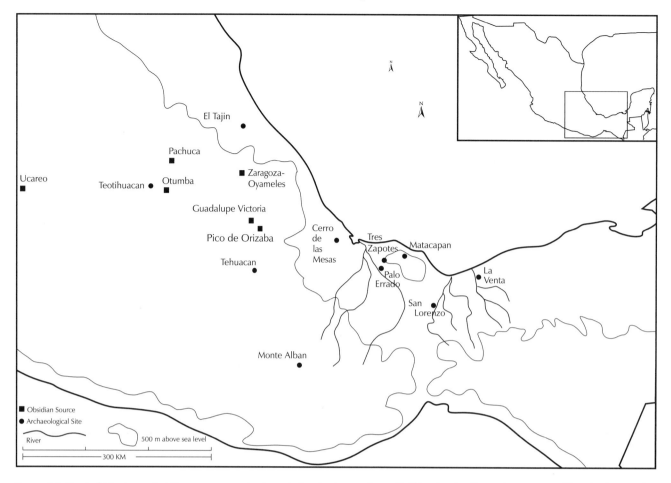

Figure 6.1 Central Mexican obsidian sources and selected sites in the southern Gulf lowlands. *Illustration prepared by Charles Knight*

tion, exchange, and service activities (Hirth 1996:224). Finally, the ideology principle identifies the beliefs that justify, rationalize, and reinforce the existing system of economic inequality. Economic ideology is particularly concerned with concepts of ownership, end-usages (for example, long-standing social obligations), and resource conversions, which allow for the development of unbalanced economic relationships (Hirth 1996:225–226).

Two common models of political economy are dubbed adaptationist and political by Brumfiel and Earle (1987). While both models focus on the principle of accumulation in attempting to explain the development of sociopolitical hierarchies (Hirth 1996:221), the context, ideology, and matrix-control principles also may be incorporated into political and adaptationist explanations. These two models, which encompass Hirth's four principles, frame the following discussion on the obsidian economy in the southern Gulf lowlands at Tres Zapotes.

Briefly, adaptationist models focus on the strategies of accumulation employed to acquire utilitarian commodities, which better enable the local population to adapt to their

environment. Such models hold that individual households will give up a certain degree of autonomy to align themselves with those individuals who control the acquisition of these strategic resources. In exchange, individual households will receive a secure and steady supply of the needed utilitarian resource from the individual(s) controlling resource accumulation (Rathje 1971, 1972; Santley 1983, 1984; Service 1962; see also Brumfiel and Earle 1987).

Different versions of the adaptationist model emphasize centralized acquisition and distribution of subsistence goods across microenvironments, centralized facilitation of market exchange, and management of subsistence production (Brumfiel and Earle 1987:2). The version most relevant to the case of obsidian exchange in the southern Gulf lowlands of Mexico proposes that centralized leadership develops to facilitate long-distance trade to accumulate non-local goods and distribute them to the general populace (Rathje 1971, 1972). Under this model, obsidian functions as a utilitarian good integral to the conduct of everyday activities, and focus is on the nature and degree of control over the exchange of the material. This model does not preclude the possibility that obsidian served as a prestige good in other parts of Mesoamerica (for example, Rice 1987a). Neither does it deny that the establishment of long-distance exchange alliances by elites to acquire prestige goods may have adaptive functions in times of resource stress (for example, Flannery 1968), but it emphasizes adaptive benefits to the society over the political aspirations of elite individuals.

Following an adaptationist model of obsidian accumulation at Tres Zapotes, the matrix-control principle may apply because certain individuals will control the flow of obsidian into the region and then distribute it to members of all social strata. Control over obsidian import may be manifest by the physical regulation of obsidian into the area by the elite based at the regional center of Tres Zapotes. In this situation political and economic power tends to be centralized in the hands of the few who control the exchange networks. Since the relevant version of the adaptationist perspective emphasizes the control over exchange rather than control over obsidian tool production, tool production may be decentralized and occur in individual households. Specialized production, where it occurs, tends to be independent, because specialists are producing for the commoner population (Earle 1987). As a result the adaptationist perspective is congruent with individual-oriented accumulation and thus addresses the context principle. Furthermore, the ideology principle justifies the involvement of elites in the acquisition of the material, and its distribution to the populace is justified in the context of the "moral economy" (Hirth 1996:221–223).

In general, political models focus on the acquisition and exchange of prestige goods and wealth (which may include "rare and highly desired subsistence goods" [Brumfiel and Earle 1987:4]) among elites to reaffirm social and political standing, as well as between the elite and non-elite to attract followers, meeting the tenets of the accumulation principle. The political strategies of wealth accumulation exploited by the elite accord two primary roles to obsidian prestige goods (Hirth 1992:22), both congruent with the ideology principle. The first role would be to legitimize the positions of the elite as political and economic leaders. In this sense an obsidian artifact would work as a "badge of authority," that "proclaim[s] the rank and status of [its] owner" (Hirth 1992:22). The "badge of authority" has no inherent value; rather, its value is symbolic and as such is not transferable. The second role holds that the value of the prestige good is transferable, making the obsidian prestige good an item of "wealth," and therefore exchangeable among elites in a regional settlement system as a means to cement political and economic ties (Brumfiel 1994:10; Brumfiel and Earle 1987:3). In a similar vein obsidian prestige goods could be used to

establish labor pools for projects undertaken by the central polity (Drennan 1987). In these situations the context principle is evoked, since control over the production of obsidian artifacts, such as prismatic blades, would be tightly controlled by the elite who would organize production through attached specialists. Obviously, elites may also employ the matrix control principle to manage the production and exchange of obsidian prestige items to enhance their social standing and political power.

In sum, the four principles of political economy are applicable to the adaptationist and political models of resource acquisition in the southern Gulf lowlands. Both models focus on the strategies employed by individuals in attracting the support of others and in developing social connections, which then become the basis of socioeconomic power (Hirth 1996:221). While they are often dichotomized in the literature, the two models are most illuminating when considered together, as will be illustrated below.

Recent Work

The RATZ project recovered 4154 obsidian artifacts from 1121 3 x 3 m surface collection units (figure 6.2). Obsidian constituted 99.5% of all chipped-stone materials recovered. Although Tres Zapotes is located near the immense basalt stone source of the Tuxtla Mountains, Mark Kruczynski's preliminary analysis of the basalt assemblage collected by RATZ suggests that this ubiquitous local resource was used for tasks different from those of obsidian (Pool 1997c:25–28). Basalt from the nearby Cerro El Vigía was used for colossal stone monuments and utilitarian items, such as *manos* and *metates*, but not for fine cutting, slicing, scraping, or carving implements. The scarcity of non-obsidian materials in the Tres Zapotes chipped-stone assemblages is not unusual for this area. Both the Matacapan (Santley 1989a; Santley et al. 1984; Santley et al. 1997) and Mixtequilla (Heller and Stark 1998; Stark et al. 1992; Stark and Heller 1991a) projects report similar proportions of obsidian in their chipped-stone assemblages. The local scarcity of chipped-stone alternatives not only necessitated some form of contact between the southern Gulf lowlands and the central highlands but also envalued an otherwise utilitarian commodity at the local level in the southern Gulf lowlands.

The dominant types of obsidian found in the southern Gulf lowlands tend to be limited to four sources: Zaragoza-Oyameles, Guadalupe Victoria, Pico de Orizaba, and Pachuca (figure 6.1). Obsidians from El Chayal, Otumba, Paredon, Ucareo, and Zacualtipan have also been recovered in the southern Gulf Coast but in limited amounts (Cobean et al. 1991; Knight 1999; Stark et al. 1992). The nearest obsidian

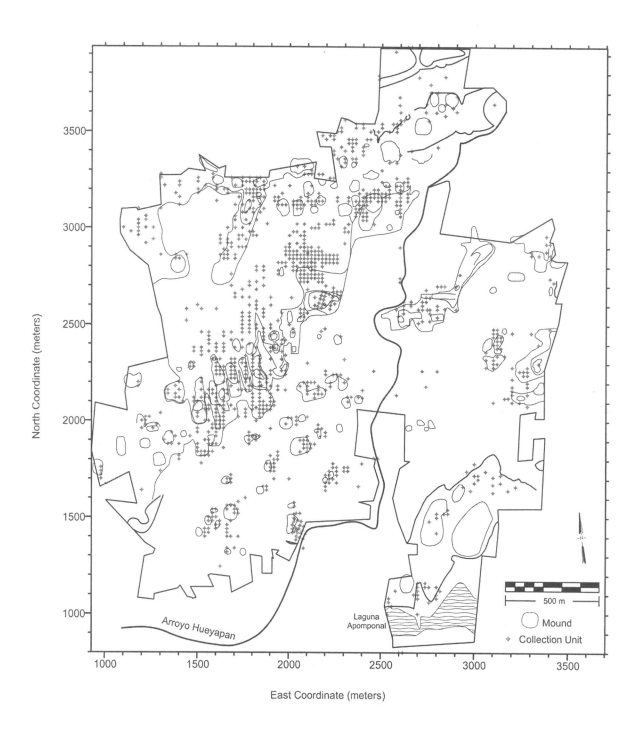

Figure 6.2 Distribution of surface collection units with at least one obsidian artifact. *Illustration prepared by Charles Knight. Base map prepared by Michael A. Ohnersorgen and Chrstopher A. Pool*

sources to Tres Zapotes are located on the Pico de Orizaba volcano, approximately 200 km west-northwest of the site on the Veracruz/Puebla border (figure 6.1). Except for the Guadalupe Victoria obsidian, the obsidian from the four main sources was of excellent quality and conducive to prismatic blade manufacture. Because of frequent inclusions, the use of Guadalupe Victoria obsidian in core-blade reduction was less common; instead, it was used primarily for producing flakes and, to a lesser extent, bifaces.

Methods

Both flake-core technology, which produces usable flakes and formalized tools such as bifaces, and core-blade technology, which produces prismatic blades, were represented in the surface obsidian assemblage at Tres Zapotes. While the presence of flakes and flake cores suggest flake-core technology, very few bifaces or unifaces were recovered from the surface materials. In general, prismatic blades and the debitage resulting from their production dominated. The classification of obsidian artifact types was based on a technological and morphological typology developed by Dan Healan and Janet Kerley at Tula, Hidalgo (Healan, Kerley, and Bey III 1983), and later adopted and modified by Kerley and Robert Santley for the Matacapan project (Santley et al. 1984), by Santley and Tom Barrett for the Tuxtlas survey (Barrett 1996), and by myself for the Palo Errado and RATZ projects (Knight 1999; Pool 1997c:24–25). This typology has been applied successfully, in one form or another, elsewhere in the Tuxtlas and surrounding regions (Knight 1999; Pool, Wright and Britt 1993: Santley, Kerley, and Kneebone 1986; Santley, Kerley, and Barrett 1995; Santley, Arnold, and Barrett 1997). The typology as it was used here was divided into ninety-one individual obsidian artifact types, which were lumped into eleven technological categories based on reduction stage (appendix A). The artifact types were thereby quantified by stage, and thus easily attributed to a point along the production-consumption (and possibly rejuvenation) continuum (figure 6.3). In this scheme, a macrocore, polyhedral core, or finished prismatic blade is referred to as a commodity, while the debris resulting from the production of that commodity is referred to as debitage or waste (Clark 1986; Clark and Lee 1984).

VISUAL CHARACTERISTICS

In addition to morphology, the obsidian materials were classified by color: three base colors (black, green, and clear) and ten subcolors, which refer to secondary colors and textural characteristics (black, gray, green, bottle clear, clear with clouds, cloudy, banded, smoky, green-blue, brown, waxy, and

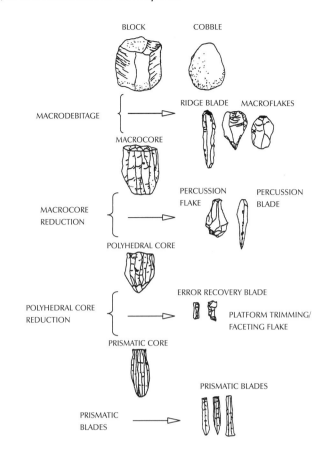

Figure 6.3 Core-blade reduction sequence. *After Santley et al. 1984*

mottled black/gray). While the reliance on visual characteristics for sourcing obsidian artifacts has been criticized because of the great variety of color and banding within single sources from elsewhere in Mesoamerica (Sheets 1977), the categorization by color has been shown to be a useful indicator of obsidian sources in the southern Gulf lowlands (see Cobean et al. 1991; Santley, Arnold, and Barrett 1997; Stark et al 1992). In each of these studies trace element analysis confirmed the initial categorization by visual characteristics. As a result, visual source analysis in the southern Gulf lowlands is a quick, inexpensive, and fairly reliable method of arriving at a general understanding of source material acquisition in the region. Instrumental Neutron Activation Analysis (INAA) of a nonprobablistic sample of ninety-nine obsidian specimens from the hinterland center of Palo Errado (Knight 1999) was used to identify sources represented in the Tres Zapotes assemblage according to their visual characteristics. INAA was performed at the University of Missouri Research Reactor (MURR) by Michael Glascock. Since I analyzed the obsidian from both Palo Errado and Tres

Table 6.1 Obsidian source categories and colors

SOURCE	COLOR-SUBCOLOR	N	%
Pico de Orizaba (PO)	Clear-Clear with Clouds	319	7.6
	SUBTOTAL	319	7.6
Guadalupe Victoria (GV)	Clear-Waxy	315	7.6
	SUBTOTAL	315	7.6
Pachuca (Pa)	Green-Clear	35	0.8
	Green-Cloudy	2	0.05
	Green-Banded	2	0.05
	SUBTOTAL	39	0.9
Zaragoza-Oyameles (Z-O)	Black-Black	1213	29.2
	Black-Grey	10	0.2
	Black-Banded	348	8.4
	Black-Smoky (translucent)	8	0.2
	Black-Brown	6	0.1
	Clear-Clear	40	1.0
	Clear-Cloudy	332	8.0
	Clear-Banded	321	7.7
	Clear-Smoky (translucent)	352	8.5
	SUBTOTAL	2630	63.3
Mixed-Ucareo (m-U)	Black-Cloudy	625	15.0
	SUBTOTAL	625	15.0
Mixed-Otumba (m-Ot)	Black-Gray, Greenish-Blue	226	5.4
	SUBTOTAL	226	5.4
TOTAL		4154	100.0

Zapotes at the same time, using the same color categories and criteria, inconsistency in the visual assignments was minimized.

In the southern Gulf lowlands, most of the chemically analyzed black and dark gray obsidian has been attributed to the Zaragoza-Oyameles source complex in Puebla, green obsidian to the Pachuca source, and clear obsidian to the Guadalupe Victoria and Pico de Orizaba sources, which lie near one another on either side of the Puebla-Veracruz border (Knight 1999; Pool 1997b; Santley, Arnold, and Barrett 1997; Stark et al. 1992). The chronology of obsidian source exploitation through time in the southern Gulf lowlands has also been documented. For the most part, clear obsidian dominates assemblages of the Early and Middle Formative periods in the southern Gulf lowlands (Cobean et al. 1991; Heller and Stark 1998; Santley, Arnold, and Barrett 1997; Stark et al. 1992). The Late Formative period, but especially the Early and Late Classic periods, witnessed an increased reliance on black and dark gray obsidian from the Zaragoza-Oyameles source (Heller and Stark 1998; Santley 1989a;

Santley, Arnold, and Barrett 1997; Stark et al. 1992). In fact, X-ray fluorescence analysis of obsidian material excavated by Stirling at Tres Zapotes found that Zaragoza-Oyameles obsidian constituted 93.4% of the obsidian assemblage (Hester, Jack, and Heizer 1971:97). Finally, at Cerro de las Mesas, Pico de Orizaba obsidian rises to prominence in the Postclassic period (Heller and Stark 1998; Stark et al. 1992).

Table 6.1 summarizes the source and color data for Tres Zapotes. Three color categories, Mixed-Ucareo, Mixed-Otumba, and Guadalupe Victoria, require special comment. In the Palo Errado INAA sample, two of twenty pieces of black-cloudy obsidian were sourced to Ucareo, and the rest to Zaragoza-Oyameles. Similarly, one of four pieces of black-gray, greenish-blue obsidian was sourced to Otumba and the rest to Zaragoza-Oyameles. Therefore, these visual categories are separated in the current analysis, although it is important to stress that the presence of Otumba and Ucareo obsidian has not been confirmed at Tres Zapotes, and most, if not all, of the pieces assigned to the black-cloudy and black-gray, greenish-blue categories at Tres Zapotes probably derive from the Zaragoza-Oyameles source. Santley et al. (1997) found that 39.6% of the obsidian sourced to Guadalupe Victoria in their INAA sample from the Tuxtlas survey had a waxy surface texture and that this texture was rare or absent in other sources. Similar specimens in the Tuxtlas survey collection indicated to me by Barrett also contained inclusions and dull blue bands. I have therefore assigned clear obsidians with these secondary characteristics (glossed as subcolor "waxy" in table 6.1) to the Guadalupe Victoria source. Other examples of chemically sourced Guadalupe Victoria obsidian have proven to be difficult to distinguish from Pico de Orizaba obsidians (Santley et al. 1997; Stark et al. 1992:229), and those assigned here to Pico de Orizaba may include some specimens from Guadalupe Victoria. The visual indeterminacy of these two sources does not invalidate the results of the study, however, because the two sources are near to one another geographically.

REDUCTION STAGE EXCHANGE AT TRES ZAPOTES

In addition to identifying the variation in source material exchanged, the type of artifact being exchanged (for example, quarried material, macrocore, polyhedral core, preform, or finished tool) was also considered. I refer to this exchange of specific technological categories as "reduction stage exchange." At Tres Zapotes obsidian from all main color categories, representing the four major sources, were utilized in prismatic blade production, albeit to varying degrees. The proportions of macrodebitage, macrocore reduction debitage, and polyhedral core reduction debitage for each source are

Table 6.2 Tres Zapotes obsidian quantities by source and stage (%)

	MD**	MCR	PCR	PB	BT	FC	FT	BR	BF	EC	UN	TOTAL
GV*	6 (1.9%)	5 (1.6%)	22 (7%)	67 (21%)	7 (2%)	32 (10%)	26 (8%)	——	2 (0.6%)	——	148 (47%)	315 (100%)
PO		1 (0.3%)	47 (15%)	109 (34%)	9 (3%)	6 (2%)	12 (4%)	1 (0.3%)	——	——	134 (42%)	319 (100%)
Pa	——	——	3 (8%)	28 (72%)	5 (13%)		1 (3%)				2 (5%)	39 (100%)
Z-O	46 (1.6%)	39 (1.6%)	370 (14%)	1643 (62%)	55 (2%)	34 (1.3%)	34 (1.3%)	3 (0.1%)	7 (0.3%)	1 (0.04%)	398 (15%)	2630 (100%)
m-U	2 (0.3%)	6 (1%)	79 (13%)	373 (60%)	12 (2%)	13 (2%)	8 (1%)	1 (0.2%)	1 (0.1%)		130 (21%)	625 (100%)
m-OT	2 (0.9%)	——	17 (7.5%)	188 (83%)	5 (2.2%)		2 (0.9%)		1 (0.4%)	——	11 (5%)	226 (100%)
TOTAL	56 (1.3%)	51 (1.3%)	538 (12.9%)	2408 (58%)	93 (2.2%)	85 (2%)	83 (2%)	5 (0.1%)	11 (0.2%)	1 (0.02%)	823 (20%)	4154 (100%)

*Sources: GV=Guadalupe Victoria, PO=Pico de Orizaba, Pa=Pachuca, Z-O=Zaragoza-Oyameles, m-U=mixed-Ucareo, m-OT=mixed-Otumba.

**Stages: MD=Macrodebitage, MCR=Macrocore Reduction, PCR=Polyhedral Core Reduction, PB=Prismatic Blades, BR=Bifacial Reduction, FT=Flake Tools, FC=Flake Core, BT=Blade Tools, Bf=Biface, Ec=Eccentrics, Un=Unidentified flakes.

presented in table 6.2. Figure 6.4 presents the surface distribution of macrodebitage and macrocore reduction debitage combined. Figure 6.5 presents the distribution for polyhedral core reduction debitage, and figure 6.6 presents the distribution of prismatic blades.

Core-blade technology was the dominant technology employed on Pachuca, Zaragoza-Oyameles, mixed-Ucareo, and mixed-Otumba obsidians, while substantial flake-core technology was utilized with the Guadalupe Victoria and Pico de Orizaba obsidians. Only three production indicators of Pachuca obsidian were recovered: a hinge recovery blade, blade shatter, and distal blade core. This suggests that at least some Pachuca obsidian entered the site as prepared polyhedral cores. In contrast, the substantial amount of polyhedral core reduction debitage (15%), the small proportion of primary reduction stage material (0.3%), and the large proportion of flakes, flake tools, and flake cores (56%) from the Pico de Orizaba source at Tres Zapotes suggests that obsidian from this source entered the site as both casual and polyhedral cores.

As elsewhere in the southern Gulf lowlands, Guadalupe Victoria obsidian was used primarily in flake-core production. In general, the poor quality and restricted cobble size of Guadalupe Victoria obsidian does not make it an attractive option for prismatic blade production on the southern Gulf coast. Nonetheless, the recovery of macrodebitage and polyhedral core debitage, in addition to the expected flakes and flake-core debris, suggests that cobbles of Guadalupe Victoria obsidian were imported for prismatic blade and expedient flake production.

The Zaragoza-Oyameles obsidian (and possibly the visually similar Ucareo and Otumba obsidians) was exchanged primarily as prepared polyhedral cores, although the presence of macroflakes and macroblades, as well as percussion flakes and blades, point to the import of blocky macrocores as well.

Blocky, poorly refined macrocores are not common in the southern Gulf lowlands, as the majority of material would have been removed at the quarry site (Pastrana 1986). Hester and his colleagues (1971:81) identified several artifacts indicative of early stage reduction at Tres Zapotes. These artifacts included ridge flakes and large "core modification debris" (Hester, Jack, and Heizer 1971:81–83, Fig. 6d, e). Macrodebitage constituted only 1.3% of the overall surface obsidian assemblage at Tres Zapotes (n=56), and 1.3% (n=10) of the surface assemblage at the nearby Early Classic center of Palo Errado (although only 0.8% [n=21] of the excavation assemblage at Palo Errado [Knight 1999]). The proportions of surface macrodebitage at Tres Zapotes and Palo Errado are similar to the proportion at Matacapan (Santley 1989a:Fig. 6), suggesting a similar pattern of reduction stage exchange. In total, fifty-six pieces of macrodebitage were recovered from the surface of Tres Zapotes, mostly composed of macroflakes but also including macroblades and ridge blades.

In sum, the Formative to Classic period exchange networks that extracted and moved Zaragoza-Oyameles obsidian to the southern Gulf lowlands concentrated on the transport of polyhedral cores. Nonetheless, the presence of Zaragoza-Oyameles macrodebitage at Tres Zapotes reflects a level of demand sufficient for block material and macrocores to sustain the transport of obsidian in an otherwise inefficient form.

PRODUCTION INTENSITY AND SCALE

Intensity and scale are important parameters to consider in assessing craft production systems. Different authors have used these terms variously, however (compare, for example, Costin 1991:15–19; Pool 1992:278–279; Rice 1987b:186, 190: Torrence 1986:89). Here I follow Pool (1992:278) in using scale to refer to gross amounts of inputs (labor, time, capital, or materials) or outputs (production and by-products). Fol-

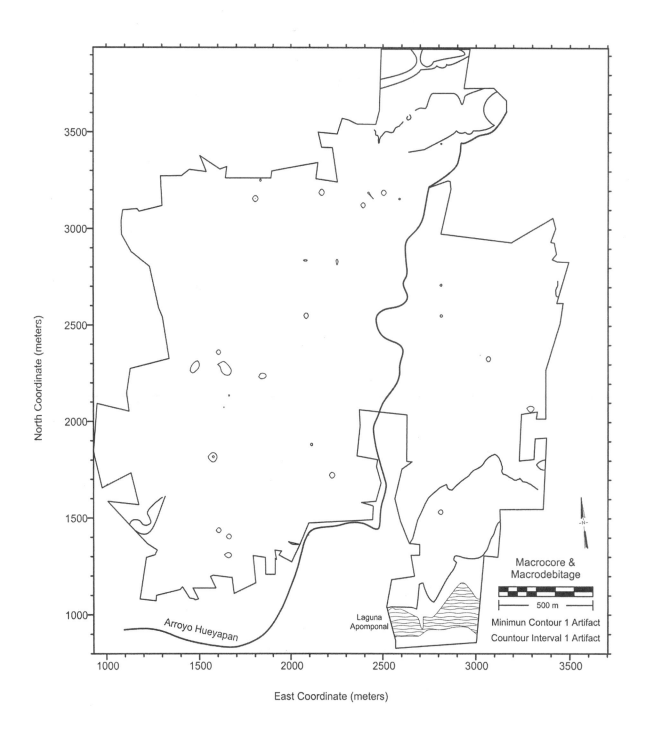

Figure 6.4 Surface distribution of macrodebitage and macrocore reduction debitage combined. *Illustration prepared by Charles Knight*

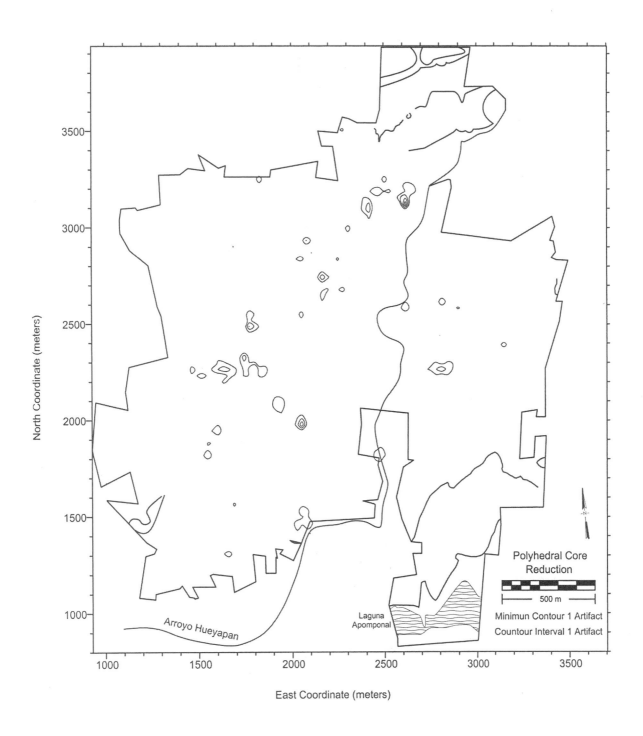

Figure 6.5 Surface distribution of polyhedral core reduction debitage. *Illustration prepared by Charles Knight*

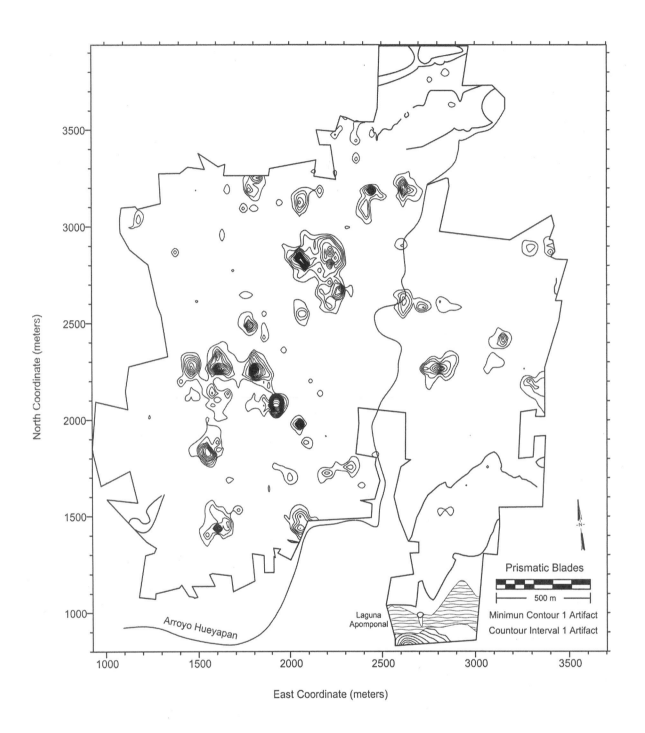

Figure 6.6 Surface distribution of prismatic blades. *Illustration prepared by Charles Knight*

lowing Costin (1991:6), I use intensity to refer more narrowly to the amount of time producers spend on their craft (see also Pool 1992: 278–289; Rice 1987:190; Torrence 1986:89). Here I divide the continuum of production intensity into three levels: nonspecialized production, part-time specialization, and full-time specialization. Nonspecialized production is defined as production for personal or household consumption, which does not require any specialized skill. Specialized production, on the other hand, is the production of goods for consumption by individuals who are not members of the producer's household (following Clark and Parry 1990).

Because it involves estimates of the amount of time devoted to a particular craft, intensity is more difficult to assess than other aspects of scale. Costin (1991:32) suggests that evidence for multiple productive activities (for example, food and lithic production) in a single household is indicative of part-time production, while a limited range of production activities probably reflects full or nearly full-time production. Such an assessment is difficult, however, with the surface data considered in this chapter.

Production scale, as defined by Pool (1992:278), is more directly accessible archaeologically, because it encompasses gross levels of material inputs and outputs. Costin (1991:15, 29), whose definition of scale focuses on the number of producers in a production unit and principles of labor recruitment, urges caution in interpreting production scale, because several variables affecting measurements of scale are seldom taken into account. For instance, the extent of production debris across a site does not necessarily correlate with production scale. Rather, it may reflect nothing more than variations in depositional activities at different loci (Costin 1991:29). The fallibility of this correlation seems to increase as the quantity of production debris under consideration increases. That is, it is more tenuous to make any connection between high frequencies of production debris and a particular production scale than it is to do so with small debris frequencies. As Costin, following Clark (1986:43), states, "when output is low, it is reasonable to rule out large-scale facilities" (1991:30). Nonspecialized (low intensity) production is expected to be small scale, because the number of consumers relying on nonspecialized output will be restricted to the immediate family. In contrast, the number of potential consumers is not limited for specialized producers, and therefore the scale of production will be more flexible, occurring along a continuum from small to large. In general, the relation between craft specialization and production scale is such that an increase in one will result in an increase in the other (Clark 1986).

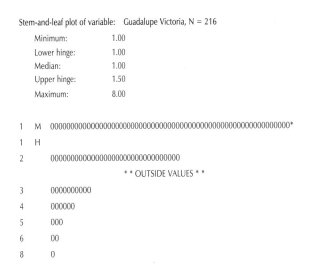

Figure 6.7 Stem-and-leaf plot of Guadalupe Victoria obsidian quantities per collection unit. *Illustration prepared by Charles Knight*

Archaeologically, we may reasonably expect that, all else being equal, increasing levels of scale and intensity should result in greater amounts of obsidian and higher ratios of production debitage to finished products within production loci. To identify the scale of obsidian artifact production at Tres Zapotes, a stem-and-leaf plot of overall obsidian quantities by source, per collection unit, was made to identify areas of the site with "unusually high" obsidian concentrations. A stem-and-leaf plot is a simple method of exploring a batch of numbers to see which cases within the batch group together (and as such are most similar) and which cases do not (Drennan 1996). The most significant digits in which variation occurs are arranged in a vertical "stem," and the digits following them for each case are arranged in horizontal "leaves." The plot may be interpreted in a fashion similar to a histogram. All surface collection units containing obsidian of a particular source were included in the stem-and-leaf plot. Unusually high concentrations are defined as those collection units in the stem-and-leaf plots that contain "outside values," defined as greater than 1.5 times the interquartile range from the upper hinge of the distribution. The obsidian assemblages, which represent these unusually high concentrations, were then analyzed in terms of production and consumption proportions.

The frequency distribution for the Guadalupe Victoria source was single-peaked, suggesting that all cases derive from a single population of obsidian frequencies (figure 6.7). Although the distribution is positively skewed, collection units having outside values (22 [10%] of the 216 cases) contained no more than eight artifacts in a 9 m^2 unit, and so do not appear to represent very high scales of production or

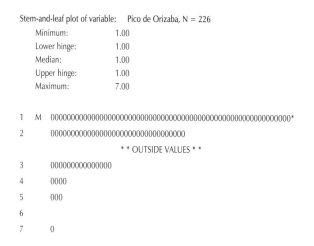

Stem-and-leaf plot of variable: Pico de Orizaba, N = 226

Minimum:	1.00
Lower hinge:	1.00
Median:	1.00
Upper hinge:	1.00
Maximum:	7.00

```
1   M   0000000000000000000000000000000000000000000000000000000000*
2       0000000000000000000000000000000000
                      * * OUTSIDE VALUES * *
3       000000000000000
4       0000
5       000
6
7       0
```

Figure 6.8 Stem-and-leaf plot of Pico de Orizaba obsidian quantities per collection unit. *Illustration prepared by Charles Knight*

Stem-and-leaf plot of variable: ZARAGOZA, N = 985

Minimum:	1.00
Lower hinge:	1.00
Median:	2.00
Upper hinge:	4.00
Maximum:	27.00

```
1   H   0000000000000000000000000000000000000000000000000000000000*
2   M   0000000000000000000000000000000000000000000000000000000000*
3       000000000000000000000000000000000000000000000000000000000*
4   H   000000000000000000000000000000000000000000000000000000000*
5       00000000000000000000000000000000000000000000000000000000
6       00000000000000000000000000000000000000000
7       000000000000000000000000
8       0000000000
                      * * Outside Values * *
9       000000000000000
10      0000000000000
11      000000
12      000000
13      000
14      00
15      00
16      00
17      00
18      000
19      0
20      0000
22      0
27      0
```

Figure 6.9 Stem-and-leaf plot of Zaragoza-Oyameles obsidian quantities per collection unit. *Illustration prepared by Charles Knight*

consumption. A very similar frequency distribution occurred with Pico de Orizaba obsidian (figure 6.8). Because both hinges of the Pico de Orizaba distribution fell at one artifact per collection, producing an interquartile range of 0, the computer program was unable to calculate a level for outside values. Because of the similar shapes of their distributions, however, it is reasonable to apply the same value of 2.5 artifacts for outside values obtained for the Guadalupe Victoria data set to the 226 collections with Pico de Orizaba obsidian. Doing so yields a figure of 10% (23) for cases with outside values.

In both the Pico de Orizaba and Guadalupe Victoria batches the collections defined as having outside values contained very few prismatic blades, and very little, if any, blade production debitage. This is not surprising for the Guadalupe Victoria obsidian, since it was primarily utilized in an expedient flake-core technology. The presence of so much Pico de Orizaba obsidian debitage unrelated to core-blade reduction may be explained in two ways. First, this debitage could reflect an expedient flake technology, suggesting an Early to Middle Formative period exploitation of this source. This interpretation is supported by the expedient use of Pico de Orizaba during the Formative period in the Mixtequilla (Heller and Stark 1998, Stark et al. 1992) and the Early to Middle Formative period in the Tuxtlas (Pool 1997b). A second explanation is that the unidentified flakes of Pico de Orizaba obsidian, which constituted 42% of the Pico de Orizaba assemblage (table 6.2), represented the detritus from core-blade reduction rather than expedient flake production. If the latter were the case, though, we would expect the proportion of prismatic blades and unidentified flakes to be similar for both Pico de Orizaba obsidian and Zaragoza-Oyameles obsidian, which was used almost entirely for core-blade reduction. Proportions presented in table 6.2 indicate that this was not the case, but rather the proportions of prismatic blades and unidentified flakes are most similar to the Guadalupe Victoria proportions, suggesting that the Pico de Orizaba obsidian assemblage best reflects a flake-core, rather than a core-blade, technology.

The collection units with Zaragoza-Oyameles obsidian, on the other hand, exhibited two fairly distinct peaks within the batch, suggesting that all cases were not related and thus were not comparable between peaks (figure 6.9). The second peak consisted of seventeen collection units with fourteen to twenty-two Zaragoza-Oyameles obsidian artifacts in each one. Zaragoza-Oyameles peak 2 obsidian data is summarized in table 6.3. Thirteen of the cases in this second peak had proportions of production indicators that fell between 7 and 25%, compared with a figure of 19% for pro-

Table 6.3 Zaragoza-Oyameles peak 2 reduction stage quantities

UNIT	MD	MCR	PCR	PB	BT	FC	FT	UN	PRODUCTION %	TOTAL
N1980 E2040	—	—	5	9	—	1	—	—	33	15
N2080 E1900	1	—	4	14	—	—	—	3	23	22
N2080 E1920	—	—	2	9	1	—	—	3	13	15
N2100 E1920	1	—	2	9	1	—	—	3	19	16
N2180 E3280	—	—	2	13	—	—	—	1	13	16
N2240 E1840	—	2	4	6	1	—	—	1	40	15
N2260 E1840	—	—	2	11	—	—	—	1	14	14
N2260 E1640	1	2	3	11	—	—	—	—	35	17
N2280 E1460	1	—	2	11	—	—	—	4	17	18
N2480 E1780	—	—	4	11	—	1	—	3	21	19
N2650 E2240	1	2	11	—	—	—	1	1	19	16
N2650 E2266	—	1	4	14	—	—	—	1	25	20
N2800 E2080	—	—	1	13	—	—	—	—	7	14
N2820 E2060	—	—	2	17	1	—	—	1	10	21
N2840 E2040	1	1	1	15	—	—	—	2	15	20
N3100 E2400	1	—	8	8	—	—	—	1	50	18
N3220 E2600	—	—	1	11	—	—	—	2	7	14

*MD=Macrodebitage, MCR=macrocore reduction, PCR=polyhedral core reduction, PB=prismatic blades, BT=blade tools, FC=flake core, FT= flake tool, UN=unidentified flakes.

duction indicators in the total Zaragoza-Oyameles assemblage. Four cases in the second peak, however, exhibited high proportions of production indicators, falling between 33 and 50% (N1980-E2040, N2240-E1840, N2260-E1640, and N3100-E2400). Most of these production indicators relate to polyhedral core reduction. Although these cases may represent relatively greater intensities or larger scales of production, the overall obsidian assemblages from these two collection units were not particularly large (n=15 to n=18) (table 6.3), and prismatic blades constituted large proportions of them as well (40 and 44%, respectively). In fact, all areas of the site that had Zaragoza-Oyameles production indicators also contained a large proportion, if not a majority, of prismatic blades. Although postdepositional activities, such as plowing, may have resulted in the mixing of domestic and production contexts, little evidence exists for intensive production of Zaragoza-Oyameles obsidian for widespread exchange.

As demonstrated in figures 6.4 and 6.5, the distribution of prismatic blade production indicators was dispersed. The large majority of production debitage was composed of obsidian from the Zaragoza-Oyameles source. Therefore, distribution of Zaragoza-Oyameles production indicators coincided with the same areas of the site that contained the highest densities of epi-Olmec and Early Classic period ceramic rims, manos, metates, other groundstone tools, and daub (see Pool 1997b:Figs. 8, 7, and 11). They also corresponded in their distribution to ceramic production indicators (see

Hoag 1997:Fig. 5.3; Hoag chapter 4; Pool 1997c:Fig. 9). This suggests that production of Zaragoza-Oyameles prismatic blades was primarily a dispersed domestic activity during the Late Formative to Early Classic period.

Obsidian and Its Role in Resource Accumulation Strategies

To facilitate the comparison of obsidian source and artifact type between non-elite and elite residential areas of Tres Zapotes, six circular zones of the site were delineated, each with a radius of 200 m (figure 6.10). The elite zones included the formal civic-ceremonial complexes at Groups 1, 2, and 3 and an elite residential district on the heavily modified southern end of Cerro Rabon. The Ranchito Group and the New Lands area represent non-elite residential zones. Raw counts of prismatic blades, production indicators, and overall obsidian artifacts from each of these zones are presented in table 6.4. The collection units within these six zones contained 337 (52%) of the 647 production indicators recovered from the surface of Tres Zapotes.

While each of the delineated zones at Tres Zapotes covers the same surface area, the intensity with which each zone was collected varied. Therefore, obsidian quantities per zone were standardized by dividing the quantity of obsidian per zone by the number of collection units within that zone. The standardized quantities and proportions per zone by source are presented in table 6.5. Group 3 contained over twice as

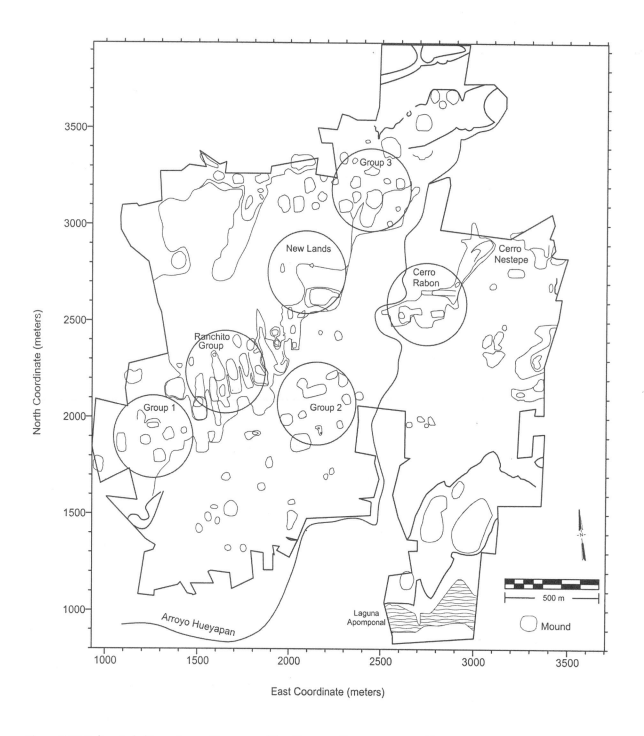

Figure 6.10 Delineated elite and non-elite zones of Tres Zapotes. *Illustration prepared by Charles Knight. Base map prepared by Michael A. Ohnersorgen and Christopher A. Pool*

Table 6.4 Raw counts of prismatic blades, production indicators, and overall obsidian artifacts from each locus

	GROUP 1 19 UNITS			GROUP 2 46 UNITS			GROUP 3 67 UNITS			CERRO RABON 30 UNITS			RANCHITO 120 UNITS			NEW LANDS 137 UNITS			
SOURCE	#pb	#pr	#ob	#pb	#pr	#ob	#pb	#pr	#ob	#pb	#pr	#ob	#pb	#pr	#ob	#pb	#pr	#ob	TOTAL
PO	0	0	2	5	4	17	17	6	28	4	1	10	7	6	37	29	4	43	137
GV	0	2	7	2	2	22	8	6	23	1	0	2	16	4	60	9	3	22	136
Pa	2	0	2	2	0	3	6	1	9	1	0	2			0	4	1	7	23
Z-O	8	1	20	36	13	78	113	63	213	49	7	72	234	75	404	369	82	502	1289
m-U	0	0	3	10	2	18	25	7	46	10	4	17	54	17	104	79	13	117	305
m-Ot	1	1	1	3	0	3	8	4	14	6	4	13	24	3	29	47	1	51	111
TOTAL		35			141			333			116			634			742		2001

#pb = quantity of prismatic blades from zone; #pr = quantity of production indicators from zone; #ob = total quantity of obsidian artifacts from zone

Table 6.5 Standardized quantities of production indicators per collection by source and zone

	GROUP 1 19 UNITS	GROUP 2 46 UNITS	GROUP 3 67 UNITS	CERRO RABON 30 UNITS	RANCHITO 120 UNITS	NEW LANDS 137 UNITS
SOURCE	#ob/unit (%)	#ob/unit (%)	#ob/unit (%)	#ob/unit (%)	#ob/unit (%)	#ob/unit (%)
PO		0.09 (19%)	0.09 (7%)	0.03 (7%)	0.05 (6%)	0.03 (4%)
GV	0.1 (50%)	0.04 (8%)	0.09 (7%)		0.03 (4%)	0.02 (3%)
Pa			0.01 (1%)			0.01 (1%)
Z-O	0.05 (25%)	0.3 (64%)	0.9 (72%)	0.2 (47%)	0.6 (74%)	0.6 (80%)
m-U		0.04 (8%)	0.1 (8%)	0.1 (23%)	0.1 (12%)	0.09 (12%)
m-O	0.05 (25%)		0.06 (5%)	0.1 (23%)	0.03 (4%)	0.01 (1%)
TOTAL	0.2 (100%)	0.47 (100%)	1.25 (100%)	0.43 (100%)	0.81 (100%)	0.75 (100%)

#ob = total quantity of obsidian artifacts from zone

many production indicators per unit as the other elite zones. It also contained almost twice as many production indicators as the two non-elite residential groups. The fact that prismatic blade production occurred in the non-elite New Lands and Ranchito Groups, however, indicates that specialized knowledge of prismatic blade production was not restricted to the elite. Indeed, including residential areas that are not among the zones discussed here, over 80% of all production indicators occurred in non-elite contexts. Nonetheless, the significant amount of production debitage occurring in Mound Group 3 indicates that there was a concentration of prismatic blade production in this elite zone, which warrants investigation through excavation.

In general, production indicators of Guadalupe Victoria, Pico de Orizaba, and Zaragoza-Oyameles obsidians were not differentiated between zones. Production indicators made of Pachuca obsidian were restricted to the Group 3 and New Lands zones, but each contained only one production indicator for this source.

Consumption

In addition to raw obsidian quantities and type, the degree of non-elite access to obsidian should be illustrated through the proportion of prismatic blades exhibiting edge retouch (see Lesure 1995:203; Santley 1989a:143). The assumption can be summarized as follows: "As the conservation of lithic raw material becomes an increasingly important consideration, reduction and resharpening techniques capable of conserving material to greater degrees will be adopted" (Hayden 1989:8). Therefore, if the elite were restricting access to prismatic blades it may be assumed that a greater proportion of retouch on existing blades would occur among the non-elite in order to stretch out their resource. Consequently, obsidian should be expected in greater quantities and with less edge retouch from elite areas of the site if it conferred some prestige advantage to those in power. Edge resharpening at Tres Zapotes was identified through macroscopic observations. Here I distinguish edge resharpening from steeper retouch to produce a scraper or backed blade; scrapers were

Table 6.6 Retouched and nonretouched prismatic blades

ZONE	RETOUCH	NO RETOUCH	TOTAL	% RETOUCH
Group 1	2	9	11	18
Group 2	8	50	58	14
Group 3	24	153	177	14
Cerro Rabon	9	62	71	15
Ranchito	33	302	335	10
New Lands	60	477	538	11

Table 6.7 Standardized quantities of total obsidian artifacts per collection unit by source and zone

	GROUP 1 19 UNITS	GROUP 2 46 UNITS	GROUP 3 67 UNITS	CERRO RABON 30 UNITS	NEW LANDS 137 UNITS	RANCHITO 120 UNITS
Clear	.5 (26%)	.9 (28%)	.8 (16%)	.4 (10%)	.5 (9%)	.8 (15%)
Zaragoza-Oyameles	1.1 (57%)	1.7 (54%)	3.2 (64%)	2.4 (62%)	3.7 (67%)	3.4 (64%)
Mixed	.2 (11%)	.5 (16%)	.9 (18%)	1.0 (26%)	1.2 (22%)	1.1 (21%)
Pachuca	.1 (6%)	.06 (2%)	.1 (2%)	.1 (2%)	.1 (2%)	0.0
TOTAL	1.8 (100%)	3.1 (100%)	4.9 (100%)	3.8 (100%)	5.5 (100%)	5.3 (100%)

identified separately in the analysis, and backed blades were absent from the surface assemblage.

Retouched and nonretouched prismatic blades were recovered in both elite and non-elite zones, although nonretouched blades dominated those assemblages (table 6.6). Importantly, frequencies of prismatic blades with retouch were greater in elite contexts (14 to 18%) than non-elite zones (10 to 11%), contrary to the expected pattern if elites had greater access to this resource. The frequency of retouch was even lower for flakes. Only three retouched flakes were recovered: two from the Ranchito Group and one from Mound Group 2. Therefore, it appears that access to new prismatic blades and flakes, and therefore fresh cutting edges, was not restricted by elites.

Obsidian source distributions were also investigated to identify differential access to obsidian. At this stage of the analysis, I lumped together clear obsidian from the Pico de Orizaba and Guadalupe Victoria sources and black obsidian from the mixed-Ucareo and mixed-Otumba categories to provide adequate cell counts for chi-square analysis (see Drennan 1996:197). Standardized quantities and proportions of the combined source categories in each zone are presented in table 6.7. The infrequent green Pachuca obsidian is included in table 6.7 for comparison but was omitted from the chi-square analysis.

Inspection of table 6.7 suggests some interesting patterns in the data. Mound Groups 1 and 2 contain higher proportions of clear obsidian and lower proportions of Zaragoza-Oyameles and mixed obsidian classes than do other zones. Standardized quantities of Zaragoza-Oyameles and mixed obsidian are also lower in Groups 1 and 2, but quantities of clear obsidian per unit are about the same for other

zones. Among the remaining zones, Group 3 and the Ranchito Group have markedly higher proportions and standardized quantities of clear obsidian than do the New Lands and Cerro Rabon zones. Although these patterns suggest significant variation in resource utilization among zones, they crosscut elite versus non-elite distinctions, implying that factors other than social class are responsible.

To obtain a detailed picture of the significance of variation in obsidian source utilization, chi-square tests of independence were performed between pairs of zones (table 6.8). For these tests, raw counts of clear, Zaragoza-Oyameles, and mixed categories were used, and Pachuca obsidian was omitted. The results of the tests indicate that frequencies of different obsidians in the non-elite residential New Lands zone are significantly different from those in the three elite civic-ceremonial zones (Groups 1, 2, and 3) but not the Cerro Rabon elite residential district. On the other hand, the non-elite residential Ranchito Group is significantly different from Group 2, but not from the other elite zones. Significant differences also occur within social class categories, between the elite Group 2 and Group 3 and Cerro Rabon, and between the New Lands zone and the Ranchito Group. Therefore, no clear-cut patterns of elite vs. non-elite use of obsidian sources—supporting a political or adaptationist argument—are apparent. Instead, the results suggest a more complex system of obsidian production and consumption, as well as the influence of variables other than status, such as chronological variation.

A factor analysis of obsidian source quantities per collection zone, using rotated loadings, identified cleavages between zones (figure 6.11). As in table 6.8 above, sources were grouped into clear, mixed, and Zaragoza-Oyameles catego-

Table 6.8 Results of χ^2 tests of unstandardized obsidian source quantities between zones

	MOUND GROUP 1	MOUND GROUP 2	MOUND GROUP 3	NEW LANDS	RANCHITO
MOUND GROUP 2	$\chi^2 = .26$ $p > .5$				
MOUND GROUP 3	$\chi^2 = 3.27$ $.2 > p > .1$	$\chi^2 = 9.64$ $.01 > p > .001$			
NEW LANDS	$\chi^2 = 14.1$ $p < .001$	$\chi^2 = 41.9$ $p < .001$	$\chi^2 = 11.94$ $.01 > p > .001$		
RANCHITO GROUP	$\chi^2 = 4.07$ $.2 > p > .1$	$\chi^2 = 13.55$ $.01 > p > .001$	$\chi^2 = .83$ $p > .5$	$\chi^2 = 13.66$ $.01 > p > .001$	
CERRO RABON	$\chi^2 = 7.4$ $.5 > p > .2$	$\chi^2 = 13.98$ $.01 > p > .001$	$\chi^2 = 4.16$ $.2 > p > .1$	$\chi^2 = 1.35$ $p > .5$	$\chi^2 = 2.82$ $.5 > p > .2$

Table 6.9 Results of χ^2 tests of flake and blade quantities between zones

SECTOR	ZONE	MOUND GROUP 1 SW	MOUND GROUP 2 SW	RANCHITO SW	MOUND GROUP 3 NE	NEW LANDS NE
SW	MOUND GROUP 1					
SW	MOUND GROUP 2	$\chi^2 = 1.79$ $.2 > p > .1$				
SW	RANCHITO	$\chi^2 = 6.7$ $.01 > p > .001$	$\chi^2 = 9.3$ $.01 > p > .001$			
NE	MOUND GROUP 3	$\chi^2 = 17.71$ $p < .001$ $p < .001$	$\chi^2 = 23.9$ $\chi^2 = 11.9$ $p < .001$			
NE	NEW LANDS	$\chi^2 = 30.4$ $p < .001$	$\chi^2 = 55.7$ $p < .001$	$\chi^2 = 45$ $p < .001$	$\chi^2 = 2.2$ $.2 > p > .1$	
NE	CERRO RABON	$\chi^2 = 10.7$ $.01 > p > .001$	$\chi^2 = 11.2$ $p < .001$	$\chi^2 = 2.8$ $.1 > p > 05$	$\chi^2 = .58$ $.5 > p > .2$	$\chi^2 = 3.9$ $.05 > p > .02$

ries. In a plot of factors 1 and 2, which explain more than 99% of the variance in the data set, Groups 1 and 2 grouped together, as did the New Lands and Cerro Rabon, and Group 3 and the Ranchito Group, paralleling the pattern suggested in table 6.7. The greatest cleavage occurred between Groups 1 and 2 and all the other zones. These groupings appear to result from the high proportions of Zaragoza-Oyameles obsidian in the northeastern section of the site and the relatively high proportions of clear obsidian in the Groups 1 and 2.

As discussed earlier, the use of obsidian from the Zaragoza-Oyameles and the clear sources in the southern

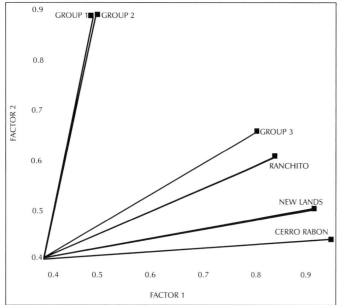

Rotated Loading matrix (ORTHOMAX, Gamma = 1.0000)

	1	2
Group 1	0.490	0.872
Group 2	0.487	0.873
Group 3	0.766	0.643
Ranchito group	0.802	0.598
New Lands group	0.868	0.497
Cerro Rabon group	0.900	0.436

"Variance explained" by rotated components

	1	2
	3.269	2.731

Percent of total variance explained

	1	2
	54.491	45.509

Figure 6.11 Factor analysis results of zone comparison based on obsidian source composition. *Illustration prepared by Charles Knight*

Gulf lowlands varies through time, corresponding to a change in reduction technology. If the spatial differences of obsidian sources identified above are, in fact, the results of different proportions of these two obsidian types (clear vs. black), we should expect to see differences in reduction technology (flake vs. prismatic blade) between the zones of the northeast sector and those from the southwest sector. Unidentified flake and prismatic blade proportions from each zone do indicate corresponding differences in technology. In the southwest sector, percentages of unidentified flakes ranged from 24 to 40%, while in the northeastern sector zones, percentages of

unidentified flakes varied from 12 to 18%. Percentages of prismatic blades varied from 3 to 53% in the southwest sector and from 53 to 73% in the northeast sector. A chi-square test of independence for frequencies of flakes and blades in the two sectors indicates that this difference is significant (table 6.9; chi square $= 17.87$, $d.f. = 1$, $p < 0.001$).

Based on surface ceramic evidence, associated sculpture, and sequences excavated by Stirling, Pool (chapter 7) argues that the occupation of mound Groups 1, 2, 3, and Cerro Rabon was contemporaneous during the Terminal Formative and Early Classic periods. This would explain the differences in obsidian source distribution. The widespread distribution of Zaragoza-Oyameles obsidian and prismatic blade technology across the site accords well with occupational contemporaneity during the Terminal Formative period and onwards. The Olmec phase or Middle Formative period occupation at Tres Zapotes occurs at several loci, the largest being centered on the terraces near mound Group 2 and the Ranchito Group, covering approximately 80 ha (Pool 1999; Pool chapter 7). Several smaller loci, or "villages," smaller than 15 ha dating to this Olmec phase are scattered about the site (Pool 1999). The larger proportion of flakes and clear obsidian from Mound Groups 1 and 2 most likely reflects this large Middle Formative period occupation.

Prismatic blade proportions in the Ranchito Group are the same as for Mound Group 3, and in fact these two cluster in the factor analysis, based on source composition. At the same time the Ranchito Group also contained a fairly large proportion of flakes and clear obsidian. This, along with the large amount of surface material (Pool 1999), suggests that the Ranchito Group was a centrally occupied area throughout the majority of site occupation.

The heavy reliance on Zaragoza-Oyameles obsidian, and its surface distribution over most of the site, corresponds to its widespread use in the southern Gulf lowlands throughout the Late Formative and Classic periods. As a result the surface distribution of Zaragoza-Oyameles at Tres Zapotes correlates strongly with the surface distribution of all other obsidian sources, except Pachuca. The distribution of Pachuca obsidian does not correspond well with the surface distribution of any of the other sources either, although the sample size of Pachuca obsidian was very small (n $=$ 39), which may have exaggerated these differences. Nonetheless, the distribution of Pachuca does differ significantly from other low frequency sources. For instance, very little Pico de Orizaba or Guadalupe Victoria obsidian was recovered east of the Arroyo Hueyapan, the area in which the highest proportions per collection unit of Pachuca obsidian were located. In contrast, no Pachuca obsidian was recovered from the Ranchito group, the area with the most obsidian from all the other sources, plus the highest frequencies of domestic refuse at the site. Pachuca obsidian was recovered from all main mound groups, plus the non-elite, residential New Lands area in the north. The great majority of the green Pachuca obsidian, though, is associated with mounded, elite plaza groups.

The production and distribution of Pachuca obsidian is known to have been under the control of the Teotihuacan elite during the Early/Middle Classic period (Charlton 1984; Santley 1983). The concentration of Pachuca obsidian tools and debitage at Mound Group 3 may reflect the direct or indirect (via Matacapan) participation of the Tres Zapotes elite in exchange networks with the central Mexican state of Teotihuacan during the Early Classic period, an association that may have cultivated some form of higher social standing. In addition the green color of Pachuca obsidian may have been ideologically charged and thus would have made it a sought after commodity for elite ritual (Stark et al. 1992:234). Whether or not this production was attached to the elite or was the result of elite household production at Tres Zapotes cannot be discerned from the surface obsidian materials alone. The low intensity of obsidian production at the site in general does not lend support to its specialized production at high levels.

Conclusions

Patterns of obsidian production and consumption at Tres Zapotes have been shown to address the four basic principles of political economy as outlined by Hirth (1996) and were incorporated into two main models of resource mobilization. The principle of accumulation, which is concerned with the strategies employed by individuals to acquire more resources to attract potential supporters, was an integral aspect in identifying how obsidian may have been used in the establishment of such supportive social networks, and thus developing sociopolitical inequality.

The context of obsidian tool mobilization, based on the intensity and scale of prismatic blade production at Tres Zapotes, did not meet the expectations for the political model. Specialized blade production was not restricted in its surface distribution. Three collection units were identified as suggesting specialized blade production but occurred in both non-elite and elite zones of the site. The intensity of specialized production was, at best, part-time; no area of the site contained surface obsidian densities even remotely close to what would be expected of full-time blade production. As a result the surface data at Tres Zapotes fits Hirth's (1996) description of an "individually oriented accumulation system," where blade production occurs at the level of the household, most likely for household consumption and limited exchange.

Access to obsidian does not appear to have afforded any greater ideological, economic, or political leverage to any specific individual, because obsidian was not restricted in its distribution. In fact, the only qualitative differences in the distribution of obsidian at Tres Zapotes resulted from the site's occupation chronology rather than from issues of accessibility. Obsidian from the Guadalupe Victoria and Pico de Orizaba sources were concentrated in the southwestern sector of the site, the area with the greatest Early and Middle Formative occupation. These two obsidian sources were also utilized to a greater degree than other obsidian sources in flake technology and were not as prevalent in prismatic blade technology as other sources were. On the other hand, prismatic blades made from the Zaragoza-Oyameles obsidian source and obsidian from both mixed categories were more prevalent in the northeastern sector of the site, which contained a more widespread Early Classic occupation. This distribution accords well with the general chronology of source exploitation and reduction technology utilized in the southern Gulf lowlands. The Ranchito Group is the exception, as it contained high proportions of debitage and tools of both flake and blade technologies from clear and black obsidians, reflecting its role as a central area of occupation throughout the history of Tres Zapotes.

Small quantities of green Pachuca obsidian tended to be concentrated in elite zones like Mound Group 3, which also contained one production indicator for this source. Considering that the long distance distribution of Pachuca obsidian is thought to have been under the control of the Teotihuacan elite (Santley 1989a), it is possible that the presence of Pachuca obsidian at Tres Zapotes suggests participation by the Tres Zapotes elite in long-distance exchange either directly with Teotihuacan or indirectly through Teotihuacan enclaves like Matacapan (Santley 1989a). While Pachuca obsidian may have brought some ritual significance to its users because of its association with Teotihuacan and its green color, it does not seem to have played any significant role in the development of sociopolitical control. Nonetheless, this aspect of the Tres Zapotes obsidian economy may be best explained in terms of the political model; the production of Pachuca obsidian prismatic blades was associated with elite practices in the civic-ceremonial loci, such as Group 3.

In sum, neither the political nor the adaptationist perspective alone appears adequate to explain the distribution of obsidian tool production and consumption at Tres Zapotes. During the Classic period, green obsidian from the Pachuca source associated with Teotihuacan may have functioned as a prestige or wealth good whose accumulation, conversion, and distribution was controlled by elites. The vast majority of obsidian artifacts in all periods, however, was produced and consumed in non-elite residential contexts. Though this pattern of wide access provides some support for an adaptationist model, there is little evidence for greater association of unusual quantities of obsidian with elite contexts, as might be expected if elites were bulking obsidian for distribution to the populace at large. In other words, with the temporally restricted exception of small

quantities of Pachuca obsidian, the current evidence for extensive elite involvement in the obsidian economy is very weak. Thus obsidian production and procurement does not appear to have played a prominent role in the development and maintenance of sociopolitical inequality at Tres Zapotes. In this regard, the theoretical dichotomy produced by the adaptationist and political models is insufficient in explaining patterns of obsidian production and consumption in this part of the southern Gulf lowlands.

Appendix A: Technology Classes of Obsidian Artifacts, 1998 Analysis

CODE	DESCRIPTION	REDUCTION STAGE
3	Percussion blades: whole	Macrocore reduction
5	Percussion blades: proximal	Macrocore reduction
7	Percussion blades: medial	Macrocore reduction
9	Percussion blades: distal	Macrocore reduction
10.1	Macroblades: whole	Macrodebitage
10.2	Macroblades: proximal	Macrodebitage
10.3	Macroblades: medial	Macrodebitage
10.4	Macroblades: distal	Macrodebitage
11	Irregular pressure blades: whole	Prismatic blades
13	Irregular pressure blades: proximal	Prismatic blades
15	Irregular pressure blades: medial	Prismatic blades
17	Irregular pressure blades: distal	Prismatic blades
19	Prismatic pressure blades: whole	Prismatic blades
21	Prismatic pressure blades: proximal	Prismatic blades
23	Prismatic pressure blades: medial	Prismatic blades
25	Prismatic pressure blades: distal	Prismatic blades
27	Ridge blade: primary	Polyhedral core reduction
29	Ridge blade: secondary	Polyhedral core reduction
27.1	Ridge blade - no cortex	Polyhedral core reduction
31	Decortication flakes: primary	Macrodebitage
33	Decortication flakes: secondary	Macrodebitage
35	Platform trimming/faceting flakes (ppf)	Polyhedral core reduction
37	Platform trimming/faceting flakes: probable	Polyhedral core reduction
39	Core trimming flakes (face of core)	Polyhedral core reduction
41	Thinning flakes	Biface reduction
43	Unidentified flakes with platforms	Flake tools
43.1	Unidentified flakes with platforms: with cortex	Flake tools
45	Unidentified flakes without platforms	Flake tools
47	Manufacturing error flakes	Polyhedral core reduction
47.1	Hinge recovery blades	Polyhedral core reduction
49	Pressure blade cores: whole	Polyhedral core reduction
51	Pressure blade cores: proximal	Polyhedral core reduction
53	Pressure blade cores: medial	Polyhedral core reduction
55	Pressure blade cores: distal	Polyhedral core reduction
57	Core truncation/section flakes	Polyhedral core reduction
59	Chunks	Flake cores
61	Stemmed blades	Blade tools
63	Large blade/flakes with lateral uni-flaking	Flake tools
65	Bifacially flaked flakes	Flake tools
67	Bifaces	Bifaces
69	Core rims: transversely struck off	Polyhedral core reduction
69.1	Core rims: not transversely struck off	Polyhedral core reduction
71	Core face flakes: transversely struck off	Polyhedral core reduction
73	Unidentified blades	Blade tools
75	Plunging blades	Polyhedral core reduction

continued

CODE	DESCRIPTION	REDUCTION STAGE
77	Eraillure flakes	Polyhedral core reduction
79	Bipolar flakes	Polyhedral core reduction
81	Blades retouched to points	Blade tools
83	Projectile points	Flake tools
87	Unifaces	Bifaces
89	Flake cores: casual	Flake cores
91	Ribbon blades	Blade tools
93	Initial series blades: whole	Polyhedral core reduction
93.1	Initial series blades: proximal	Polyhedral core reduction
95	Indirect percussion flakes	Flake tools
97	Platforms removed in manufacturing error	Polyhedral core reduction
99	Blade shatter	Polyhedral core reduction
101	Notched blades	Blade tools
103	Stemmed points: bifacially flaked flake	Flake tools
105	Pressure flakes	Blade tools
107	Macrocore platform flakes	Macrodebitage
109	Notching/retouching flakes	Flake tools
111	Percussion microblades	Blade tools
113.1	Macroflakes: whole	Macrodebitage
113.2	Macroflakes: proximal	Macrodebitage
113.3	Macroflakes: fragment	Macrodebitage
115	Microblade cores	Polyhedral core reduction
117	Eccentrics	—
119	Biface hinge removals	Flake tools
121	Needle blades: bifacially retouched	Blade tools
123	Macrocores	Macrodebitage
125	Core rims from distals	Polyhedral core reduction
127	Alternate flakes	Flake tools
129	Blade eccentrics: bilobal and trilobal	Blade tools
131	Longitudinal blade core fragments	Polyhedral core reduction
135	Other	—
136	Percussion flake: whole	Macrocore reduction
137	Percussion flake: proximal	Macrocore reduction
138	Percussion flake: fragment	Macrocore reduction
141	Bifacial Reduction Flake	Bifaces
150	Unidentified flake	Undetermined
150.1	Unidentified flake: fragment	Undetermined
152	Rejuvenated core blades: proximal	Polyhedral core reduction
152.1	Rejuvenated core blades: whole	Polyhedral core reduction
153	Platform overhang flake	Polyhedral core reduction
156	Tongued flakes	Polyhedral core reduction
157	Lateral rejuvenation flakes	Polyhedral core reduction
158	Distal rejuvenation flake: core bottom	Polyhedral core reduction
160	Rejuvenation flake	Polyhedral core reduction
161	Rejuvenation blade	Polyhedral core reduction
162	Wedge	Polyhedral core reduction

7

CENTERS AND PERIPHERIES

Urbanization and Political Economy at Tres Zapotes

Christopher A. Pool

As DOCUMENTED IN THE OTHER CHAPTERS OF THIS VOLUME, the RATZ project has produced a large body of survey data on settlement and craft production at Tres Zapotes. In this concluding chapter, I draw on these studies to discuss the political and economic processes that may have fostered the particular form of urbanism expressed during the Late to Terminal Formative apogee of the site.

The nature of lowland urbanism is a long-standing problem in Mesoamerican research. Although most of us have moved beyond debates over whether or not lowland centers were truly urban, the processes that produced variations in the size and form of lowland centers remain poorly understood. Moreover, the fact that the bulk of research on the organization of lowland centers has been carried out in the larger sites of the Maya lowlands suggests that we have still not thoroughly sampled the range of variation that may have existed in lowland urbanism.

The southern Gulf lowlands of Veracruz and Tabasco constitute the second largest lowland region in Mesoamerica, exceeded only by the vast Maya lowlands. Several large sites in the southern Gulf lowlands clearly fit a broad definition of the urban center as a place in which a variety of integrative institutions and activities are centralized and which both serves and is served by a hinterland from which it is differentiated in size and population density (Blanton 1978; Fox 1977; Sanders and Webster 1988; Wirth 1938). These sites differ from large Maya urban centers in the scale, plan, and construction of their formal architecture, which is usually smaller, less concentrated, and built of earth and clay. While these contrasts have been recognized for the better part of a century, only since 1982 have surveys and systematic surface collection programs revealed the relationship between formal architecture and residential occupation at centers like Cerro de las Mesas, Matacapan, and San Lorenzo (Cyphers 1997; Santley, Ortiz, and Pool 1987; Stark 1991, 1999; Symonds and Lunagomez 1997). These recent data indicate that, in addition to offering a contrast to Maya urbanism, the southern Gulf lowlands encompass considerable variation in size, form, and organization among themselves.

Of all the concepts employed in settlement archaeology, perhaps the most pervasive is that of the center and its complement, the periphery. In Mesoamerica, these concepts have structured much of our analysis at scales ranging from intrasite to supraregional levels. In the Maya lowlands, for example, the term center has been applied at the intrasite level to "aggregates and nucleated arrangements of pyramids, big platforms, palaces, and other buildings that were the foci of Maya political and religious life" (Willey 1981:391; compare Haviland 1981). At the same time, center (often modified by adjectives such as urban or ceremonial) has been used as a neutral term lacking some of the connotations of city to refer to sites that occupy the upper levels of regional central place hierarchies and that both serve and exploit their surrounding hinterlands. In addition, we have recently seen several applications of core-periphery models at the supraregional scale, including world systems theory (for example, Blanton and Feinman 1984; Chase-Dunn and Hall 1992; Santley and Alexander 1992, 1996; Schortman and Urban 1987, 1992).

I do not intend to argue that center-periphery patterns of organization are figments of our imagination; there is more than ample empirical evidence and theoretical justification for their existence. Invariably, however, center-periphery models invoke specific assumptions about the organization of economic and political hierarchies in space; I can think of no example where the periphery is believed to have controlled the center. Moreover, the pervasiveness of center-periphery models at different organizational scales reflects to some degree our expectation that social, political, and economic hierarchies tend to coincide spatially and organizationally. Indeed, when dealing with complex societies we are so conditioned to thinking in terms of centers and peripheries that we often find it difficult to accommodate settlements and settlement systems that do not square with our expectations (for example, Chase 1986; Crumley 1979, 1995; Stark 1999).

At Tres Zapotes, distributions of habitational remains, craft production loci, and formal architecture challenge the center-periphery model for intrasite organization. Here I use an approach based in the concept of "bundled continua of variation" (de Montmollin 1989; White 1995) to interpret settlement pattern data from Tres Zapotes. I am particularly concerned with assessing settlement patterns along two continua of variation: nucleation and centralization. Nucleation is essentially a spatial phenomenon, referring to the geographical clustering of populations, activities, and their physical manifestations. In contrast, centralization is an organizational phenomenon whereby authority, power, and responsibility for providing services are concentrated in the hands of a relatively few persons, groups, and/or institutions. By analytically decoupling these interacting processes we can achieve greater precision in our characterization of ancient urbanism and greater insight into the processes responsible for its variability.

Population nucleation, usually operationalized as the density of population residing within a settlement ("residential density" in Drennan's [1988] terminology), is widely recognized as an important variable in urban settlement. Indeed, some have employed it as one of two key quantitative variables for defining urbanism (the other being overall population size) (for example, Sanders and Price 1968:47). The rationale for this position is that, in the absence of efficient modes of transportation, craftspeople and merchants need to be close to markets (Sanders and Price 1968:46). Today, functional criteria tend to be favored for defining urban centers, and Drennan (1988) has pointed out that relatively small, nonurban settlements in Formative Mesoamerica often had higher residential densities than later urban centers. Nevertheless, nucleation of population remains a significant dimension for characterizing variation in urban forms. In the Mesoamerican case, this variation is often recognized in the contrast between nucleated highland centers and more dispersed lowland centers, as well as variation within lowland settlement patterns (for example, Sanders and Price 1968:165; Sanders and Webster 1988; Stark 1999).

The centralization of administrative, economic, and religious functions is a second, and arguably more important, variable in the development of urbanism. The physical manifestations of centralization include the buildings and other facilities utilized and the distinctive residues produced by participants in these integrative functions. At the intrasite level, the concepts of nucleation and centralization may coincide in that greater degrees of control may be facilitated by spatial nucleation of formal architecture (temples, palaces, plazas, and so forth) and craft production loci. Because centralization also implies the servicing of broader segments of the population and greater control over resources, however, under higher levels of centralization facilities should not only be concentrated but also much larger than functionally similar facilities in less centralized societies.

Late to Terminal Formative Settlement Organization

In chapter 2, Michael Ohnersorgen and I outlined the growth of Tres Zapotes from the Middle Formative period to the Late Formative period and its decline in the Classic period. In this chapter I focus in greater detail on the organization of settlement and craft production during the site's apogee, broadly defined as corresponding to the Hueyapan and Nextepetl phases of the Late and Terminal Formative periods.

RESIDENTIAL SETTLEMENT

In combination, the surface and subsurface distributions of low mounds and intervening areas of nonmounded occupation associated with diagnostic ceramics of the Hueyapan and Nextepetl phases indicate a concentric pattern of residential occupation during the site's apogee (figure 7.1). Total surface ceramic densities, largely attributable to these phases, often exceed 20 sherds per m^2 in a residential core covering 180 ha. In the surrounding 325 ha of less intensive occupation sherd densities rarely surpass 10 sherds per m^2 (compare figures 2.10, 7.1). Hueyapan phase ceramic densities in auger tests on the alluvial plain lend further support to this concentric pattern, which was modified somewhat with the Nextepetl phase abandonment of portions of the floodplain (figures 2.14, 3.10) (chapter 3).

Comparison of surface sherd densities with surveys conducted at Matacapan and at Cerro de las Mesas suggests that the residential core at Tres Zapotes exhibits unusually intensive occupation for the southern Gulf lowlands. The average systematic transect collection from the 1995 survey, which encompasses the residential core of Tres Zapotes, had a sherd density of 11.84 per m^2. The 1996 survey, which covered the eastern periphery, averaged 3.3 sherds per m². In contrast, a similar surface collection strategy at Matacapan yielded average sherd densities of 3 to 4 sherds per m², equivalent to densities in the peripheral zone of Tres Zapotes (Santley et al. 1984:14; Santley and Ortiz 1985:3). At Cerro de las Mesas only rim sherds from mounds and artifact concentrations were collected. Rim sherd densities on the Cerro de las Mesas mounds averaged 0.37 per m², about one-third the average of 1.2 rim sherds per m² from mounds and concentrations at Tres Zapotes (Stark and Heller 1991a:6). The contrasts in sherd densities are all the more impressive when one considers that recent deposition in the alluvial plain and widespread use of terraces for pasture should, if anything, lower average surface densities at Tres Zapotes.

FORMAL ARCHITECTURE

Temples, plazas, and palaces are the setting for many of the centralized ritual, administrative, and economic activities that characterize urban centers. Consequently, formal architectural complexes provide one of the most direct indicators of urban organization. At Tres Zapotes, formal architecture is concentrated in four plaza groups designated Group 1, Group 2, Group 3, and the Nestepe Group (figures 2.9, 7.1). Each plaza group contains one or more conical mounds at one or both ends of the plaza and a longer mound along one side of the plaza. The long mounds probably represent elite residences, as they typically exhibit higher surface ceramic densities than do the conical mounds. With their greater height and smaller summit areas, the conical mounds presumably functioned as bases for temples. It appears then, that the plaza groups served as loci for ritual and elite residential activities. In contrast, an architectural complex on the southern edge of Cerro Rabon contains a series of platforms arranged on a natural terrace whose rectilinear outline suggests extensive modification by filling. Heavy concentrations of coarse utilitarian pottery in combination with fine decorated wares suggest that Cerro Rabon functioned primarily as an elite residential complex.

Stirling's excavations revealed multiple construction stages in mound 5 in Group 1, mound 8 in Group 2 and mound 23 in Group 3 (figure 2.9) (Drucker 1943a:25–26; Weiant 1943:6, 13, Map 8). In each case, the ceramic assemblages of the construction phases suggest that these mound groups were in use from the Late Formative into the Classic period (Pool 2000a:147). Monuments associated with Groups 1, 2, and 3 further support their Late to Terminal Formative use. The Nestepe Group has not been excavated, but the few surface sherds recovered from its long mound suggests its use in the Late and Terminal Formative periods as well. An Olmec colossal head discovered in the plaza of the group suggests that this location had a long history of political and/ or ritual activities. Diagnostic rims recovered from a residential terrace immediately east of the Nestepe Group provide additional evidence for long-term continuity of occupation in its immediate vicinity from the Middle Formative period onward. In addition, surface collections reveal that Cerro Rabon was occupied continuously over the course of the site's history. Thus the evidence at hand suggests broad contemporaneity for the major groups of formal architecture during the Late Formative through Classic periods, although the intensity of their use and their specific functions may have varied at different points in their history.

With respect to the distribution of residential occupation, Group 2 clearly occupies the center of the Late to Terminal Formative site, and the activities carried out there may have served to integrate the community as a whole (figures 2.9, 7.1). The other plaza groups are located in the peripheral zone, however, and they do not appear to have formed centers for their own, separate, residential nuclei. Interestingly, nearest neighbor distances measured from the centers of the four plaza groups are very consistent, ranging from 945 to 985 m. At 1.16, the calculated nearest neighbor statistic does not differ much from a random distribution, but the arrangement of Group 1, Group 3, and the Nestepe Group around Group 2 appears anything but random.

All of the formal architecture is rather modest in scale, and no single mound group clearly dominates the others in terms of the height of its mounds or the volume of its constructions. For example, at 12 m high and 100 m across, the conical Mound 23 in Group 3 is as tall and twice as broad as Mound 8 in Group 2. Likewise, the filling and leveling of the elite residential terrace on Cerro Rabon may surpass the volume of Mound 9 in Group 2, the largest single mound at the site.

Thus Tres Zapotes does not exhibit the massive central concentration of formal construction seen in many Classic Mayan sites or in such Formative and Classic Gulf Coast centers as La Venta, Laguna de los Cerros, and Matacapan. Rather, the scale and dispersion of its formal architecture argue against strong centralization of administrative and ritual functions at Tres Zapotes in the Late Formative through Classic periods.

CRAFT PRODUCTION

Data concerning the organization of craft production constitute a third important line of evidence regarding the character of urban centers. Craft production data for Tres Zapotes

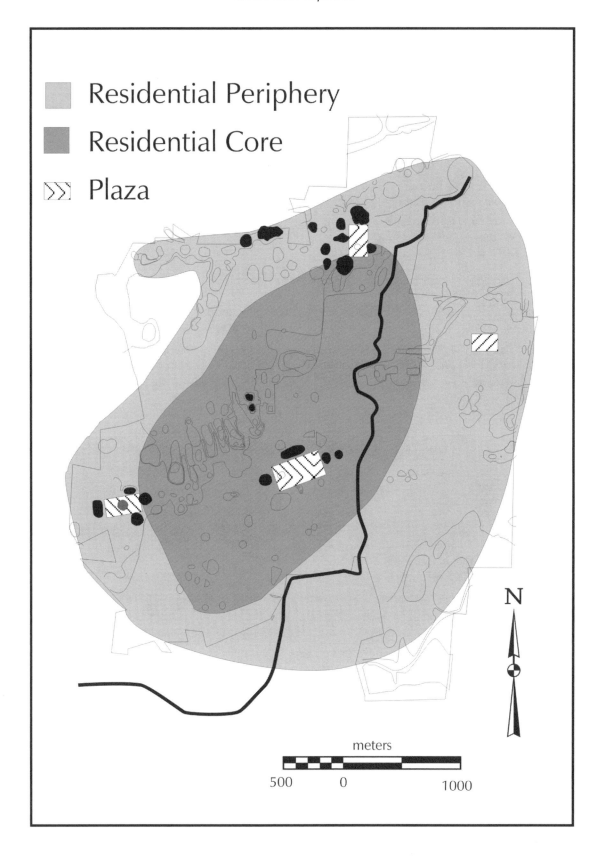

Figure 7.1 Map of Tres Zapotes showing area of residential core, plaza groups, and elite residential zone. *Illustration prepared by Christopher A. Pool*

have been detailed in this volume by Hoag (chapter 4), Pool (chapter 5), and Knight (chapter 6). Here I make only some general observations.

Evidence for ceramic production at Tres Zapotes includes high ceramic densities, deformed waster sherds, and fragments of kilns. In south-central and southern Veracruz, kilns or kiln fragments have now been reported from Matacapan, Bezuapan, La Mojarra, and the Mixtequilla, but with the exception of Terminal Formative kiln fragments from Bezuapan, all of these date from the Classic period (Arnold et al. 1993; Santley, Arnold, and Pool 1989; Pool 1997a; Diehl 1997). Our criteria are therefore biased toward the identification of Terminal Formative and Classic Period ceramic production. Reliance on kiln fragments may also introduce some bias toward identifying more intensive or specialized production loci, but evidence from Matacapan shows that kilns were employed by domestic households, as well as in more intensive settings (Pool 1990, 1997a, 2000b; Santley et al. 1989).

The distribution of kiln debris and wasters discussed by Hoag suggests that small-scale ceramic production may have been common in domestic contexts at Tres Zapotes. The evidence from either of these artifact classes alone must be interpreted cautiously, however, because it is possible that other processes, including the burning of houses, could produce occasional pieces of vitrified daub or overfired ceramics that might mimic residues of ceramic production. The double criterion I employ in chapter 5, which requires the presence of an overt indicator of production in conjunction with higher ceramic density, provides for more secure identification of ceramic production areas but introduces a bias toward more intensive modes of production.

Despite our different analytic biases, Hoag and I concur that most production occurred in residential contexts, with considerably less production carried out by attached specialists in elite contexts. In the latter part of the site's apogee, during the Terminal Formative Nextepetl phase, independent specialist production encompassed a range of scales and intensities and was concentrated in the residential core of the site. Production area assemblages contain all or most of the wares attributable to this phase, and product specialization appears to have been relatively low. During the Classic period, production areas were more widely dispersed, and specialized production emphasized a particular ware, Fine Orange, indicating an increase in product specialization despite less concentration of production areas.

Knight's technological and spatial analysis of obsidian (1999; chapter 6), paints a similar picture for the production of this commodity. Knight's study also provides additional insights into long-distance exchange and intrasite consumption patterns, although it is more difficult to distinguish diachronic patterns in the obsidian assemblage. Most of the obsidian consumed at Tres Zapotes came from the Zaragoza-Oyameles complex (63–84%). The range of values for the usually black to dark gray Zaragoza-Oyameles obsidian is owing to the possible presence of an undetermined amount of visually similar obsidian from the Ucareo and Otumba sources, suggested by their presence in a sample from the hinterland site of Palo Errado subjected to INAA analysis (Knight 1999:108–113). Clear obsidian from the Pico de Orizaba and Guadalupe Victoria sources together make up about 15% of the assemblage. Green obsidian from Pachuca comprises only about 1% of the assemblage. Most of the Zaragoza-Oyameles obsidian entered Tres Zapotes as prepared polyhedral cores for prismatic blade production, although some blocky macrocores were imported as well. Pico de Orizaba obsidian was imported as polyhedral and casual flake cores, and the identifiable Guadalupe Victoria obsidian appears to have been exchanged as raw cobbles for the manufacture of expedient flakes and prismatic blades.

Distributions of cores and debitage suggest that production was widespread and associated predominantly with domestic occupation both for clear obsidian from Pico de Orizaba and Guadalupe Victoria and black or dark gray Zaragoza-Oyameles obsidian. Likewise, Knight's analysis of consumption patterns for different obsidian types indicates wide access to most sources by elites and non-elites alike. The exception is green Pachuca obsidian, which is more strongly associated with elite contexts in formal architectural groups. Because of its scarcity, its association with the prestigious Central Mexican city of Teotihuacan, and the symbolic associations of its green color, elites may have restricted access to this commodity. Overall, however, Knight concludes that control over the production, exchange, or consumption of obsidian contributed little to the power base of elites at Tres Zapotes.

Mark Kruszczynski (1998; Pool 1997c:25–28) has completed a preliminary analysis of the groundstone assemblage at Tres Zapotes. Over 97% of the groundstone industry, including flakes, modified raw material, and unworked stone, come from nearby basalt sources in the Tuxtla mountains, especially the Cerro el Vigía volcano, the slopes of which extend to within 5 km of Tres Zapotes. Basalt implements, including manos, metates, mortars, pestles, and *molcajetes* (chile grinders) are distributed throughout all parts of Tres Zapotes. Celts and axes are slightly more common in areas of less intensive occupation, perhaps because of their use in field clearing (Pool 1997c:28). The distribution of basalt flakes and unmodified cobbles is strongly associated with areas of residential occupation (Pool 1997c:28, Fig. 11). Although this pattern could reflect widespread production of groundstone implements, we suspect that most of the cobbles were used in architectural construction as wall footers and platform fill. Such uses are documented in Stirling's excavations (Weiant 1943:10–11, Maps 7, 10). Many of the ubiquitous basalt flakes may have been broken from architectural elements and finished tools by recent plowing. More secure production indicators, including eight unfinished metates and two pics like those used for metate manufacture in highland Chiapas (Hayden 1987:49–71), are scarce at Tres Zapotes. Those we have found occur in three distinct zones, all associated with residential occupation (Pool 1997c:28).

In general, then, craft production at Tres Zapotes appears to have been primarily a household activity. The association of some ceramic and obsidian production indicators with formal architectural groups may suggest that clients supplied elite patrons with these crafts, but there is very little evidence for high levels of elite control over their production. In other words, the data on craft production at Tres Zapotes suggests the existence throughout the site's history of a horizontally integrated economy with relatively low levels of craft specialization and broad access to goods across classes. In this regard, Tres Zapotes parallels some models of economic integration developed for the Maya area (Blanton et al. 1993:197–200; Fedick 1988; Potter and King 1995; Rice 1987a) and the Mixtequilla (Stark and Heller 1991b; Stark 1992).

Discussion

To summarize, Late to Terminal Formative settlement at Tres Zapotes combined nucleation of residential occupation with dispersal of elite and ceremonial architecture. In addition to their spatial dispersion, formal architectural groups exhibit little functional differentiation; all plaza groups appear to have contained both ceremonial and elite residential structures. This combination of spatial dispersal and functional uniformity suggests weak centralization of political authority. Terminal Formative ceramic production appears to exhibit a range of scales and intensities and was differentiated into attached and independent contexts. Larger and more intensive ceramic production areas were evidently concentrated within the site's residential core, which may be expected as a result of higher densities of residential occupation. By the same token, as Classic occupation broke up into discrete concentrations, specialized ceramic production appears to

have become more dispersed. Temporally specific loci of Late and Terminal Formative lithic production are more difficult to identify, but currently there is little evidence for the concentration of obsidian production in restricted areas of the site, and most craft production appears to have been conducted in household contexts. In general then, the organization of craft production suggests little centralization, corroborating the settlement evidence for a horizontally integrated society, at least at the intrasite level.

The combination of nucleated residential core, dispersed formal architecture, and dispersed craft production appears to be unusual among major Formative and Classic centers in the southern Gulf Coast lowlands. La Venta, Laguna de los Cerros, Cerro de las Mesas and Matacapan all contain large central concentrations of mounds, platforms, and plazas, which dwarf any one of the plaza groups at Tres Zapotes (Bove 1978; Gonzalez Lauck 1996; Santley, Ortiz Ceballos, and Pool 1987; Stark 1999:213–215). Cyphers (1997:102) reports that most artificial mounds on the summit of the San Lorenzo plateau postdate the major Early Formative occupation of the site, and most of the low mounds there may not be intentional pre-Hispanic constructions at all. Extensive modification of the plateau, however, suggests an expenditure of labor far exceeding anything at Tres Zapotes (Cyphers 1997:102–106). At each of these sites, religious and political authority appears to have been much more centralized than at Tres Zapotes.

Comparable data on residential settlement patterns are much harder to come by for the southern Gulf lowlands, but they suggest considerable variability in their degree of nucleation. For example, La Venta seems to have contained a dispersed complement of non–elite households, while San Lorenzo was apparently surrounded by a large area of dense settlement (Gonzalez, Lauck 1996:75, 80; Cyphers 1997:106). Matacapan has been described as a highly nucleated site (by myself, among others), and occupational remains are certainly more concentrated there than in the surrounding countryside, but as I note above, densities of surface sherds and low residential mounds there are considerably less than at Tres Zapotes (Santley 1994:Fig. 11; Santley and Ortiz 1985:14, Figs. 4, 5; Santley, Ortiz Ceballos, and Pool 1987).

Systematic data on craft production are even more scarce, but those that exist indicate quite variable patterns of organization. At San Lorenzo, obsidian blades and flakes were evidently produced at the household level, but Cyphers (1996:66) describes the recycling of sculpture into groundstone implements and the production of multiperforate ilmenite cubes as activities seemingly conducted "at an industrial scale of manufacture." The association of at least one monument recycling workshop with elite architecture further suggests centralized control over this craft (Cyphers 1996:66). Obsidian working was also relatively unspecialized at Matacapan (Santley, Ortiz Ceallos, and Pool 1987:43), but Classic period ceramic production exhibited a high degree of differentiation, with widely varying scales, intensities, and contexts represented (Arnold et al. 1993; Santley, Arnold, and Pool 1989; Pool 1990, chapter 5). Notably, the largest, most intensive production areas are located on the fringes of the site. The nature of interaction between elites and craft producers at Matacapan is not known, but even though portions of the ceramic industry can be described as nucleated, it appears that organizationally the ceramic production system was not highly centralized. In their broad outlines, the distributions of residential occupation and formal architecture at Tres Zapotes appear to parallel those of the Mixtequilla to the west of the Papaloapan estuary more closely than any of these more easterly centers (Stark 1991, 1992, 1997, 1999). In the Mixtequilla, concentrations of public architecture dating primarily to the Late Formative and Classic periods are distributed at close intervals throughout a nearly continuous distribution of dispersed residential occupation that extends over much of the 62 km² surveyed by Stark and her associates. As at Tres Zapotes, Late Formative occupation was concentrated in the vicinity of formal architectural groups at Cerro de las Mesas, but Stark and Heller (1991b:54) characterize the distribution of residential mounds at Cerro de las Mesas as "not particularly densely packed," and residential mounds grew even more dispersed in the Classic period (Stark and Curet 1994:276–281). In addition, the production of pottery, obsidian, and possibly cotton was widely distributed throughout residential zones as well as in the centers (Stark and Heller 1991b:54; Stark et al. 1998).

Stark (1997, 1999) has proposed that several mound groups in the vicinity of Cerro de las Mesas may have constituted a "capital zone"—"an extensive area with dispersed formal groups that, together, constituted an administrative and service core" (Stark 1999:201). Under this model, new complexes are built within the capital zone, in part as a process of succession in rulership. New complexes may eclipse the older ones as active foci of power, but the older complexes continue to serve significant integrative functions (Stark 1999:203–204).

A similar situation may have characterized some periods at Tres Zapotes. If, however, the plaza groups functioned simultaneously for a time as the foci of ritual, administration, and elite residence, as current evidence suggests, then the political system may have been organized more as a confederacy, with several elite lineages sharing and negotiating ruling authority.

FACTORS AFFECTING SETTLEMENT ORGANIZATION

How can we account for the variation in patterns of site organization and craft production on the southern Gulf coast? First, we must recognize the range of variation we are talking about. Although the sites reviewed above exhibit different degrees of population nucleation, all of them would probably be considered dispersed settlement as compared to large highland centers. I would be very surprised if average population densities in site cores exceeded 25 people per hectare, except perhaps on the terraces surrounding San Lorenzo (Cyphers 1997; compare Drennan 1988:280–281). In addition, the inferred functions of formal architecture, as well as iconographic and epigraphic themes expressed in monuments at these sites, indicate that all would fall into Sanders and Webster's (1988) regal-ritual type of urban center. Therefore, we are talking about variation within a restricted range.

Drennan (1988) reviewed several possible causes of variation in residential density in Mesoamerica, including community size, swidden agriculture, defense, political control, and economic central-place functions (see also de Montmollin 1989:76–115 for various causes of centralization, including politically "forced settlement"). Arguing that compact settlement was the more normal pattern because of its numerous advantages for social, political, and economic organization, Drennan concluded that none of these causes explained variation in residential density as fully as did investment in labor-intensive agriculture, which favors dispersed settlement. In contrast, Stark and Heller (1991b:56) view residential dispersion and relatively weak political systems in the Mixtequilla as the result of a combination of factors that may have included relatively low agricultural risk, which supported household autonomy and reduced the need for economic interdependence between patrons and clients. Nevertheless, Stark (1999:221) suggests that early cotton production and export to the Mexican highlands may have contributed to regional centralization of wealth and development of a persistently important capital zone.

Other authors have also addressed the evolution of sociopolitical hierarchy in the southern Gulf lowlands, which should be reflected in the functional and distributional characteristics of formal architecture. For the Olmec, control over scarce resources, including fertile levee lands and imported basalt and obsidian, have been offered as the economic bases for emerging elites (Coe 1981a; Coe and Diehl 1980b:151–152; Rathje 1972). In discussing the organization of Classic period political and economic systems at Matacapan, Santley (1989b, 1994:262–263) has argued that efficient water transport on the Río Catemaco and the presence of an enclave of foreigners from Teotihuacan contributed to greater commercialization at Matacapan than is typical for regal-ritual centers. Regionally, Santley (1994) argued that the extractive and export economy of Matacapan was organized as a dendritic central–place system, accounting for the site's Middle Classic primacy.

The variation in site organization and craft production exhibited by the centers described above suggests that the process of urbanization in the southern Gulf lowlands responded to many factors that varied in space and time. Two related factors appear to have been particularly important at Tres Zapotes and account for some of the formal variation in centers across the region. These are ecological variation and the degree to which elites could control access to strategic resources, including agricultural land, basalt, and obsidian.

Unlike San Lorenzo and La Venta, where control over scarce, fertile levee lands and access to distant basalt sources may have contributed to the development of hierarchical political systems, Tres Zapotes is located in a broad area of fertile luvic phaeozem soils and near a massive source of basalt, Cerro el Vigía (figure 1.2). The extensive distribution of these resources would have reduced the ability of emergent elites to control access to them, contributing to the weak political hierarchy reflected in the modest size and dispersed pattern of formal architecture. Periodic flooding of the Arroyo Hueyapan valley would have maintained soil fertility, resulting in low levels of agricultural risk and encouraging household autonomy, as in the Mixtequilla. As a nonlocal resource, obsidian could have provided an economic basis for hierarchical institutions through control of its production and distribution, but the existence of multiple entry points for obsidian (and other imports) via the tributaries to the Papaloapan estuarine system would have undermined the ability of any one group to monopolize its import and regional distribution. Matacapan may provide one example of an export economy that allowed elites to overcome the tendency for locally extensive resource availability to dampen the development of hierarchical political structures, but Tres Zapotes lacked a foreign enclave disposed to organize production systems for nonlocal exchange.

On the other hand, residential occupation appears to have been more nucleated in Tres Zapotes than in most centers in the southern Gulf lowlands. The weak development

of specialized craft production at Tres Zapotes tends to argue against economic activities as a strong centripetal force acting to nucleate population. If anything, the reverse appears to have been the case; the few cases of more intensive ceramic production appear to have developed in response to the nucleation of settlement (chapter 5). Defense may have been a factor favoring nucleation in the Late Formative, as increasing regional population may have fostered competition for land and other resources. Certainly, warfare is a prominent theme in the inscription of the Terminal Formative stela from La Mojarra (Justeson and Kauffman 1993:1703), but we know too little about the frequency and intensity of warfare—or, for that matter, regional population densities—to evaluate the role of defense in nucleating population in the Tres Zapotes region. Furthermore, in the absence of a strong political hierarchy, forced resettlement does not appear to offer a likely explanation for residential nucleation (compare de Montmollin 1989:76–115).

How then to explain residential nucleation at Tres Zapotes? Part of the answer appears to lie in its ecological setting. The luvic phaeozems of the Arroyo Hueyapan valley constitute the largest local expanse of fertile, easily worked soils penetrating the low sedimentary uplands on the flanks of the Sierra de los Tuxtlas. Occupation of the upper reaches of phaeozem soils in this valley would have given the inhabitants access to the basalt sources required to make the implements necessary for processing agricultural products, as well as the best soils for growing them. Under these conditions, relatively intensive occupation of the upper Arroyo Hueyapan valley is to be expected. If Drennan is correct about the "normality" (1988:284) of concentrated settlement in Mesoamerica, then with the need for labor-intensive agriculture reduced by the annual replenishment of soil fertility in the Arroyo Hueyapan valley, the establishment of the civic-ceremonial complexes at Tres Zapotes would have provided the slight additional attraction required to nucleate residential population.

Conclusion

The concentration of population, formal architecture, and sculpture at Tres Zapotes leave little doubt that it functioned as a central place with respect to its hinterland in the Late and Terminal Formative periods. Internally, however, the association of residential nucleation with dispersal of formal architecture tends to blur the lines between traditional notions of site center and site periphery. In this chapter I have considered spatial nucleation and organizational centralization as interacting but analytically separable processes that respond differently to factors affecting demographic, political, and economic systems in ancient urban centers. In the specific case of Tres Zapotes, this perspective has helped to suggest possible causes for quite different patterns in the distributions of residential occupation, formal architecture, and craft production. Additionally, comparison of Tres Zapotes with other Formative and Classic period sites of the Gulf lowlands suggests that the development of urbanism in this region responded to a variety of local and exogenous factors that resulted in a diversity of urban forms.

Understanding the causes and implications of this variation constitutes a key problem for research into the political economy of the southern Gulf lowlands. Although the Maya lowlands will doubtless continue to be a productive source for comparisons, understanding of the causes and consequences of lowland settlement patterns will not be advanced by simply shoehorning the Gulf coast data into Mayan models or by shoving all lowland centers into regal-ritual or dispersed ceremonial pigeonholes. What is needed, rather, is careful documentation of specific Gulf settlement patterns through surveys designed to facilitate intersite and interregional comparisons and interpreted with a clear understanding of the evidential biases inherent in different research designs. I believe I speak for the other contributors to this volume when I express the hope that the studies we have presented will contribute to the design and interpretation of future surveys.

BIBLIOGRAPHY

Abascal, R.
1976   Los Primeros Pueblos Alfareros Prehispánicos. In *El Proyecto Arqueológica de Puebla-Tlaxcala*. Vol. 1: *Suplemento de Comunicaciones* no. 3, 40–52. Puebla, Mexico.

Abrams, E.M.
1996   The evolution of plaster production and growth of the Copan Maya state. In *Arqueología Mesoamericana: Homenaje a William Sanders*, vol. II, edited by A.G. Mustache, J.R. Parsons, R.S. Santley, and M.C. Serra Puche, 193–208. Mexico City: Instituto Nacional de Antropologiá e Historia.

Abrams, E.M., and A.C. Freter
1995   A Late Classic lime-plaster kiln from the Maya center of Copan, Honduras. *Antiquity* 70:422–428.

Arnold, P.J., III
1990   The organization of refuse disposal and ceramic production within contemporary Mexican houselots. *American Anthropologist* 92:915–932.

1991   *Domestic ceramic production and spatial organization: A Mexican case study in ethnoarchaeology.* Cambridge: Cambridge University Press.

Arnold, P.J., III, and R.S. Santley
1993   Household ceramics production at Middle Classic period Matacapan. In *Prehispanic domestic units in western Mesoamerica: Studies of the household, compound, and residence*, edited by R.S. Santley and K.G. Hirth, 227-248. Boca Raton: CRC Press.

Arnold, P.J., III, C.A. Pool, R.R. Kneebone, and R.S. Santley
1993   Intensive ceramic production and Classic-period political economy in the Sierra de los Tuxtlas, Veracruz, Mexico. *Ancient Mesoamerica* 4:175–191.

Ashmore, W., ed.
1981   *Lowland Maya settlement patterns*. Albuquerque: University of New Mexico Press.

Balkansky, A.K., G.M. Feinman, and L.M. Nicholas
1997   Pottery kilns of ancient Ejutla, Oaxaca, Mexico. *Journal of Field Archaeology* 4:1–22.

Barrett, T.P.
1996   Formative obsidian on the Gulf Coast of Mexico: Industry development in the Tuxtlas region. Paper presented at the 61st Annual Meeting of the Society for American Archaeology, New Orleans, LA.

Beals, R.L.
1944   *Houses and house use of the Sierra Tarascans*. Institution of Social Anthropology Publication 1. Washington, DC: Smithsonian Institution.

Bernal, I.
1969   *The Olmec world*. Berkeley: University of California Press.

Blanton, R.E.
1978   *Monte Alban: Settlement patterns at the ancient Zapotec capital*. New York: Academic Press.

1998   Beyond centralization: Steps toward a theory of egalitarian behavior in archaic states. In *Archaic states*, edited by G.M. Feinman and J. Marcus, 135–172. Santa Fe, NM: School of American Research Press.

Blanton, R.E., and G.M. Feinman
1984   The Mesoamerican world system: A comparative perspective. *American Anthropologist* 86:673–682.

Blanton, R.E., G.M. Feinman, S.A. Kowalewski, and P. Peregrine
1996   A dual-processual theory for the evolution of Mesoamerican civilization. *Current Anthropology* 37:1–15.

Blanton, R.E., S.A. Kowalewski, G.M. Feinman, and J. Appel
1982   *Monte Alban's hinterland, Part I: The prehispanic settlement patterns of the central and southern parts of the Valley of Oaxaca, Mexico*. Memoirs of the Museum of Anthropology 15. Ann Arbor: University of Michigan.

Blanton, R.E., S.A. Kowalewski, G.M. Feinman, and L.M. Finsten
1993   *Ancient Mesoamerica: A comparison of change in three regions*, 2nd edition. Cambridge: Cambridge University Press.

Bordaz, J.
1964   Pre-Columbian kilns at Peñitas, a Post-Classic site in Coastal Nayarit, Mexico. Ph.D. dissertation. Department of Anthropology, Columbia University, New York. Ann Arbor: University Microfilms.

Bove, F.J.
1978   Laguna de los Cerros: An Olmec central place. *Journal of New World Archaeology* 2(3):1–56.

Brumfiel, E.M.
1994   Factional competition and political development in the New World: An introduction. In *Factional competition and political development in the New World*, edited by E.M. Brumfiel and J.W. Fox, 3-13. Cambridge: Cambridge University Press.

Brumfiel, E.M., and T. K. Earle
1987   Specialization, exchange and complex societies: An introduction. In *Specialization, exchange and complex societies*, edited by E.M. Brumfiel and T.K. Earle, 1-9. Cambridge: Cambridge University Press.

Cabrera Castro, R.

1988   Horno Ceramico Posteotihuacano en el Palacio de Atetelco. *Arqueología* 4:47–75.

Canto Aguilar, G.

1986   Proposiciones para el Estudio de Talleres de Producción Cerámica. In *Unidades Habitacionales Mesoamericas y Sus Areas de Actividad*, edited by L. Manzanilla, 41–58. Universidad Nacional Autonoma de Mexico, DF.

Charlton, T.H.

1984   Production and exchange: Variables in the evolution of a civilization. In *Trade and exchange in early Mesoamerica*, edited by K. Hirth, 17–42. Albuquerque: University of New Mexico Press.

Chase, D.Z.

1986   Social and political organization in the land of cacao and honey: Correlating the archaeology and ethnohistory of the Postclassic lowland Maya. In *Late lowland Maya civilization: Classic to Postclassic*, edited by J.A. Sabloff and E.W. Andrews V, 347–377. Albuquerque: University of New Mexico Press.

Chase, J.E.

1981   The sky is falling: The San Martin Tuxtla volcanic eruption and its effects on the Olmec at Tres Zapotes, Veracruz. *Vínculos* 7:54.

Chase-Dunn, C.K., and T.D. Hall

1992   *Core-periphery relations in precapitalist worlds*. Boulder, CO: Westview Press.

Clark, J.E.

1986   From mountains to molehills: A critical review of Teotihuacan's obsidian industry. In *Economic aspects of prehispanic highland Mexico*, edited by B.L. Isaac, 23–74. Research in Economic Anthropology Supplement 2. Greenwich, CT: JAI Press.

1987   Prismatic blades and Mesoamerican civilization. In *The organization of core technology*, edited by J.K. Johnson and C.A. Morrow, 259–284. Boulder, CO: Westview Press.

Clark, J.E., and T.A. Lee, Jr.

1984   Formative obsidian exchange and the emergence of public economics in Chiapas, Mexico. In *Trade and exchange in early Mesoamerica*, edited by K. Hirth. 235–274. Albuquerque: University of New Mexico Press

Clark, J.E., and W.J. Parry

1990   Craft specialization and cultural complexity. *Research in Economic Anthropology* 12:289-346.

Clewlow, C.W., Jr.

1974   *A stylistic and chronological study of Olmec monumental sculpture.* Contributions of the University of California Archaeological Research Facility 19. Berkeley: University of California Archaeological Research Society.

Clewlow, C.W., Jr., R.A. Cowan, J.F. O'Connell, and C. Benemann

1967   *Colossal heads of the Olmec culture.* Contributions of the University of California Archaeological Research Facility 4. Berkeley: University of California Archaeological Research Society.

Cobean, R.H., J.R. Vogt, M.D. Glascock, and T.L. Stocker

1991   High-precision trace-element characterization of major Mesoamerican obsidian sources and further analysis of artifacts from San Lorenzo Tenochtitlan, Mexico. *Latin American Antiquity* 2:69–91

Coe, M.D.

1961   *La Victoria: An early site on the Pacific Coast of Guatemala.* Papers of the Peabody Museum of Archaeology and Ethnology 53. Cambridge: Harvard University.

1965a   Archaeological synthesis of southern Veracruz and Tabasco. In *Archaeology of southern Mesoamerica, part 2*, edited by G.R. Willey, 679–715. Handbook of Middle American Indians, vol. 3 (R. Wauchope, general editor). Austin: University of Texas Press.

1965b   The Olmec style and its distribution. In *Archaeology of southern Mesoamerica, part 2*, edited by G.R. Willey, 716–775. Handbook of Middle American Indians, vol. 3 (R. Wauchope, general editor). Austin: University of Texas Press.

1981a   Gift of the river: Ecology of the San Lorenzo Olmec. In *The Olmec and their neighbors*, edited by Elizabeth P. Benson, 15–21. Washington, DC: Dumbarton Oaks.

1981b   San Lorenzo Tenochtitlan. In *Archaeology*, edited by J.A. Sabloff, 117–146. Supplement to the Handbook of Middle American Indians, vol. 1 (VICTORIA REIFLER BRICKER, GENERAL EDITOR). Austin: University of Texas Press.

Coe, M.D., and R.A. Diehl

1980a   *In the land of the Olmec.* Vol. 1: *The archaeology of San Lorenzo Tenochtitlán.* Austin: University of Texas Press.

1980b   *In the land of the Olmec.* Vol. 2: *The people of the river.* Austin: University of Texas Press.

Cook, R.A.

1997   Reconstruction as a tool for exploring archaeological data: Multiple interpretations of the past at the incinerator site, Montgomery County Ohio. Paper presented at the 62nd Annual Meeting of the Society for American Archaeology, Nashville, TN.

Costin, C.L.

1991   Craft specialization: Issues in defining, documenting, and explaining the organization of production. In *Archaeological method and theory*, vol. 3, edited by M. Shiffer, 1–56. Tucson: University of Arizona Press.

Costin, C.L., and M. Hagstrum

1995   Standardization, labor investment, skill, and the organization of ceramic production in late prehispanic highland Peru. *American Antiquity* 60:619–639.

Cowgill, G.L.

1990   Toward refining concepts of full-coverage survey. In *The archaeology of regions: A case for full-coverage survey*, edited by S.K. Fish and S.A. Kowalewski, 249–259, Washington, DC: Smithsonian Institution Press.

Crumley, C.L.

1979   Three locational models: An epistemological assessment of anthropology and archaeology. In *Advances in archaeological method and theory*, vol. 2, edited by M.B. Schiffer, 141–173. New York: Academic Press.

1995   Heterarchy and the analysis of complex societies. In *Heterarchy and the analysis of complex societies*, edited by R.M. Ehrenreich, C.L. Crumley, and J.E. Levy, 1–5. Archaeological Papers of the American Anthropological Association 6. Arlington, VA: American Anthropological Association.

Curet, A.

1993   Regional studies and ceramic production areas: An example from La Mixtequilla, Veracruz, Mexico. *Journal of Field Archaeology* 20:427–440.

Cyphers, A.

1982   Tres Zapotes y la Cronología Olmeca. *Revista Mexicana de Estudios Antropológicos* 28:11–31. Sociedad Mexicana de Antropología, Mexico.

1996   Reconstructing Olmec life at San Lorenzo. In *Olmec art of ancient Mexico*, edited by E.P. Benson, and B. de la Fuente, 61–71. Washington, DC: National Gallery of Art.

1997   Olmec architecture at San Lorenzo. In *Olmec to Aztec: Settlement patterns in the ancient gulf lowlands,* edited by B.L. Stark and P.J. Arnold III, 96–114. Tucson: University of Arizona Press.

Daneels, A.

1997   Settlement history in the lower Cotaxtla basin. In *Olmec to Aztec: Settlement patterns in the ancient Gulf lowlands*, edited by B.L. Stark and P.J. Arnold III, 206–252. Tucson: University of Arizona Press.

de la Fuente, B.

1973   *Escultura Monumental Olmeca.* Mexico, DF: UNAM.

1981   Toward a conception of monumental Olmec art. In *The Olmec and their neighbors*, edited by E.P. Benson, 83–94. Washington, DC: Dumbarton Oaks.

de Montmollin, O.

1989   *The archaeology of political structure: Settlement analysis in a Classic Maya polity.* Cambridge: Cambridge University Press.

Deal, M.

1998   *Pottery ethnoarchaeology in the central Maya highlands.* Salt Lake City: University of Utah Press.

Diehl, R.A.

1997   Informe Técnico Final: Investigaciones Arqueológicas en La Mojarra, Veracruz, Mexico Temporada 1995. Report to the Instituto Nacional de Antropología e Historia, Mexico, DF.

Diehl, R.A., A. Vargas González, and S. Vásquez Zárate

1997   Proyecto Arqueológico La Mojarra. In *Memoria del Coloquio Arqueología del Centro y Sur de Veracruz,* edited by S. Ladrón de Guevara González and S. Vásquez Zárate, 197–210. Veracruz: Universidad Veracruzana, Xalapa.

Downum, C.E., and G.B. Brown

1998   The reliability of surface artifact assemblages as predictors of subsurface remains. In *Surface archaeology*, edited by Alan P. Sullivan III, 111–123. Albuquerque: University of New Mexico Press.

Drennan, R.D.

1987   Regional demography in chiefdoms. In *Chiefdoms in the Americas*, edited by R.D. Drennan and C.A. Uribe, 307–334. Latham: University Press of America.

1988   Household location and compact versus dispersed settlement in prehispanic Mesoamerica. In *Household and community in the Mesoamerican past,* edited by R.R. Wilk and W. Ashmore, 273–293. Albuquerque: University of New Mexico Press.

1996   *Statistics for archaeologists: A commonsense approach.* New York: Plenum Press.

Drucker, P.

1943a   *Ceramic sequences at Tres Zapotes, Veracruz, Mexico.* Bureau of American Ethnology Bulletin 140. Washington, DC: Smithsonian Institution.

1943b   *Ceramic stratigraphy at Cerro de las Mesas, Veracruz, Mexico.* Bureau of American Ethnology Bulletin 141. Washington, DC: Smithsonian Institution.

1952   Middle Tres Zapotes and the Preclassic ceramic sequence. *American Antiquity* 17:258–260.

1981   On the nature of Olmec polity. In *The Olmec and their neighbors,* edited by E.P. Benson, 29–47. Washington, DC: Dumbarton Oaks.

Ekholm, G.

1945   Review of *An introduction to the ceramics of Tres Zapotes, Veracruz, Mexico; Ceramic sequences at Tres Zapotes, Veracruz, Mexico;* and *Ceramic Stratigraphy at Cerro de las Mesas, Veracruz, Mexico. American Antiquity* 11(1):63–64.

Earle, T.K.

1981   Comment on P. Rice, Evolution of specialized pottery production: A trial model. *Current Anthropology* 22(3):230–231.

1987   Specialization and the production of wealth: Hawaiian chiefdoms and the Inka Empire. In *Specialization, exchange and complex societies*, edited by E.M. Brumfiel and T.K. Earle, 64–75. Cambridge: Cambridge University Press.

1997   *How chiefs come to power.* Stanford: Stanford University Press.

Erickson, C.L.

1995   Archaeological methods for the study of ancient landscapes of the Llanos de Mojos in the Bolivian Amazon. In *Archaeology in the lowland American tropics: Current analytical methods and applications,* edited by P.W. Stahl, 66–91. Cambridge: Cambridge University Press.

Fay, G.E.

1970   *Indian house types of Sonora, Mexico.* Museum of Anthropology Miscellaneous Series 14. Greeley: University of Northern Colorado.

Fedick, S.L.

1988   Prehistoric Maya settlement and land use patterns in the upper Belize River area, Belize, Central America. Ph.D. dissertation, Department of Anthropology, Arizona State University, Tempe.

Feinman, G.M.

1999   Rethinking our assumptions: Economic specialization at the household scale in ancient Ejutla, Oaxaca, Mexico. In *Pottery and people: A dynamic interaction*, edited by J.M. Skibo and G.M. Feinman, 81–98.

Feinman, G.M., and A. Balkansky

1997   Ceramic firing in ancient and modern Oaxaca. In *The prehistory and history of ceramic kilns*, edited by Prudence M. Rice, 129–148. Westerville, OH: American Ceramic Society.

Flannery, K.V.

1976   The early Mesoamerican house. In *The early Mesoamerican village*, edited by Kent V. Flannery, 16–24. New York: Academic Press.

Flannery, K.V., J. Marcus, and W.O. Payne

1994   *Early Formative pottery of the Valley of Oaxaca.* MEMOIRS OF THE MUSEUM OF ANTHROPOLOGY 27. PREHISTORY AND HUMAN ECOLOGY OF THE VALLEY OF OAXACA 10. Ann Arbor: University of Michigan.

Foster, G.M.

1955   *Contemporary pottery techniques in southern central Mexico.* Middle American Research Institute Publication 22. New Orleans: Tulane University.

Fox, R.

1977   *Urban anthropology.* Englewood Cliffs, NJ: Prentice Hall.

Fry, R.E.

1972   Manually operated post-hole diggers as sampling instruments. *American Antiquity* 37(2):259–261.

García, E.

1981   *Modificaciones al Sistema de Clasificación Climática Koeppen.* Instituto de Geografía, Mexico, DF: UNAM.

Gerhardt, J.C., and N. Hammond

1991   The community of Cuello: The ceremonial core. In *Cuello, an early Mayan community in Belize*, edited by N. Hammond, 98–117. Cambridge: Cambridge University Press.

Gómez-Pompa, A.

1973   Ecology of the vegetation of Veracruz. In *Vegetation and vegetational history of Latin America,* edited by A. Graham, 73–148. Amsterdam: Elsevier.

González Lauck, R.

1996   La Venta: An Olmec capital. In *Olmec art of ancient Mexico,* edited by E.P. Benson and B. de la Fuente, 73–81. Washington, DC: National Gallery of Art.

Grove, D.C.

1994   La Isla, Veracruz, 1991: A preliminary report with comments on the Olmec uplands. *Ancient Mesoamerica* 5:223–230.

Hall, B.A.

1994   Formation processes of large earthen residential mounds in La Mixtequilla, Veracruz, Mexico. *Latin American Antiquity* 5:31–50.

Haviland, W.A.

1981   Dower houses and minor centers at Tikal, Guatemala: An investigation into the identification of valid units in settlement hierarchies. In *Lowland Maya settlement patterns,* edited by W. Ashmore, 89–117. Albuquerque: University of New Mexico Press.

Hayashida, F.

1999   Style, technology and state production: Inka pottery manufacture in the Leche Valley. *Latin American Antiquity* 10:337–352.

Hayden, B.

1987   Traditional metate manufacturing in Guatemala using chipped stone tools. In *Lithic studies among the contemporary highland Maya,* edited by B. Hayden, 9–119. Tucson: University of Arizona Press.

1989   From chopper to celt: The evolution of resharpening techniques. In *Time, energy, and stone tools*, edited by R. Torrence, 7–16. Cambridge: Cambridge University Press.

Hayden, B., ed.

1987   *Lithic studies among the contemporary highland Maya.* Tucson: University of Arizona Press.

Healan, D.M., J.M. Kerley, and G.J. Bey III

1983   Excavation and preliminary analysis of an obsidian workshop in Tula, Hidalgo, Mexico. *Journal of Field Archaeology* 10:127–145

Hendry, J.C.

1992   *Atzompa: A pottery producing village in southern Mexico in the mid-1950s.* Nashville, TN: Vanderbilt University Press.

Heller, L., and B.L. Stark

1998   Classic and Postclassic obsidian tool production and consumption: A regional perspective from the Mixtequilla, Veracruz. *Mexicon* 5(20):119–128.

Hester, T.R., R.N. Jack, and R.F. Heizer

1971   The obsidian of Tres Zapotes. In *Papers on Olmec and Maya archaeology*, 65–132. Contributions of the University of California Archaeological Research Facility 13. Berkeley: University of California Archaeological Research Facility.

Hirth, K.G.

1992   Interregional exchange as elite behavior: An evolutionary perspective. In *Mesoamerican elites*, edited by D.Z. Chase and A.F. Chase, 18–29. Norman: University of Oklahoma Press.

Hirth, K. G.

1996   Political economy and archaeology: Perspectives on exchange and production. *Journal of Archaeological Research* 4(3):203–235

Hoag, E.

1997   An analysis of the burned earth materials from Tres Zapotes, Veracruz, Mexico. M.A. thesis, Department of Anthropology, University of Cincinnati, Cincinnati, OH.

Hoag, E., and C.A. Pool

2000   Building a ceramic kiln: An ethnographic example from San Isidro, Veracruz, Mexico. Paper presented at the 65th Annual Meeting of the Society for American Archaeology, Philadelphia, PA.

Holl, A.

1987   Mound formation processes and societal transformations: A case study from the Perichadian plain. *Journal of Anthropological Archaeology*, 6:122–158.

Howell, T.

1993   Evaluating the utility of auger testing as a predictor of subsurface artifact density. *Journal of Field Archaeology* 20:475–484.

INEGI (Instituto Nacional de Estadística, Geografía e Informática)

1984a   Carta Uso de Suelo y Vegetación, 1:250,000, Coatzacoalcos, E15-1-4. Secretaría de Programación y Presupuesto, Instituto Nacional de Estadística, Geografía e Informatica, Dirección General de Geografía, Mexico, DF.

1984b   Carta Edafológica, 1:250,000, Coatzacoalcos, E15-1-4. Secretaría de Programación y Presupuesto, Instituto Nacional de Estadística, Geografía e Informática, Dirección General de Geografía, Mexico, DF.

1984c   Carta Topográfica, 1:50,000, Tres Zapotes, E15A72. Secretaría de Programación y Presupuesto, Instituto Nacional de Estadística, Geografía e Informática, Dirección General de Geografía, Mexico, DF.

Justeson, J.S., and T. Kauffman

1993   A deciperment of epi-Olmec hieroglyphic writing. *Science* 259:1703–1711.

Kachigan, S.K.

1991   *Multivariate statistical analysis. A conceptual introduction.* New York: Radinus Press.

Kelly, I.T., and A. Palerm

1952   *The Tajin Totonac. Part 1: History, subsistence, shelter, and technology.* Institute of Social Anthropology Publication 13. Washington, DC: Smithsonian Institution.

Kievit, K.

1994   Jewels of Ceren. *Ancient Mesoamerica* 5:193–208.

Killion, T.W.

1990   Cultivation intensity and residential site structure: An ethnoarchaeological examination of peasant agriculture in the Sierra de Los Tuxtlas, Veracruz, Mexico. *Latin American Antiquity* 1:191–215.

1992   Residential ethnoarchaeology and ancient site structure: Contemporary farming and prehistoric settlement agriculture at Matacapan, Veracruz, Mexico. In *The gardens of prehistory*, edited by T.W. Killion, 119–149. Tuscaloosa: University of Alabama Press.

Kintigh, K.W.

1990   Comments on the case for full-coverage survey. In *The archaeology of regions: A case for full-coverage survey,* edited by S. K. Fish and S.A. Kowalewski, 237–242. Washington, DC: Smithsonian Institution.

Klima, B.

1963   *Dolni Vestoniče.* Prague: Nakladatelstvi Ceskoslovenske Akademie Ved.

Knight, C.

1999   The Late Formative to Classic period obsidian economy at Palo Errado, Veracruz, Mexico. Ph.D. dissertation, Department of Anthropology, University of Pittsburgh. Ann Arbor: University Microfilms.

Kowalewski, S.A., G.M. Feinman, L. Finsten, R.E. Blanton, and L.M. Nicholas

1989   *Monte Alban's hinterland, Part II: Prehispanic settlement patterns in Tlacolula, Etla, and Ocotlan, the Valley of Oaxaca, Mexico.* Memoirs of the Museum of Anthropology 23. Ann Arbor: University of Michigan.

Krotser, P.H.

1974   Country potters of Veracruz, Mexico: Technological survivals and culture change. In *Ethnoarchaeology,* edited by C.B. Donnan, 131–146. Monograph 4. Los Angeles: UCLA Institute of Archaeology.

1980   Potters in the land of the Olmec. In *In the land of the Olmec.* Vol. 2: *The people of the river*, edited by Michael D. Coe and Richard A. Diehl, 125–138. Austin: University of Texas Press.

Kruszczynski, M.A.

1998   Basalt exploitation and craft production at Tres Zapotes and its hinterlands: A preliminary report. Paper presented at the 63rd Annual Meeting of the Society for American Archaeology, Seattle, WA.

Lackey, L.M.
1982   *The pottery of Acatlán. A changing Mexican tradition.* Norman: University of Oklahoma Press.

Landon, J.R.
1991   *Booker tropical soil manual.* New York: Longman

Lesure, R.G.
1995   Paso de la Amada: Sociopolitical dynamics in an Early Formative community. Ph.D. dissertation, Department of Anthropology, University of Michigan. Ann Arbor: University Microfilms.

Lewis, B.S.
1996   The role of attached and independent specialization in the development of sociopolitical complexity. *Research in Economic Anthropology* 17:357–388.

Lowe, G.W.
1989   The heartland Olmec: Evolution of material culture. In *Regional perspectives on the Olmec,* edited by Robert J. Sharer and David C. Grove, 33–67. Cambridge: Cambridge University Press.

Marcus, J.
1983   On the nature of the Mesoamerican city. In *Prehistoric settlement patterns,* edited by E. Vogt and R. Leventhal, 195–242. Albuquerque: University of New Mexico Press.

Marcus, J., and K.V. Flannery
1996   *Zapotec civilization: How urban society evolved in Mexico's Oaxaca Valley.* London: Thames and Hudson

McIntosh, R.J.
1974   The excavation of mud structures: An experiment from West Africa. *World Archaeology* 9:185–199.

Melgar, J.M.
1869   Antigüedades Mexicanos. *Boletín de la Sociedad Mexicana de Geografía y Estadística* 2o ep. 1:292–297. Mexico, DF.
1871   Estudio Sobre la Antigüedad y el Origen de la Cabeza Colosal de Tipo Etiópico que existe en Hueyapam. *Boletín de la Sociedad Mexicana de Geografía y Estadística* 2o ep. 3:104–109. Mexico, DF.

Milbrath, S.
1979   *A study of Olmec sculptural chronology.* Studies in Pre-Columbian Art and Archaeology 23. Washington, DC: Dumbarton Oaks.

Millet, L.A.
1979   Rescate Arqueológico en la Región de Tres Zapotes, Veracruz. Tésis profesional, Escuela Nacional de Antropología e Historia, Mexico, DF.

Moore, J.D., and J.L. Gasco
1990   Perishable structures and serial dwelling from coastal Chiapas. *Ancient Mesoamerica* 1:205–212.

Ortiz Ceballos, P., and Santley, R.S.
1988   La Cerámica de Matacapan, Ms. on file, Department of Anthropology, University of New Mexico, Albuquerque.

Ortiz Ceballos, P.
1975   La Cerámica de los Tuxtlas. Tesis de licenciatura. Facultad de Antropologia, Universidad Veracruzana, Jalapa, Mexico.

Parsons, J.R.
1990   Critical reflections on a decade of full coverage regional survey in the Valley of Mexico. In *The archaeology of regions: A case for full-coverage survey,* edited by S.K. Fish and S.A. Kowalewski, 7–31. Washington, DC: Smithsonian Institution Press.

Pastrana, A.
1986   El proceso de trabajo de la obsidiana de las minas de Pico de Orizaba. *Boletin de Antropología Americana* 13:133–145

Payne, W.O.
1982   Kilns and ceramic technology of ancient Mesoamerica. In *Archaeological ceramics,* edited by J.S. Olin and A.D. Franklin, 189–192. Washington, DC: Smithsonian Institution Press.

Peacock, D.P.S.
1982   *Pottery in the Roman world: An ethnoarchaeological approach.* London: Longman.

Pike, K.L.
1980   *A Mixtec lime oven.* Dallas: SIL Museum of Anthropology.

Pool, C.A.
1990   Ceramic production, resource procurement, and exchange at Matacapan, Veracruz, Mexico. Ph.D. dissertation, Department of Anthropology, Tulane University. Ann Arbor: University Microfilms.
1992   Integrating ceramic production and distribution. In *Ceramic production and distribution: An integrated approach,* edited by G.J. Bey III and C.A. Pool, 275–313. Boulder, CO: Westview Press.
1993   Excavation of Late Formative houselots at Bezoapan, Veracruz. Paper presented at the 58th Annual Meeting of the Society for American Archaeology, St. Louis, MO.
1995   La Cerámica del Clásico Tardío y el Postclásico en la Sierra de los Tuxtlas. *Arqueología* 13/14:37–48.
1997a   Prehispanic kilns at Matacapan, Veracruz, Mexico. In *The prehistory and history of ceramic kilns,* edited by W.D. Kingery and P.M. Rice, 149–172., Westerville, OH: American Ceramic Society.
1997b   The spatial structure of formative houselots at Bezuapan. In *Olmec to Aztec: Settlement patterns in the ancient Gulf lowlands,* edited by B.L. Stark and P.J. Arnold III, 40–67. Tucson, AZ: University of Arizona Press.
1997c   Tres Zapotes archaeological survey: 1995 field season. Report submitted to the National Science Foundation. Washington, DC.
1999   Tres Zapotes: An Olmec secondary center? Paper presented at the 64th Annual Meeting of the Society for American Archaeology, Chicago, IL.
2000a   From Olmec to epi-Olmec at Tres Zapotes, Veracruz, Mexico. In *Olmec art and archaeology in Mesoamerica,* edited by J.E. Clark and M.E. Pye, 137–153. Washington, DC: National Gallery of Art.
2000b   Why a kiln? Firing technology in the Sierra de los Tuxtlas, Veracruz, Mexico. *Archaeometry* 42:1.

Pool, C.A., and G.M. Britt
2000   A ceramic perspective on the Formative to Classic transition in southern Veracruz, Mexico. *Latin American Antiquity* 10(2):139–161.

Pool, C.A., and R.S. Santley
1992   Middle Classic pottery economics in the Tuxtla Mountains, southern Veracruz, Mexico. In *Ceramic production and distribution: An integrated approach,* edited by G.J. Bey III and C.A. Pool, 205–224. Boulder, CO: Westview Press.

Pool, C.A., and C.J. Wendt
2000   Ceramic chronology and settlement history at Tres Zapotes. Paper presented at the Midwestern Mesoamerican Conference, University of Illinois, Champagne-Urbana.

Pool, C.A., P. Wright, and G.M. Britt
1993   Formative houselot structure in Bezoapan, Veracruz, Mexico. Report submitted to the H.J. Heinz III Charitable Trust, Pittsburgh.

Potter, D.R., and E.M. King
1995   A heterarchical approach to lowland Maya socioeconomies. In

Heterarchy and the analysis of complex societies, edited by R.M. Ehrenreich, C.L. Crumley, and J.E. Levy, 17–32. Archaeological Papers of the American Anthropological Association 6. Arlington, VA: American Anthropological Association.

Porter, J.B.
1989   The monuments and hieroglyphs of Tres Zapotes, Veracruz, Mexico. Ph.D. dissertation, Department of Anthropology, University of California, Berkeley.

Pugh, M.S.
1981   An intimate view of archaeological exploration. In *The Olmec and their neighbors*, edited by E.P. Benson, 1–14.

Rathje, W.L.
1971   The origin and development of Classic Maya civilization. *American Antiquity* 36:275–285
1972   Praise the gods and pass the metates: A hypothesis of the development of lowland rainforest civilizations in Mesoamerica. In *Contemporary archaeology*, edited by M. Leone, 365–392. Carbondale, IL: Southern Illinois University Press.

Redman, C.L.
1973   Multistage fieldwork and analytical techniques. *American Antiquity* 38:61–79.

Rendon, S.
1950   *Modern pottery of Riotenco San Lorenzo, Cuauhtitlan*. Middle American Research Institute, Publication 15. 251–268. New Orleans: Tulane University.

Reynolds, J.K.
1979   Residential architecture at Kaminaljuyu. In *Settlement pattern excavations at Kaminaljuyu, Guatemala*, edited by Joseph W. Michels, 223–275. State College: Pennsylvania State University Press.

Rice, P.M.
1987a   Economic change in the lowland Maya Late Classic period. In *Specialization, exchange, and complex societies*, edited by E.M. Brumfiel and T.K. Earle, 76–85. Cambridge: University Press Cambridge.
1987b   *Pottery analysis: A source book*. Chicago: University of Chicago Press.

Roler, K., and B.L. Stark
1992   Recognizing poor households in the archaeological record: A case study from southern Veracruz, Mexico. Paper presented at the 57th Annual Meeting of the Society for American Archaeology, Pittsburgh, PA.

Roscoe, J.
1965   *The Baganda: An account of their native customs and beliefs*. 2nd edition. London: Frank Cass & Co. Ltd.

Rye, O.
1981   *Pottery technology: Principles and reconstruction*. Washington, DC: Taraxacum Press.

Sanders, W.T., and B. J. Price
1968   *Mesoamerica: The evolution of a civilization*. New York: Random House.

Sanders, W.T., and D. Webster
1988   The Mesoamerican urban tradition. *American Anthropologist* 90:521–546.

Santley, R.S.
1983   Obsidian trade and Teotihuacan influence in Mesoamerica. In *Highland-lowland interaction in Mesoamerica: Interdisciplinary approaches*, edited by A. Miller, 69–124. Washington, DC: Dumbarton Oaks.
1984   Obsidian exchange, economic stratification, and the evolution of complex society in the Basin of Mexico. In *Trade and exchange in early Mesoamerica*, edited by K.G. Hirth, 43–86. Albuquerque: University of New Mexico Press.

1989   Obsidian working, long-distance exchange, and the Teotihuacan presence on the south Gulf Coast. In *Mesoamerica after the decline of Teotihuacan A.D. 700–900,* edited by R. Diehl and J. Berlo, 131–151. Washington, DC: Dumbarton Oaks.
1989   Urbanization at Matacapan: Testing the goodness of fit of the regal-ritual and administrative models. Paper presented at the 54th Annual Meeting of the Society for American Archaeology, Atlanta, GA.
1992   A consideration of the Olmec phenomenon in the Tuxtlas: Early formative settlement pattern, land use, and refuse disposal at Matacapan, Veracruz, Mexico. In *The gardens of prehistory*, edited by Thomas W. Killion, 150–183. Tuscaloosa: University of Alabama Press.
1994   The economy of Ancient Matacapan. *Ancient Mesoamerica* 5:243–266.

Santley, R.S., and R.T. Alexander
1992   The political economy of core-periphery systems. In *Resources, power, and interregional interaction*, edited by E.M. Schortman and P.A. Urban, 23–49. New York: Plenum Press.
1996   Teotihuacan and Middle Classic Mesoamerica: A precolumbian world system? In *Arqueología Mesoamericana: Homenaje a William T. Sanders*, edited by A.G. Mastache, J.R. Parsons, R.S. Santley, and M.C. Serra Puche, 173–194. Mexico, DF: INAH and Arqueología Mexicana.

Santley, R.S., P.J. Arnold III, and T.P. Barrett
1997   Formative period settlement in the Tuxtlas Mountains. In *Olmec to Aztec: Settlement patterns in the ancient Gulf lowlands*, edited by B.L. Stark and P.J. Arnold III, 174–206. Tucson: University of Arizona Press.

Santley, R.S., P.J. Arnold III, and C.A. Pool
1989   The ceramics production system at Matacapan, Veracruz, Mexico. *Journal of Field Archaeology* 16:107–132.

Santley, R.S., T.P. Barrett, M.D. Glascock, and H. Neff
1997   Prehispanic obsidian procurement in the Tuxtla Mountains, southern Veracruz, Mexico. Paper presented at the 62nd Annual Meeting of the Society for American Archaeology, Nashville, TN.

Santley, R.S., J.M. Kerley, and T.P. Barrett
1995   Teotihuacan period lithic assemblages from the Teotihuacan Valley. In *The Teotihuacan Valley project final report. Vol. 3: The Teotihuacan period occupation of the Valley, Part 2. artifact analysis*, edited by W.T. Sanders, 466–497. Occasional Papers in Anthropology 20. Matson Museum of Anthropology, University of Pennsylvania.

Santley, R.S., J.M. Kerley, and R.R. Kneebone
1986   Obsidian working, long-distance exchange, and the politico-economic organization of early states in central Mexico. In *Economic aspects of prehispanic highland Mexico*, edited by B.L. Isaac, 101–132. Research in Economic Anthropology Supplement 2. Greenwich, CT: JAI Press.

Santley, R.S., and P. Ortiz Ceballos
1985   Reporte Final de Campo Proyecto Matacapan: Temporada 1983. *Cuadernos del Museo* 4:3–91. Jalupa: Universidad Veracruzana

Santley, R.S., P. Ortiz Ceballos, T.W. Killion, P.J. Arnold, and J.M. Kerley
1984   *Final field report of the Matacapan archaeological project: The 1982 season*. Latin American Institute Research Paper Series 15. Albuquerque: University of New Mexico.

Santley, R.S., P. Ortiz Ceballos, and C.A. Pool
1987   Recent archaeological research at Matacapan, Veracruz: A summary of the results of the 1982 to 1986 field seasons. *Mexicon* 9(2):41–48.

Santley, R.S., and C.A. Pool
1993   Prehispanic exchange relationships among central Mexico, the Valley of Oaxaca, and the Gulf Coast of Mexico. In *The American Southwest and Mesoamerica: Systems of prehistoric exchange*, edited by J.E. Ericson and T.G. Baugh, 179–211. New York: Plenum Press.

Scarborough, V.L.
1983   A Preclassic Maya water system. *American Antiquity* 48(4):720–744.

Schortman, E.M., and P.A. Urban
1987   Modeling interregional interaction in prehistory. In *Advances in archaeological method and theory*, vol. 11, edited by M.B. Schiffer, 37–95. New York: Academic Press.

1992   *Resources, power, and interregional interaction*. New York: Plenum Press.

Schuldenrein, J.
1991   Coring and the identity of cultural resource environments: A comment on Stein. *American Antiquity* 56(1):131–137.

Service, E.R.
1962   *Primitive social organization*. New York: Random House.

Shaffer, G.D.
1982   Attempts at maximizing anthropological knowledge of prehistoric buildings. *Antropología Contemporanea* 5:141–146.

Sheets, P.D.
1977   The analysis of chipped stone artifacts in southern Mesoamerica: An assessment. *Latin American Research Review* 12(1):130–158.

1992   *The Ceren site*. Fort Worth: Harcourt Brace Jovanovich.

Sheets, P.D., H.F. Beaubien, M. Beaudry, A. Gerstle, B. McKee, C.D. Miller, H. Spetzler, and D.B. Tucker
1990   Household archaeology at Ceren, El Salvador. *Ancient Mesoamerica* 1:81–90.

Siegel, P.E.
1995   The archaeology of community organization in the tropical lowlands: A case study from Puerto Rico. In *Archaeology in the lowland American tropics: Current analytical methods and applications*, edited by Peter W. Stahl, 42–65. Cambridge: Cambridge University Press.

Sinopoli, C.M.
1988   The organization of craft production at Vijayanagara, South India. *American Anthropologist* 90(3):580–597.

1991   *Approaches to archaeological ceramics*. New York: Plenum Press.

Smyth, M.P.
1998   Surface archaeology and site organization: New methods for studying urban Maya communities. In *Surface archaeology*, edited by Allan P. Sullivan III, 43–60. Albuquerque: University of New Mexico Press.

Soto, M., and L. Gama
1997   Climas. In *Historia Natural de los Tuxtlas*, edited by E. González Soriano, R. Dirzo, and R.C. Vogt, 7–23. Mexico, DF: UNAM.

Stark, B.L.
1984   An ethnoarchaeological study of a Mexican pottery industry. *Journal of New World Archaeology* 6:4–14.

1985   Archaeological identification of pottery-production locations: Ethnoarchaeological and archaeological data in Mesoamerica. In *Decoding prehistoric ceramics*, edited by B.A. Nelson, 158–194. Carbondale, IL: Southern Illinois University Press.

1989   *Patarata pottery: Classic period ceramics of the south-central Gulf Coast, Veracruz, Mexico*. Anthropological Papers of the University of Arizona 51. Tucson: University of Arizona Press.

1990   The Gulf Coast and the central highlands of Mexico: Alternative models for interaction. *Research in Economic Anthropology* 12:243–285.

1991   Survey methods and settlement features in the Cerro de las Mesas region. In *Settlement archaeology of Cerro de las Mesas, Veracruz, Mexico*, edited by B.L. Stark, 39–48. Monograph 34. Los Angeles: UCLA Institute of Archaeology.

1992   Ceramic production in prehistoric La Mixtequilla, south-central Veracruz, Mexico. In *Ceramic production and distribution: An integrated approach*, edited by G.J. Bey III and C.A. Pool, 175–204. Boulder, CO: Westview Press.

1997   Discusión de dos aspectos del patrón de asentamientos en la Mixtequilla. In *Memoria del Coloquio Arqueología del Centro y Sur de Veracruz*, edited by S. Ladrón de Guevara González and Sergio Vásquez Zárate, 211–222. Veracruz, Mexico: Universidad Veracruzana, Xalapa.

1999   Formal architectural complexes in south-central Veracruz, Mexico: A capital zone? *Journal of Field Archaeology* 26(2):197–225.

2000   Pottery production and distribution in the Gulf lowlands of Mesoamerica. Paper presented at the 65th Annual Meeting of the Society for American Archaeology, Philadelphia, PA.

Stark, B.L., ed.
1991   *Settlement archaeology of Cerro de las Mesas, Veracruz, Mexico*. Monograph 34. Los Angeles: UCLA Institute of Archaeology.

Stark, B.L., ed.
2000   *Classic period Mixtequilla, Veracruz, Mexico: Diachronic insights from residential investigations*. State University of New York, Albany: Institute for Mesoamerican Studies.

Stark, B.L., and L.A. Curet
1994   The development of Classic period Mixtequilla in south-central Veracruz, Mexico. *Ancient Mesoamerica* 5(2):267–287.

Stark, B. L., and L. Heller
1991a   Cerro de las Mesas revisited: Survey in 1984-1985. In *Settlement archaeology of Cerro de las Mesas Veracruz, Mexico*, edited by Barbara L. Stark, 1–25. Monograph 34. Los Angeles: UCLA Institute of Archaeology.

1991b   Residential dispersal in the environs of Cerro de las Mesas. In *Settlement archaeology of Cerro de las Mesas, Veracruz, Mexico*, edited by B.L. Stark, 49–58. Monograph 34. Los Angeles: UCLA Institute of Archaeology.

Stark, B.L., L. Heller, M.D. Glascock, J.M. Elam, and H. Neff
1992   Obsidian-artifact source analysis for the Mixtequilla region, south-central Veracruz, Mexico. *Latin American Antiquity* 3(3):221–239

Stark, B.L., L. Heller, and M.A. Ohnersorgen
1998   People with cloth: Mesoamerican economic change from the perspective of cotton in south-central Veracruz. *Latin American Antiquity* 9(1):7–36.

Stein, G.J., and J.M. Blackman
1993   The organizational context of specialized craft production in early Mesopotamian states. *Research in Economic Anthropology* 14:29–59.

Stein, J.K.
1986   Coring archaeological sites. *American Antiquity* 51(3):505–527.

1991   Coring in CRM and archaeology: A remainder. *American Antiquity* 56(1):138–142.

Stenholm, N.A.
1979   Identification of house structures in Mayan archaeology: A case study at Kaminaljuyu. In *Settlement pattern excavations at Kaminaljuyu, Guatemala*, edited by Joseph W. Michels, 31–182. State College: Pennsylvania State University Press.

Stirling, M.W.
1940   *An initial series from Tres Zapotes, Vera Cruz, Mexico.* National Geographic Society Contributed Technical Papers 1(1). Washington, DC: National Geographic Society.
1943   *Stone monuments of southern Mexico.* Bureau of American Ethnology Bulletin 138. Washington, DC: Smithsonian Institution.
1965   Monumental sculpture of southern Veracruz and Tabasco. In *Archaeology of southern Mesoamerica, Part 2,* edited by Gordon R. Willey, 716–738. Handbook of Middle American Indians, vol. 3 (Robert Wauchope, general editor). Austin: University of Texas Press.

Sullivan, A.P., III
1988   Prehistoric southwestern ceramic manufacture: The limitations of current evidence. *American Antiquity* 53(1):23–35.

Symonds, S.C., and R. Lunagómez
1997   Settlement system and population development at San Lorenzo. In *Olmec to Aztec: Settlement patterns in the ancient gulf lowlands,* edited by B.L. Stark and P.J. Arnold III, 144–173. Tucson: University of Arizona Press.

Thompson, J.E.S.
1941   *Dating of certain inscriptions of non-Maya origin.* Carnegie Institution of Washington, Division of Historical Research, Theoretical Approaches to Problems 1. Cambridge.

Torrence, R.
1986   *Production and exchange of stone tools:Prehistoric obsidian in the Aegean.* Cambridge: Cambridge University Press.

Urban, P.A., E.C. Wells, and M.T. Ausec
1997   The fires without and the fires within: Evidence for ceramic producing facilities at the Late Classic site of La Sierra, Naco Valley, northwestern Honduras, and its environs. In *The prehistory and history of ceramic kilns,* edited by W.D. Kingery and P.M. Rice, 173–194. Westerville, OH: American Ceramic Society.

Valenzuela, J.
1945   Las Exploraciones Efectuadas en los Tuxtlas, Veracruz. *Anales del Museo Nacional de Arqueología, Historia y Etnología* 3:83–107.

van der Leeuw, S.
1976   *Studies in the technology of ancient pottery.* Amsterdam: Organization for the Advancement of Pure Research.

Van de Velde, P., and H.R. Van de Velde
1939   The black pottery of Coyotepec, Oaxaca, Mexico. *Southwest Museum Papers* 13:7–43.

Wauchope, R.
1938   *Modern Maya houses: A study of their archaeological significance.* Washington, DC: Carnegie Institution of Washington.
1950   A tentative sequence of Pre-Classic ceramics in Middle America. *Middle American Research Records* 1(14):211–250.

Weiant, C.W.
1943   *An introduction to the ceramics of Tres Zapotes, Veracruz, Mexico.* Bureau of American Ethnology Bulletin 139. Washington, DC: Smithsonian Institution.
1952   Reply to Middle Tres Zapotes and the Pre-Classic ceramic sequence. *American Antiquity* 18(1):57–59.

Wendt, C.J.
1998   Intra-community settlement organization at Tres Zapotes: The perspectives from a sub-surface testing program. M.A. thesis, Department of Anthropology, University of Kentucky, Lexington.

White, J.C.
1995   Incorporating heterarchy into theory on socio-political development: The case from southeast Asia. In *Heterarchy and the analysis of complex societies,* edited by R.M. Ehrenreich, C.L. Crumley, and J.E. Levy, 101–123. Archaeological Papers of the American Anthropological Association 6. Arlington, VA: American Anthropological Association.

Willey, G.R.
1956   Problems concerning prehistoric settlement patterns in the Maya lowlands. In *Prehistoric settlement patterns in the New World,* edited by G.R. Willey. Viking Fund Publications in Anthropology 23. New York: Wenner Gren Foundation for Anthropological Research.
1981   Maya lowland settlement patterns: A summary review. In *Lowland Maya settlement patterns,* edited by W. Ashmore, 385–415. Albuquerque: University of New Mexico Press.

Willey, G.R., W.R. Bullard, Jr., J.B. Glass, and J.C. Gifford
1965   *Prehistoric Maya settlements in the Belize Valley.* Papers of the Museum of Archaeology and Ethnology 54. Cambridge: Harvard University.

Williams, H., and R.F. Heizer
1965   *Sources of rocks used in Olmec monuments.* Contributions of the University of California Archaeological Research Facility 1. Berkeley: University of California Archaeological Research Facility.

Winter, M.C., and W.O. Payne
1976   Hornos para Cerámica Hallados en Monte Albán. *Instituto Nacional de Antropología e Historia, Boletin,* Epoca II(16):37–40.

Wirth, L.
1938   Urbanism as a way of life. *American Journal of Sociology* 44:3–24.

Zeidler, J.A.
1995   Archaeological survey and site discovery in the forested neotropics. In *Archaeology in the lowland American tropics: Current analytical methods and applications,* edited by P.W. Stahl, 7–41. Cambridge: Cambridge University Press.